A
Thousand
Cuts

ADVANCE PRAISE FOR THE BOOK

'*A Thousand Cuts* is a harrowing, sobering and ultimately inspiring autobiography of Professor T.J. Joseph, who in 2010 became the victim of a brutal terrorist assault, accused of blasphemy after setting an exam question that enraged fundamentalists. This book is an important reminder of the pernicious effect of religious extremism and the duty of every person to speak out against those who would silence free expression'—Shashi Tharoor

'No sensitive human being can finish reading Prof. T.J. Joseph's *A Thousand Cuts* without a lump in his/her throat. On the one hand, it narrates a harrowing tale of the inhuman torments this innocent, much-loved teacher and his family had to undergo for a crime he had never even dreamt of; on the other, it comes out as a strong indictment of hate-driven religious fundamentalism that goes to absurd lengths to find heresy where none exists, the tragic collusion of political parties and religious heads with the agents provocateurs, the brutalized and corrupt police system in the country, and even the non-judicious judiciary that often refuses to look into the facts of the case. There is excruciating agony here, but also black humour and irony that enliven and lighten the narrative even at the height of anguish. A moving testament of our unkind times and a textbook for the secular-minded seekers of truth and justice in our inhuman times'—K. Satchidanandan

'The saga of the question paper that led to the manhunt and assault of Prof. T.J. Joseph, after the crime of blasphemy was foisted on him, and its consequences on him and his family, including complete isolation, was penned down by him in Malayalam. The poignant tale, with its sense of urgency and helplessness, has been sensitively translated as *A Thousand Cuts*, and the reader can experience the trauma of the author as he recalls and relives those days which changed his life'—Rana Safvi

A
Thousand
Cuts

AN INNOCENT QUESTION
AND DEADLY ANSWERS

T.J. JOSEPH

Translated by NANDAKUMAR K.

VINTAGE

An imprint of Penguin Random House

VINTAGE

USA | Canada | UK | Ireland | Australia
New Zealand | India | South Africa | China

Vintage is part of the Penguin Random House group of companies
whose addresses can be found at global.penguinrandomhouse.com

Published by Penguin Random House India Pvt. Ltd
4th Floor, Capital Tower 1, MG Road,
Gurugram 122 002, Haryana, India

First published in Vintage by Penguin Random House India 2021
This edition is published by Penguin Random House India Private Ltd
by arrangement with DC Books

10 9 8 7 6 5 4 3 2

The views and opinions expressed in this book are the author's own and the facts
are as reported by him which have been verified to the extent possible, and the
publishers are not in any way liable for the same.

As on the date of publication of this book, Mr Kurian and Mr Kuriakose have
challenged the Kerala State Human Rights Commission order before the Hon'ble
High Court of Kerala. The order of Kerala State Human Rights Commission has
been stayed by the high court. The matter is still pending before the Hon'ble High
Court of Kerala.

ISBN 9780670094455

Typeset in Adobe Jenson Pro by Manipal Technologies Limited, Manipal
Printed at Replika Press Pvt. Ltd, India

www.penguin.co.in

To my Salomi . . .

PART I

I

A Momentous Question

19 March 2010. Father Manuel Pichalakkat came into the Malayalam department just as I was getting ready to head to class post the lunchbreak. Besides me, he was the only other teacher in our department.

As Father Pichalakkat—his legal name was Raju Jacob—was also the college bursar, he had been assigned a private room for official business. His principal duty was to manage the college's financial matters.

During 1993–95, he had been my student in the postgraduate course in Malayalam at Nirmala College, Muvattupuzha. I had always fancied that of all his teachers, he felt closest to me.

In 2006, he was appointed as lecturer in the Malayalam department in Newman College, Thodupuzha, and two years later, he assumed the position of the bursar. That was also the year in which I received a promotion and joined the college as head of the Malayalam department from Nirmala College. I shall never forget his genuine and solicitous, almost devout, regard for his ex-teacher as he led me to the department room—then shared by the Malayalam and Hindi departments—and to my desk, which he himself proceeded to wipe clean of non-existent dust.

The second semester's second internal examination for undergraduate students was due the following week. It was the last day for setting the Malayalam question paper. Father Pichalakkat had to set the question papers for the BSc and BA classes; and I, for the BCom students. I had already passed on to him the questions for the lessons I had taught in the BSc and BA classes. For the BCom classes, Father Pichalakkat taught the text, *Navakam*. I was waiting for questions from him to add to the ones I had in mind for the text, *Ezhuththola*. Burdened as he was with his many duties, he had delayed turning in the questions. He had come in now to do so. I accepted the questions without even a glance, as I was already late for class.

After the lecture, I felt like a cup of tea. I had no class for the next hour. But it was also the last period of the day—time that I could use to prepare the question paper. I decided to forgo that cup of tea and returned to the room.

Questions from both texts had to be included in the paper, though for groups which had different weightages. If I had prepared my questions already, it would have been easy to mix up the questions and set the entire question paper. However, reluctant to write them down twice, I was forming my own questions only then.

Setting a question paper is not to be taken lightly; it needs creativity. A person who sets purposeful questions in humanities must surely undergo the painful throes of creativity. Which is why most teachers tend to take refuge in question papers of previous years. This shortcut is what makes students believe that if they learn the answers to questions that have appeared over the previous decade, high marks are theirs for the taking.

I have never been in favour of copy-pasting from old question papers. In over twenty-five years of my career as a teacher, not once have I done it. When I am setting a question paper, the only two things in front of me are the syllabus and the prescribed texts.

In front of me was *Ezhuththola*, a text created to help students avoid the usual pitfalls in the use of the language and to engender in them chaste diction. I prepared a few questions under the heading 'Correct the Errors'. Next, I needed questions from the chapter 'Punctuation'. It describes each of the punctuation marks and gives examples of their usage. How does one prepare engaging questions on this? It wouldn't suffice if I set questions to use each of the signs in isolation. After some thought, I decided: 'Rewrite the passage below with appropriate punctuations.' Then I pondered over a passage that would be appropriate for this exercise.

In Malayalam, for direct speech, the practice is to use a colon after the speaker's name (e.g., Rama:). Therefore, I felt a dialogue would be appropriate here. A dialogue that I knew by heart rose up in my mind.

Thirakathayute Reethisastram (Methodology of Screenplay)—a compilation of essays by prominent Malayalam filmmakers on scriptwriting, edited by P.M. Binukumar—is a Kerala Bhasha Institute publication, prescribed as a reference text for BA and MA courses in Malayalam of Mahatma Gandhi University. One of the essays in it is 'Screenplay: Discoveries of a Believer' by filmmaker and social worker P.T. Kunju Muhammed. A dialogue within the text suggested itself as the one that I should use for the question on punctuations.

In the article, Kunju Muhammed postulates that the structure, the energy, and the impetus for a script can be found within one's own environment. He narrates the story of a mad man from his native place, who formed the inspiration for a scene in his movie *Garshom* where the protagonist is speaking with God. Kunju Muhammed quotes the mad man as he holds a dialogue with God.

Mad man: Creator, Creator . . .

God: What is it, sonofabitch?

Mad man: A mackerel—if one cuts it, how many pieces will there be?

God: You dawg, how many times do I have to tell you it's three?

The mad man is doubling up as God in this conversation.

While at Nirmala College, I taught a class on 'Theatre and Cinema' in the final semester of the MA Malayalam course. P.T. Kunju Muhammed's mad man story would be discussed in the sessions on movie scriptwriting.

The dialogue between God and the mad man appeared to me as a great example of the 'black humour' used in modern literature and on which I was doing research. The mad man is a symbol for the entire human race. That conversation took root in my mind as a piece of literature that encompassed the ambiguity of the human condition for which even God had no solution. I started quoting it in postgraduate classes whenever modern literature and black humour came up for discussion.

On the occasions that mackerel was the fare at home, I would amuse myself by declaiming this piece of dialogue, so much so that even my wife and children learnt it by rote.

I put it down in the question paper. I did have fleeting thoughts about the appropriateness of God calling someone a sonofabitch.

However, abuses are as essential to language as endearments. A besotted lover addressing his beloved as his treasure and a wife calling her abusive husband Kaalan (vernacular for Yama, the God of Death) are embellishments in the use of language. It is such figurative usage, beyond their literal sense, that gives energy and life to language.

If Mahakavi Vyloppilli Sreedhara Menon's masterpiece of a poem 'Kutiyozhikkal' (Eviction) has words such as slut, whore, harlot, etc., it is because these words are not proscribed in literature.

Take the Bible, and how John the Baptist and Jesus Christ utter these words in different ways. In Matthew 23:33, Jesus abuses Pharisees, saying, 'You snakes! You brood of vipers!' out of intolerance. However, In Matthew 3:7, when John the Baptist addresses those who arrive to be baptised as a 'brood of vipers', it is not out of wrath, but sympathy.

I also remembered reading in ecology warrior Kallen Pokkudan's autobiography[1] that, in North Malabar, 'sonofabitch' is used as a term of endearment.

I decided to include the whole conversation between the mad man and God in the question paper. In any case, this was not a question for students of religious studies. For students of literature, shouldn't all characters, whether gods, demons, devils, angels, devas, asuras or incarnations, be of equal standing?

Although the cream of the students with intelligence and imagination are absorbed into the BCom course, a modicum of brilliance is also required for the study of literature. I prefer to have discourses with students possessing these faculties. I had thought that, after the examination, when the marked answer sheets were returned to the students, I could elaborate on the dialogue between God and the mad man, and make the session more literary.

I was still pondering over that piece of dialogue. In Kunju Muhammed's article, the dialogue comes after the mad man's backstory has been narrated. Here, when the backstory could not be told, I rationalized, wouldn't it be better if a name were given to the interlocutor? Usually in Kerala, the community that refers to God as padachchon, meaning the Creator, is Muslim. I should choose a Muslim name, I decided. The writer who had narrated the mad man's tale was himself a Muslim. I took out the initials of his name first. That left 'Kunju Muhammed'.

That's too long. Muhammed. That should suffice.

With my handwritten question paper, I moved to the DTP centre—a small room adjacent to the college library. The DTP operator was a twenty-seven-year-old girl who had been working there for nine years as a daily-wager. I showed her the question on punctuation and instructed her not to add any punctuation marks to it. After reading the dialogue, she laughed and asked me if I had written it myself. Gratified that the humour in it could make her laugh, I told her that it was taken from a book, and then proceeded to the canteen for a cup of tea.

When I returned, she was still keying in the question paper. I proofread while she typed.

I went back to my room with the printout and my hand-written questions. I read through once more to check if any errors had crept in. I noticed that she had missed putting 'Malayalam' in the heading. I added it by hand, stencil-style. I wrote down the figure '35' on the reverse of the printout as the number of photocopies to be taken, although there were only thirty-two students. I went to the principal's room and handed it in. The last bell, indicating that classes were over, sounded at that moment.

2

The Apprehensions of Faith

25 March 2010. It must have been some time past 8 p.m.—dinner time at home. Father Pichalakkat called me on my mobile phone.

'There's talk that there is some problem with our BCom semester question-paper,' he said.

I asked anxiously, 'What kind of problem?'

'There's some issue with the question you had set for punctuation.'

'Who told you this, Father?'

'It has come on Indiavision channel.'

I was flabbergasted.

'Did you see the news, Father?'

'No, a relative of mine from the Gulf who saw the news called me.'

Indiavision is a channel that was founded by a member of the Muslim community.

I explained to Father Pichalakkat that the extract in the question was taken from a book published by the Kerala Bhasha Institute, aided by the Union Ministry for Human Resource Development, and my reason for choosing it.

'Then it's okay,' he said, and disconnected the line. His assurance didn't put my mind at ease, though. A few other concerns rushed into my mind.

The second internal assessment examinations for the undergraduate courses were conducted on 23–24 March 2010. The tests were an hour-and-a-half long—two tests in the morning, and one in the afternoon. The Malayalam test took place between 11.30 a.m. and 1 p.m. on 23 March.

I had invigilation duty that afternoon. As I walked towards Hall No. C1–06 where the test was to be conducted, a Muslim girl student of second-semester BCom approached me and asked, 'Did you set the question paper for Malayalam?'

'Yes,' I replied.

'Would you be marking the papers too?'

'Yes.'

'I have answered the punctuation question after changing the names of the persons in it. Would that be a problem?'

'It doesn't matter what names have been used. As long as the punctuation marks are correct, you will get marks.'

By that time, we both had entered the hall. Later, when she came to hand over her answer sheet, I said softly, 'There is a story behind that question. I shall narrate it in the class.'

My next class for second-semester BCom was on Friday, 26 March. Using my free time on Wednesday and Thursday, I marked all their papers. All except one had answered the question on punctuation in a regular fashion. Three of the students were Muslims.

The girl who had approached me had not only changed the names, but had also put down her reasons for doing so: 'Sir, I am answering in this way since my faith doesn't permit me to write such a conversation with the names as they are.'

She had changed the names to *aniyan* (younger brother) and *chettan* (older brother). Since not all the punctuations were correct, I gave a weightage of only 75 per cent to that answer. I looked at the answer sheet. It appeared as if she had started to answer using the names in the question paper but her faith had not permitted her to write about a God who addressed someone as a 'sonofabitch'. Would God, the embodiment of love and the most merciful, call anyone by such an abusive term? She had then tried to write the conversation, omitting God's dialogue. Then she scratched out the names that had been written initially and put in new names. Thus had she protected her faith.

'Well, well,' I said to myself, 'though a believer, she is smart.'

At that moment, I recalled another incident. During my time at Nirmala College, there had been a major overhaul of the MA Malayalam syllabus. For the fourth semester, theatre and cinema was introduced as a new subject. When I was a student, cinema was not a subject of study. At an academic level, cinema was marked as an 'untouchable' subject. Thus, although literature students had to learn everything from Kathakali to Kakkarissi Natakam (a folk theatre form), not a single screenplay was part of the syllabus. However, cinema was, even then, the most popular art form among students like me. All discussions on it would happen outside the classroom.

As cinema gained primacy worldwide as the most popular form of art and entertainment in modern times, not merely its screenplays, even its technical aspects became subjects of study in universities. That was how dramaturgy and filmmaking got included in MG University's MA Malayalam Literature syllabus. The curriculum required comparative studies to be undertaken. Prof. T.J. Thomas, our head of department, knew that I had a passion for cinema and plays, and put me in charge of the new subject.

As someone who had written and directed plays during my schooldays, my adolescent dreams had been centred on becoming a playwright and actor like N.N. Pillai. Although I had not made it my vocation, I occasionally directed and acted in amateur plays and kept my connection to the stage alive, until I became a lecturer.

One who has watched enough plays will be able to write and direct plays. At the same time, however many movies one may see, one will not get the nous or capability to direct a movie, since it is a highly technical art form. One can work in this field only if one learns the essentials of its technical side.

I had helped in the scripting of a few movies through some of my friends in the field. I had been to studios in Chennai and was familiar with dubbing and editing. However, I decided that I should start teaching classes on cinema only after learning about this art thoroughly. So, on holidays, I would visit film and TV serial shooting locations in Ernakulam, Thiruvananthapuram, and Palakkad at my own expense, working as an assistant and doing sundry other jobs without remuneration. After listening to my suggestions on editing, dubbing, and mixing, the director of a mega serial in Malayalam was keen to hand over its post-production work to me. Since that was neither my métier nor my purpose, I declined graciously and returned to my students to teach them theatre and cinema.

Since, in those days, there was a dearth of good reading and reference material in Malayalam about cinema, my classes were the only source of information for my students; no one missed my classes if they could help it. Also, because the students liked both cinema and stage plays, and they may have been keen to learn about their technical side, they stayed engaged and the classes were lively and participative.

For the students who had so diligently worked in the course, I wanted to screen some of the celebrated movies of world cinema. The college had an LCD projector and therefore I went to Ernakulam and bought CDs of *Rashomon, Bicycle Thieves, Pather Panchali,* and other famous movies. These were screened for my students in the seminar hall which is adjacent to the library.

One day, Iranian director Majid Majidi's *The Color of Paradise* was being screened. It's an artfully wrought but popular movie featuring the heart-rending story of a blind child named Mohammad. Since I had to go to another class, I stepped out a few minutes after the movie had begun. As I walked towards the department, I saw a student who should have been watching the movie coming towards me. A Muslim girl, she had a ready smile on her face, which deepened the dimples on her cheeks. Her essays on cinema were of a high standard. Her interventions in the seminar on 'Acting in Theatre and Cinema' were also commendable.

As she walked past, I asked her, 'Why . . . aren't you going to watch the movie?'

'I don't like it,' she said. The smile on her face vanished.

'Don't you like movies?' I was curious.

She said impassively, 'Movies are haram for us.'

I stood there, confounded. Then a deep sadness descended over me like a fog.

When I had recovered sufficiently, I thought, 'It's a good thing that classes are over for the day. How would I have been able to lecture about cinema in front of her?'

As I sat ruminating gloomily on such challenges from religious fundamentalism and conservative faith faced by earnest and progressive college teachers, the mobile phone rang again. It was a journalist. He was trying to verify the story aired by a TV channel. I explained the thought process behind the impugned question.

As soon as I hung up, I immediately telephoned Dr T.M. Joseph, the principal of Newman College. I was reluctant to call him so late, but fortunately he had not gone to sleep. After telling him of the news on the TV channel, I explained the details about the formulation of the question. From his reaction I could gauge that he already knew about the matter.

'Shouldn't we speak to the manager?' I asked him.

'Not now. He must have gone to sleep. I'll contact him in the morning.'

He ended the call.

3

A Criminal Is Born

26 March 2010. I was woken up from a disturbed sleep by the ringing of my phone. I rubbed my sleepy eyes and looked at the screen—it was Father Pichalakkat.

'The college yard is teeming with the police,' he blurted out without preamble. There was no fear or concern in his voice, only amusement. So, his words didn't upset me. I looked at the wall-clock; it was only getting to 6 a.m.

Before I could speak, he said, 'Sir, I think it would be better if you didn't come to college today.'

'Why?' I asked evenly.

'Things may blow up if you come.'

'How "blow up"? I haven't done anything wrong. Then why fear?' I tried to argue without acrimony.

'Whatever it is, you shouldn't come to the college today.' There was an uncharacteristic edge to his voice.

'Are you worried about the police presence? If they are there, isn't it for our protection?'

'I wouldn't count on it.' He sounded irascible.

'Shouldn't I be present to explain the background and relevance of the question? Shouldn't we remove their misapprehensions?'

'It's not you alone who should do this. We are all there.'

I thought his words made sense. Since I was the question-setter, it would be better if the others in the faculty set up the defence. I had explained everything to Father Pichalakkat and the principal. And they were eloquent enough to impress this upon the interlocutors. Trusting them, I said, 'If in your opinion, I shouldn't come to the college, let it be so.'

'I'll call you later,' he said and cut the line.

The next call came almost immediately—Dr Sankararaman, a professor in the physics department, and a close friend of mine. He lived close to the college. His words were full of alarm and concern. Things weren't looking good. The talk was that the Prophet had been insulted and posters had been stuck on the college walls.

'The Prophet has been *insulted*?!'

I was stunned. In the next moment, a flash of lightning seared through my mind. It was the realization that the truncation of P.T. Kunju Muhammed's name to 'Muhammed' was being misinterpreted to create the controversy. I went numb.

'I had used the name Muhammed in the question paper. Nevertheless, isn't that a common name? If it were to connote the Prophet's name, shouldn't it have been Nabi (Arabic for Prophet and used thus in Malayalam) or Mohammad Nabi?' My voice was tremulous.

'All that is true. But if they create this false propaganda, who knows where this will end up?' He sounded distressed. He rang off saying he would call later.

He called again in a short while. He told me that notices had been distributed in mosques in and around Thodupuzha exhorting the faithful to protest. He also advised me to get in touch with the member of Parliament from Idukki, P.T. Thomas, the candidate of the United Democratic Front alliance in which the Muslim League was a constituent.

P.T. Thomas and I have known each other from the time we were teenagers. We have even broken bread together and slept under the same roof. I told him about the controversy and requested him to call the Muslim community leaders in Thodupuzha to remove their misapprehensions and help avoid any untoward incidents.

Then I called K.I. Antony, a local leader in Thodupuzha, and appealed to him to intervene. He had been my colleague in Nirmala College, a professor in the Malayalam department.

The next call that I received was from Thodupuzha Deputy Superintendent of Police K.G. Simon. I narrated the background of the controversial question, and my non-culpability in the whole matter.

After that, there was a call on my landline—an unknown Muslim from Thodupuzha. After hearing the pronouncements in the mosque and exhortations to the community to protest, he had somehow discovered my number and called to find out the truth. I clarified the matter to him and he seemed satisfied.

His parting words were: 'Thank you, sir. I understand the situation completely. The question now is: How can this be relayed to everybody here? Moreover, there are people in my community hell-bent on fomenting trouble.'

I noticed a cup of black tea that someone had brought to me while I was busy on the telephone. I decided to drink it although it had gone cold. But before I could take a sip the phone rang again. It was a senior professor from the college, who I knew had connections with police officers in Thodupuzha. He advised me to move out of my house and stay away for some time.

'Do you think someone may attack me?'

'Not only that, there is also a possibility that the police may arrest you.'

'Why? What crime have I committed?'

'Irrespective of that, there is a move to do that.'

'Where did you get this information, sir? From the police department?'

'You may consider it so. Anyway, don't let them arrest you now.'

He had always been my well-wisher. I felt that I must heed his advice.

Thereafter, everything happened on a war footing. I rushed through my ablutions; I asked my wife, Salomi, to pack a bag with a change of clothes. By the time I got dressed, she had come in with another cup of tea.

'No,' I refused, not wanting to waste time. I decided to stay with a friend in Ernakulam and told my wife and son not to reveal my whereabouts. Should anyone enquire about me, they should tell them I had left for Thodupuzha town. I asked my son, Mithun, to drop me off at the Muvattupuzha bus terminal.

4

The Accused Goes Underground

A bus to Ernakulam was ready to leave. Wanting to leave Muvattupuzha with no further loss of time, I boarded it although it was going via Kakkanad, a route that is not the most comfortable. I suddenly remembered that my cousin, Joycy, a novelist, had retreated to a lodge in Kakkanad to complete his book. I bought a ticket only up to Kakkanad.

By the time we reached Kakkanad, it was 9.30 a.m. I realized that I was starving, so I went into one of the restaurants nearby. However, I found that I had no appetite. I ordered a cup of tea and took out my phone to call Joycy. Then I remembered my friend Philip Edayar, who stayed in Edappally. Although I had been to his house before, I couldn't recall the route. When I called, he was at home. Asking him for directions, I told him briefly that I was in a serious situation and would explain everything after reaching his place. He instructed me to board any bus headed to Ernakulam and alight at the Alumchuvadu stop. He picked me up on his motorbike.

As soon as we reached his place, I asked him to switch on the TV. One of the channels was telecasting live the scenes in Thodupuzha in connection with the question-paper controversy. Without my having to narrate anything, Philip understood everything. Protest marches, from as far away as Erattupetta, Aluva, and Perumbavoor, were headed towards Newman College. The police were preventing them from entering the college. There was a press release by the college management announcing my suspension as the Malayalam department head. However, the protestors did not disperse and continued to mill around the college entrance.

My state of mind was like that of a person—too straitlaced to undo the top button of his shirt even at the height of summer—being stripped naked without warning. Although I was mortified by the suspension order, I consoled myself with the thought that if it helped in mollifying the protestors, it was a good move.

Apart from the two of us, only Philip's aged mother was at home. She was a cancer survivor who had undergone surgery a few times. I gulped down the tea she brought me.

The principal's announcement on the news broadcast about the dialogue having been an extract from MG University's reference text, written by P.T. Kunju Muhammed, had somewhat appeased the crowd. This gave me some solace. I used the respite to call home.

My house had been surrounded by police. The college manager, Reverend Father Thomas Malekudi, had telephoned to tell Mithun to ensure that I made myself scarce and avoided the college campus as there was a strong likelihood that the police would arrest me. I told my wife and son that I had taken refuge with Philip and that they should call me only on his landline number. Then I called Dr Sankararaman to check on the situation in the college. It seemed that things were still fraught.

More shocks awaited me. The pro vice chancellor appeared on TV, repudiating the fact that any book of P.T. Kunju Mohammed was a prescribed reference text of the university. I felt dejected that people in high places should make such an announcement without checking its veracity; it was disquieting since this could lead to the worsening of an already bad situation. The State Assembly was in session on that day. When the issue of the question paper was raised on the floor of the House, the minister of education, unaware, or perhaps uninformed, of the truth, chose to respond emotionally. The cherry on the top was the collector's order to prosecute me for non-bailable offences. That left me dumbfounded.

Philip tried to comfort me, 'Isn't it the courts that decide whether to give bail or not?' When I had heard non-bailable offences, I was under the impression that I could never get bail. Philip's observation disabused me of that notion.

I called Joy Mathew, a professor of commerce in our college. He was a graduate in law and had good knowledge of the Code of Criminal Procedure and the like. As a good friend of mine, he had maintained a respectable distance from the police and the protestors. Yet, he kept himself informed and constantly evaluated the situation. He assured me that I need not be exercised over the case and that he would do all that was required for me to obtain anticipatory bail. We decided to approach advocate N.M. Mathew, the husband of one of the retired professors from our college, and have him file the bail application. When Joy Mathew said that he was Thodupuzha's leading criminal lawyer and things would go smoothly with him handling my case, I felt reassured. He, however, cautioned me that it may take a couple of days for the bail order to come, and I shouldn't fall into the hands of the police until then.

Where would I hide for two days? It wasn't enough that I merely avoid the police because if I were to inadvertently run into any of the fanatics, my very life would be in danger! Philip's house was no longer safe—I had made a number of calls from the landline.

I had some friends in Mulavukad in Vypeen Island—actually they were Joycy's friends—but I didn't have their contact numbers. Philip called Joycy and told him that I was in trouble, and that he should come over urgently.

It was close to 1 p.m. when I called Joy Mathew again, anxious to know the developments in Thodupuzha. The news was that the protestors were forcibly closing shops and creating an atmosphere of intimidation. Furthermore, the news that the protestors had toppled an idol near a Krishna temple had infuriated the Hindus, who had now congregated in large numbers. I prayed fervently that it wouldn't lead to a communal riot and that not a drop of blood be spilled.

Just as I hung up, my phone rang. I misread the number as that of the professor who had advised me to flee my house. It turned out to be the Muvattupuzha DySP, Sabu Mathew. After introducing himself as the son-in-law of Xavier, the former principal of Nirmala College, he told me that my life was in danger and that if I could tell him where I was, he would come and rescue me. I felt that this was a ruse to arrest me. I quickly replied that I would return the call, cut the line and switched off my phone.

I regretted having answered the call. I had nightmarish visions of the cyber cell department of the police tracking me down, leading to my arrest. I had to get away. I had only Rs 800 on my person. If Joycy had come, I could have borrowed some money from him. I got Philip to ring him again. 'I'm just leaving' was what he said. I felt disappointed and angry.

By this time, Philip's mother had set the table for lunch. I was in no mood to eat, but Philip insisted I eat something and dragged me to the table saying that we would finish lunch by the time Joycy arrived.

I looked at the spread on the table. Despite her illness, Philip's mother had made a lot of dishes for my sake. I served myself some rice and a curry made with thick buttermilk and started to eat. However, the food refused to go down my throat. It took great effort to swallow the first morsel. Saying that I was unable to eat, I drank some water and rose from the table. As they could appreciate my mental turmoil, neither Philip nor his mother pressed me to eat.

I telephoned Joy Mathew again and asked him to tell my friend, T.A. Joy, a lecturer in Nirmala College, Muvattupuzha, to take my wife and son to his home. I also gently reminded him that remaining underground was not easy and that he should expedite my bail application.

He assured me that it would be done soon. 'Because of the current tense situation, it may not happen today. I assure you it will be done tomorrow. Don't call me on this number again. Call on Bindu's number.' He gave me the telephone number of his wife, Bindu, an engineer in BSNL.

His words assuaged my fears to a great extent. Suddenly I felt confident that I could face the adversity with courage. As the gloom lifted, I could see the humour in my situation. I smiled and told myself, 'From this moment, the accused goes underground.'

The sound of an approaching vehicle made me peep through the curtains timidly, fully expecting to see a police jeep; thankfully it was only Joycy's car. As he hadn't watched TV, he had no idea what had happened. As soon as he was brought up to date, he looked at me rather helplessly.

'I need to stay in hiding somewhere, out of sight of the police and the fanatics,' I said.

'But where?' asked Joycy, befuddled.

Before writing his novel *Harbour*, Joycy and I had made boat trips all along the waterways in and around Kochi, in search of a setting for the novel. I asked if he could take the help of some of his friends and arrange for me to hide out in one of the islets we had seen during that trip.

'That won't work,' he said.

'Then where else?'

'Shall we go to some lodge near Thrippunithura?' That suggestion didn't appeal to me.

'Drop me off at a bus stop. The rest we'll decide later,' I said.

We bid Philip and his mother goodbye and left quickly.

'What about Alappuzha?' I asked, when we got into the car.

He didn't reply. I myself discarded the idea presuming that the lodging and boarding charges could be expensive. Upon my asking, he gave me the names of a couple of cheap lodges in Thiruvananthapuram. By that time, we had reached Vyttila junction. He parked the car a little away from the bus stop.

'This is a four-road junction. You can go in any direction. Don't tell me where you plan to go. If the police ask me, I may blurt it out.'

'Okay. So be it.'

Appreciating his sincerity, I asked, 'Do you have any money on you?'

He handed over the Rs 2000 he had with him. That brought the total amount in my pocket to Rs 2800, sufficient to see me through two or three days, provided I scrimped a bit.

As I got out of the car, Joycy said, 'Just one thing: don't make any calls from where you are staying or even the same town. It would be worth it to even travel two or three hours to make a call.'

'Okay, you can leave now,' I said, seeing him off.

I stood at the crossroads as if it were the centre of the earth.

5

Georgekutty, the Novelist

If I say that I had no idea where to go, that would not be true. When Joycy shot down my idea of weathering the storm in some islet near Mulavukad, the next place that sprang to my mind was Palakkad. Only after setting my heart on Palakkad, had I discussed other possible locations with Joycy. Why I had chosen Palakkad needs an explanation, which I shall give in due course.

I had not mentioned Palakkad to Joycy because I knew his nature as well as he knew himself. I also knew that should the police question him, he would spill everything. Therefore, I had decided that if I was going anywhere other than a place arranged by him, I wouldn't breathe a word of it to him.

I still believed that whatever one does, it should be done as faultlessly as possible. I was going underground for the first time in my life. The only other person who knew that I was now at this bus stop was Joycy—the only chink in my armour. I started to view even him with suspicion. Although I had watched him drive away, I wondered whether, out of natural human curiosity, he had doubled back and hidden himself to stealthily see where I was headed.

I didn't want to leave anything to chance. I took a bus headed towards Fort Kochi, that is in the opposite direction, and paid the minimum charge. I got off at the second stop, crossed the road and hopped on a bus going the other way, towards Aluva.

Like the proverbial ostrich with its head in the sand, I kept my face averted, gazing at the view outside the window and studiedly avoiding the eyes of the other passengers on the bus. As the bus progressed along the national highway bypass, I noticed police jeeps parked on the side of pocket roads opening out into service roads off the highway. Perhaps the police had been drawn to the Edappally area by the signals from the mobile phone I had used while I was at Philip's house. Whatever it was, I got a smidgen of the sense of gratification that fugitives feel when they get away from right under the noses of the police.

From Aluva I took a bus to Angamaly, and then on to Thrissur. The torrid summer breeze dehydrated and enervated me; my lips felt dry and my throat, parched. I alighted at the Thrissur bus terminal with the intention of slaking my thirst, but then I saw that a bus for Palakkad was ready to depart. It was almost 6 p.m. and the next bus could probably be another half hour away. I hurriedly clambered aboard the bus, which had started to move. Thankfully, the bus had vacant seats; up until then, I had to mostly stand through my journey. I occupied a seat meant for two passengers and bought a ticket to Palakkad.

It was almost nightfall when I reached my destination. The first thing I did upon disembarking from the KSRTC bus was to seek out a restaurant. My eyes alighted on Indian Coffee House across the terminal. I was like the hornbill, a perennially thirsty bird in Malayali folklore. After washing up, I gulped down the glass of water the waiter placed before me. My breath caught in my throat, but I somehow managed to gasp out my order, 'Two chapattis and a vegetable curry.'

As soon as the waiter left, I took the jug of water and poured myself another two or three glasses of water, so much so that my bloated stomach had no place for the food which the waiter eventually brought to me. Nonetheless, as starving was not an option, I slowly finished my meal. When the waiter appeared with the bill, I asked, 'Is there a cheap lodge nearby?'

'There is Sithara Guest House. Their rates are comparatively cheap,' he answered.

'Is it close by?'

'Half a kilometre,' he replied as he swung around to deliver the bill to the adjacent table.

'How are the rooms? Do they have all amenities?'

'The rooms are okay. But there are no restaurants nearby,' was his parting shot as he moved away to another table.

I was at the counter paying my bill when he hurried over to me and indicated the direction I should take. I was not surprised by his hospitality and thoughtfulness despite his punishing schedule. I knew it was typical of Palakkad's denizens—I have experienced their friendly, helpful and goodhearted nature before.

My previous visits to Palakkad were in connection with the TV and movie shootings, staying in hotels there and in Nenmara. Along with my local friends, I have spent many nights out in the open—in the paddy drying grounds and flat rocks of Kollengode and Panangattiri—gazing at the night sky, enjoying the music of the wind rustling through the palmyra leaves, and falling asleep in that tranquillity.

One day, I remember, I had ordered breakfast at a middling restaurant in Palakkad. The ghee roast dosa was singed at the edge, and since I dislike the charred taste, I left that bit uneaten. The manager noticed this. He summoned the waiter and ordered him to give me another dosa although I told him that the portion I had eaten had been sufficient for me. When I returned to the table after washing my hands, I found that I had been billed only for the tea which I had had with the dosa. Despite my determination to pay for the dosa, the manager refused to take the money. There have been many such extraordinary and humbling experiences in Palakkad.

Apart from their goodwill, it was my belief that the cost of living here was lower than in other towns and cities. The lightness of my pocket played a crucial role in my choice of a bolthole.

I eventually reached Sithara Guest House which, fortunately, had rooms available. The tariff for a room with TV was Rs 240, and Rs 200 without TV.

The man at the reception counter asked, 'Sir, haven't you stayed here before?'

I replied in the affirmative, deciding that this was neither the time nor the place for disarming honesty. He must have found my features similar to those of someone who had stayed there earlier. I had no quarrel with that.

As I started to write my name in the vernacular in the register, the incognito-director in me tugged hard at the reins and made me quickly transform the first syllable I had put down for Joseph to Georgekutty. Thus, in the guise of a writer from an interior village in Idukki who planned to write a novel set in Palakkad, I jauntily followed the bellboy (a misnomer for a gentleman over sixty, who had the sacred sandalwood paste smeared across his forehead) to room number 102.

I liked the room—the bathroom was clean; it had an intercom telephone; and TV. It was a steal for Rs 240. The elderly staff member brought in a jug of water and a glass. I switched on the TV and surfed the channels. After a look at the news flash 'Prohibitory Orders in Thodupuzha Following Question Paper Controversy', I went in for a bath and then emerged feeling invigorated. But soon enough, like seeds sprouting after the summer rain, fretful thoughts started to crop up in my mind.

I expected the police or fanatics to barge into my room, to either put me in manacles or assassinate me. More than that, thoughts of my family troubled me. How had this calamity that had swept in with the force of a tsunami affected them? Had they moved to my friend's home? Or had they decided to stick it out at our own place? How could they have any peace in a house which was under twenty-four-hour surveillance by the police? Wouldn't they be worried about me? Salomi and Mithun knew fully well what I had been accused of; but my daughter, Amy, who was in the hostel, wouldn't know the truth. How much distress would news from secondary sources cause her?

I broke down and wept.

I felt someone within me chide me for crying like a coward. I got up resolutely and washed away my tears and along with them, my worries.

I drank a glass of water and lay down to sleep.

I started to recite my nightly prayer, one that I had composed for myself. One part of it was: 'O God, control my thoughts. My words and deeds should be truthful, just, and appropriate.' When I recited that part, my eyes welled up again. I asked God: 'Why have You forsaken me, when I have always prayed to You thus? Why did You let me frame that question that has become so controversial? Couldn't You have set another one?'

God remained silent.

6

An Affair with Pappadams

I slept lightly, waking up the next morning at 6 a.m. I brushed my teeth and went out of the lodge. A few minutes' walk brought me to a Milma milk-vending booth, which was also serving tea. After a cup of tea, I went in search of a telephone booth. In my pocket was the telephone number of Joy Mathew's wife, Bindu.

Bindu herself answered the phone.

'I am T.J. Joseph. May I speak to Joy Mathew?'

'Sir hasn't returned yet; he left yesterday.'

'Then, I shall call later.'

'All right.' The line was disconnected.

Joy Mathew hadn't reached home! This could mean that he had been up all night preparing my anticipatory bail application along with the lawyer. It would possibly be filed today. I felt my tension abate.

On my way back to the lodge, I picked up a copy of the *Malayala Manorama* daily. I opened it only after shutting the door behind me in my room.

Even though it was the Palakkad edition, 'Question-paper Controversy: Prohibitory Orders in Thodupuzha' was front-page news. The protests had turned violent, prompting the Idukki collector to impose prohibitory injunctions. According to the police, I had disappeared. There was also a picture of a procession by local political leaders to re-establish communal amity.

In my fifty-two years, this was the first news item about me—that too, front-page news. A medallion of recognition for twenty-five years of sincere, committed, distinguished service as a teacher! Why are newspapers named *Manorama* (one who delights the mind) and such like, I lamented. Mine, for one, was far from delighted. I didn't read the rest of the news.

The nearest restaurant was Indian Coffee House. The distance was more than half a kilometre. As someone living incognito, I ought not to be seen walking around at large. I decided that I would skip breakfast even though I was hungry. I could save some money too.

At 1 p.m. I finally headed for Indian Coffee House. It was crowded. Their lunch menu didn't offer a wide choice. Sambar had been replaced by another curry; the only other dish was rasam. I was given a pappadam too.

The person sitting beside me, a conductor on a private bus, was apparently a regular here. He was wolfing down his lunch in a hurry. He offered me his pappadam; he explained that he was allergic to the baking soda used in its preparation. I was not too fond of pappadam either; I usually crumbled it into the sambar to enhance the saltiness. The Palakkad style of cooking wasn't exactly tickling my palate. I thought I should accept his pappadam; in any case, he was offering it voluntarily. After all, wasn't the entire citizenry of Palakkad my host?

After pulverizing the two pappadams and sprinkling it over the rice, I started tucking into the meal. I did get the feeling that the pappadam-maker had been over-generous with the baking soda. However, I couldn't share the sentiment because, by then, the conductor, who had finished his meal, had left the place.

By the time I washed up and gargled after the meal, my tongue was tingling, throat itching and my lips felt puffy. It wasn't only for the bus conductor, the Palakkad pappadam had turned into an allergen for me as well.

As I walked back to the lodge, I could feel my lips swelling even more. Strangely enough, when I reached the room and looked in the mirror, they didn't look too bad. Nonetheless, those pappadams effectively fended off my other anxieties for the next few hours.

As soon as the pappadams' dalliance with me abated, my mind was again inundated with questions about my anticipatory bail. I set off from the lodge again and walked farther than I had done that morning till I came across another telephone booth.

'Hello.' I felt relieved when I heard Bindu's voice at the other end.

'I'm T.J. Joseph . . . wanted to know where things stand now . . . is Joy Mathew back?' the words tumbled out of me in a rush.

Bindu replied in a guarded whisper, 'I'm in the office now. Sir had called. Said the bail application will be filed either today or on Monday. One more thing . . . please don't call me like this.'

'Just one more thing . . .' I spoke hurriedly, '. . . my wife and son?'

'They've left for Murickassery. Salomi's brother has taken them.'

'Please delete my calls from your mobile.'

'I shall do,' she said and disconnected swiftly.

As I strolled back to the lodge, my heart felt light. My wife and son were safe with my mother-in-law and brother-in-law, Saju. Their house was beside the Murickassery police station. Their neighbours were the policemen living in the police quarters. What was there to fear?

My own situation was different. I was lost in the wilderness of uncertainty. How was I to get out? Preoccupied with these worrying thoughts, I ended up losing my way.

Should I ask someone for directions? I decided against it. I was supposed to be invisible. Should I hire an autorickshaw? But then, I shouldn't tell him to take me to Sithara Guest House. I could ask to be taken to the KSRTC bus terminal from where I knew my way back.

I flagged down an autorickshaw. All through the ride, I kept throwing furtive glances at the driver. If at some point he realized that he had transported a fugitive, what would his statement to the police be? He would say that he had dropped me off at the KSRTC terminal. And what would the police make of that? That I had reached Palakkad and taken a bus out of Palakkad. With that, their investigations in Palakkad would end.

I returned to the lodge, deeply regretting having used up Rs 15 for auto fare out of my meagre funds—not out of carelessness, but out of abundant caution.

Back within the four walls of my room, my anxieties kicked into a higher gear. Why had Bindu asked me not to call? Did she sound scared?

Was she under police surveillance? If they suspected her, wouldn't they be checking her mobile? Had she deleted my calls? Even if her call register was clean, wouldn't the police's cyber cell be able to figure out her call history? Wouldn't it be clear to them that my calls to her originated from Palakkad?

Even though the calls had been made from a public booth, it had been a blunder to make the calls from here. That too twice. Joycy had expressly warned me against it. I had disregarded his long years of experience saving many of his protagonists from the clutches of the police or villains who were in hot pursuit, by having them go underground. Feeling conscience-stricken and deeply disturbed, I paced the room.

Suddenly, I decided I should leave Palakkad; I didn't feel safe here anymore. But go where?

Where would I find another inexpensive and inconspicuous refuge like this lodge? Wandering around in the open, looking for a new safe house, could be risky because those in pursuit could recognize me.

I experienced the acute insecurity of fugitives forced unexpectedly to flee their hole-in-the-wall. Yet, I was determined to move out. As for the rest, I would cross that bridge when I came to it.

When I checked out, I didn't know where I was headed. Crossing the road towards the KSRTC terminal, I noticed a private bus parked by the roadside. The destination board read Guruvayoor. I got on board, the last passenger to do so.

The bus was crowded; even standing room was limited. A swift appraisal of my fellow passengers confirmed that most of them seemed to be returning to their villages after a visit to the city. They all had homes to return to, destinations to reach, I mused. Lucky people; I envied them.

I got a seat after about an hour and a half of travel. Night had surreptitiously fallen. I hadn't boarded this bus entirely without forethought. It was common knowledge that the police seldom raided hotels and lodges close to places of worship and medical colleges. I had also seen cheap lodges in the vicinity of the Guruvayoor temple.

By the time the bus reached Guruvayoor, it was past 10 p.m. The well-lit road and the flow of worshippers meant there was no need to ask for directions. A cup of strong tea at one of the wayside stalls re-energized me.

I strolled up and down a few times, sizing up the hostelry on either side. I went into what seemed to be the oldest among them—modest, double-storeyed, with a tiled-roof. I asked the sleepy gentleman at the reception if a room was available. He nodded in reply.

'How much for a single room?'

He yawned, releasing thick alcohol fumes into the air and said, 'One hundred and seventy-five.'

That I liked. 'I'll take it.'

'There's just one hitch. The room is on the first floor and the toilet and bathroom on the ground floor.'

'Don't you have one with an attached bathroom?'

'No.'

I muttered that it wouldn't work and walked out.

When I checked with a better-looking lodge, the rent was Rs 350. When, willy-nilly, I decided to take it, the lodge keeper wanted an ID proof.

I didn't have one on me, not that I could have shown it to him even if I did.

'I have no ID card. When I have come to see the Lord, why would I need ID cards and things like that?' I demanded ingenuously.

'To see Guruvayoorappan, you don't need it; to get a room here, you do,' he replied blandly. 'If you have a driving licence that should be enough.'

'I have one, but it's not with me.' I looked at him beseechingly, hoping for some sympathy.

'Then I can't give you a room.'

I tried to bluff: 'I stayed here two years ago. At the time, there were no such demands.'

'It has only been a year since ID proof has been made compulsory. It is mandated by the police. If we don't comply, we'll be screwed.'

I had no quarrel with the need for such rules. Nevertheless, I left the place realizing that even good rules could turn into impossible hurdles in one's life.

Now where to?

The precarious state of my finances precluded my selecting one of the posh hostelries. Should I return to the first one even if it meant the inconvenience of having the bathroom on a floor below?

The 'receptionist' was standing in front of that lodge. He looked lit up; he must have gulped down two more drinks. He was swaying slightly too.

As soon as I reached him, I said, 'I need the room.'

'Show me your ID.' He stretched out his hand towards me.

'Can't I get a room without an ID?' I wheedled.

'Without your ID, you won't get a room anywhere in Guruvayoor,' he said, swaying some more. He looked at me narrow-eyed with suspicion, 'Who are you anyway? Where do you work? Are you a policeman? You're quite tall and look strong.'

It was true that I was bigger than he was.

'I am not the police,' I said guardedly.

'There's a dormitory near the temple run by the *devaswom* (the temple administration). You could try there. Even if you show an ID, since you are single and without your family, getting a room in the lodge could be difficult—'

'Okay.' I started to walk towards the temple.

After a short distance, I saw a paid bathroom. The charge was Rs 7. I had a bath, extracted a fresh mundu from my bag and put it on.

I asked around for the dormitory, but no one could direct me to it. Then I saw that there were people sitting or sleeping near the public wedding platform. The floor looked clean. I settled down, with my bag as my pillow.

Exhausted by the journey and with the soporific effect of the bath, I fell asleep almost immediately. However, my peaceful repose was short-lived. I was woken up by loud clanging sounds and opened my eyes to see security guards beating their truncheons against the steel fence around the wedding platform to wake us up and force us to vacate the place. My watch showed it was 2 a.m. Everyone cleared out quickly. The cleaners appeared and started to sweep the area.

I went out, wondering what to do next. The people who had been driven out had taken their place in the queue to enter the sanctum sanctorum. Facing the sanctum sanctorum, I said, 'My Krishna, although I haven't come to see you, it pains me to go away without seeing you after having come this far. My times are bad. Otherwise, I would've been rash enough to try . . .'[1]

After bidding goodbye to the Lord, I walked on in the direction of the KSRTC bus terminal. It was deserted. At the information counter, I asked about the timing of the bus to Thrissur. I got a lackadaisical reply that services for all destinations started only after 4 a.m.

I meant to find a lodge in Thrissur and stay there.

Since the waiting room was deserted, I hesitated to sit there alone. Only after a few other passengers went in did I join them. Although I had thought I could sit there and catch some shut-eye, the mosquitoes, which seemed to have taken a vow to scourge, didn't allow me any.

7

Lookout Notice

When my bus reached Thrissur, it was still dark. I tried many of the modest lodges near the KSRTC terminal. Most of them had no vacant rooms; those that had, were very shabby.

Exhausted, I eventually decided to take a single room in one of them but was asked again to produce an ID card. I said I had no ID card but did not leave the place.

Two young men arrived just then, asking for a room. The manager asked for their IDs, but they too had none. He refused them a room. After they left, he muttered, as if to himself, but audible to me: 'They don't even have a towel with them, forget a bag, and they want a room! Who knows what kind of criminals they are? We often have police officers staying with us.'

That statement about the police scared me and I decided not to take a room there. But perhaps because the manager felt that I was a gentleman compared to those young men, he pushed the register towards me and asked me to enter my details.

Fearful that if I now refused the room, he would get suspicious and summon the police, I put down my details in the register. This time I was T. Srinivasan, Thekkekuttu House, Ettumanoor, Kottayam. And I signed in as Srinivasan.

He summoned the bellboy and handed over the key. I didn't like the room at all. In addition to being shabby, there was no air circulation and although it was small room, there were two beds. Two beds in a single room?

After my ablutions, I lay down. Although I had had a bath, I felt warm. I switched on the ceiling fan; it had no regulator and it swung and swayed causing a small racket. Sleep tarried at the door, afraid to come in.

I rang for the bellboy, gave him Rs 10, and ordered tea. He returned with half a cup, and pocketed the balance Rs 5 as a tip for himself. The accountant in me chided that this was wanton profligacy in my current financial state.

After having the tea, I lay on the bed, thinking—there was no dearth of time to think.

Staying in this lodge was risky. Policemen were staying on the upper floors. To have food, I would need to step out. It was close to the bus station; chances of being recognized were high. I felt suffocated, especially with the lack of ventilation. Should I leave? And go where? Who would give me a room without an ID?

If only I could find a room like the one in Sithara Guest House. I had not been asked for an ID card because I looked familiar. Otherwise, I would have been denied a room there as well. I heartily regretted leaving that place.

Why shouldn't I go back? If the police had some suspicions following my phone calls, they must have made enquiries already and not found me there. Or, they may never check.

I was done with hunting for rooms.

When I went to the reception, the same person was at the counter. I placed the key on the counter and told him I was leaving.

He looked at the room number on the key and the register and asked, 'Was it a double room?'

'No. A single room. I was told the rent was Rs 180.'

'How many beds were there in the room?'

'There were two. But I needed only one.'

He nodded as if he understood it all.

'The room given to you is a double room. The rent is Rs 320.'

'That is a mistake from your side. I asked for a single room. You should rectify it,' I argued.

'If I change it in the register, they'll suspect hanky-panky. I've not been working here for even a month.'

I felt angry and sad.

'Why should I be penalized for your mistake? I will only pay the single room rate.'

How could I bear losing Rs 140 from my rapidly thinning purse?

'Brother, if you won't pay it, I will have to pay it and I am paid a pittance here.'

From his conciliatory tone, I realized one thing: I would have to bear the charges for a double room. I had already paid an advance of Rs 500. If I put my foot down now and created a scene, a crowd would gather. I knew I was telling the truth, but the register would belie my assertion. Apart from this, I was supposed to be keeping a low profile. I would have to suffer many iniquities.

'You do what you want.'

He did what he wanted. I lost Rs 140.

It was almost 11 a.m. when I reached Palakkad. I was famished. I went into Indian Coffee House; it was too early for lunch and I made do with two idlis for temporary relief, planning to return after a couple of hours.

The sun was blazing hot. As I approached the main road that led towards Sithara, I saw a police jeep exit the lodge's compound. That unnerved me. Had they come in search of me? Now that they had left, I steeled myself to face whatever was in store and walked into the reception.

Three men stood at the reception counter. I looked at them; they stared back in silence. Was there something amiss? I gathered my courage and asked them, 'Has anyone come here asking for me?'

Although I knew what I meant, they didn't. They said nothing.

'I'm Georgekutty. I was asking if anyone had come asking for Georgekutty.' They exchanged glances but didn't reply, their expressions impassive.

'A friend said he would come at ten o'clock. I was delayed. It's now eleven-thirty. That's why I asked.'

They said no one like that had come. I was relieved.

That also made me realize something. When one is a fugitive, one will suspect anything and everything—one becomes paranoid.

'You have a room, don't you?'

The receptionist nodded. The room given this time was 105; with the same layout as the previous one. I felt greatly relieved and at peace.

Almost as if I had been left adrift and had now managed to return home safely.

The bellboy was a different one. A pair of spectacles adorned his face instead of sandal paste, and he was about ten years younger than the previous one.

'What's your name?' I tried to get friendly.

'Suleiman.' He brought in a jug of water and a glass.

'Which place do you belong to?'

He told me, and added, 'I'm the owner's neighbour,' before asking, 'What about your food, sir?'

'I'll have it outside.'

'All right.' He left the room.

I switched on the TV and flipped through all the channels. It was all unimportant news as far as I was concerned. I lay down but kept the TV on. The drone of the newsreaders could be heard occasionally in my sleep.

By the time I woke up, it was 1.30 p.m. Lunch was beckoning. I got ready to leave. The news was still on, but no longer uninteresting. My photo filled the screen. The police had put out a lookout notice for Prof. T.J. Joseph, head of the Malayalam department of Newman College, Thodupuzha, who was absconding after the question-paper controversy erupted.

The news shook me to the core. I had never expected my photo to be published in the media. The police, more than anybody else, should be aware that if religious fundamentalists were to recognize me, my life would be in danger. Yet, they had done this! Why? The notice had been issued by Manoj Abraham, the Kochi City police commissioner. He was an IPS officer. Where was his common sense?

I immediately understood the imperatives: A mob, which didn't care about the truth, was baying for my blood. In an apology of a democracy, the interests of the mob got weightage over anything else even if those interests were born out of ignorance, against truth and flagrantly unethical. Vote banks comprise such mobs. They shoulder the chair of power.

I recalled the Jewish high priest Caiaphas in the Bible who had recommended that it was expedient that an innocent man should die to appease the mob. The government and the police had adopted the law of the jungle in my case. They had no need to take me alive. If they got my corpse, all the better. Problem solved!

I imagined how the news of my death would come out. Someone informs the police of a dead body seen somewhere. 'What a relief, we have got our man.' They issue a press release. The press and TV media get into a feeding frenzy. 'Suicide or murder?' Debates turn into carnivals. The dam of conjectures and untruths bursts, inundating the public.

The other scene.

My wailing wife; my children unable to contain their grief; my friends and relatives engulfed by their sorrow; my gloomy students; the disinterested, dispassionate general public; and then, those who were rejoicing.

Eventually, the dust would settle.

After a few days, my wife and children would return to their normal lives. That's how the world works.

But how would they survive? Mine was the only income in the family. I shouldn't worry; after my death, they would get family pension. Being under suspension doesn't affect the pension. I too had read the Kerala Service Rules. It says that if the person dies while under suspension, the period of suspension should be counted as part of his service. Was it possible that my death could benefit my family more?

I realized that the issue of the lookout notice would have resulted in my photo being pasted in railway stations, airports, and bus terminals. Now life in hiding would become more and more difficult. I could be killed by a crazed fanatic at any point.

What if the police reached me before a zealot did? Arrest, lock-up, interrogation, court-appearance, cross-examination, all of this would follow, and none of them fazed me. I had the courage to face anything. Or I would find the courage when the time came.

After all the torment, what if the court punished me? I would have neither a job, nor my pension. Which meant, for my family, my death was the better option.

So, should I die? Didn't that make more sense?

I looked at the fan above me.

If I were to kill myself, would my wife understand the rationale behind my decision? And my children? Father, we didn't expect this of you. What cowardice . . . such a shame! Would they be spared that lifelong sorrow? Can family pension or other benefits ever be able to wash off the stigma? What will the thousands of students whom I have taught think of me? I have enjoined them, both overtly and through example, to go forward in the arena of life without losing their composure before their opponents and always displaying great sportsmanlike spirit.

That me . . . ? It would be such a disgrace. But then, what crime have I committed to turn tail and flee?

A congregation of imbeciles, instead of reaching into the infinity of knowledge, withered into the darkness of blind faith and raised a hue and cry. A non-Malayali collector, with little or no knowledge of the language, immediately passed an order to prosecute me. Police officers without powers of discrimination, sensibility and discernment registered the complaint. And now, in effect consigning me to my death, they have released the lookout notice including my photo.

Would all this be possible in a country with a thriving, mature democracy? Shouldn't proceedings have been instituted against me after an official enquiry by someone with superior knowledge and experience in language and literature to find out if I—a professor with over twenty-five years of experience—had erred in setting a question for my students?

Was this justice?

Was this the administration of justice?

Let the powers of evil and the morons who sing hosannas to them, ready to do their bidding, pave my path with thorns and nettles of myriad miseries. I shall tread this path, however painful the journey. I was determined.

I am not getting out of this room. After pinning up their lookout notices, let the police and the feckless media wait.

After drinking two glasses of water to temporarily alleviate my pangs of hunger, I marked the start of a hunger campaign.

8

Ottapalam Railway Station

The lookout notice meant the police had intensified their search for me. I expected the police to discover me any time. That would bring down the curtain on my game of hide-and-seek.

Unlike the boisterous game of my childhood, today, there was only me doing the hiding and the entire police force, seeking.

If I were to be taken into custody, I would probably not get to bathe for a couple of days at least, so I always sat ready after my bath. Everything, except for one set of clothes, was kept packed. I put my toiletries back in the bag immediately after using them. I was ready to leave within the minute if the police came for me.

I placed a few blank sheets of paper, with folded margins, and a pen on the table. This was to give the hotel staff the impression that I was a writer. From Sunday, 28 March, when the lookout notice had come out, I hadn't stirred out of my room. I used the water in the jug to fill my tummy.

Unsure of how long this starvation diet would have to continue, I tried to conserve my energy. I lay down most of the time.

Monday, 29 March. I had a bath as soon as I woke up. My yawn reminded me of the bed coffee I was missing. I decided to substitute it with water. I poured out the remaining half a glass of water from the jug and as I picked it up to drink, I espied a mosquito larva in it. Dawn was still some time away and I hadn't the heart to bother the room boy at that ungodly hour. I flicked away the larva, christened it bed coffee, and drank the water.

When Suleiman came in that day, I had him fetch an extra jug of water. Hunger didn't trouble me much; whenever it made its presence felt, I subdued it with glasses of water.

My anticipatory bail application was due that day and, in all probability, would be heard on the same day. The court would be in session from 11 a.m. Whether or not the court granted my bail, the TV news was bound to carry it. I turned on the channel Indiavision, whose coverage of the controversy was the most fervid. Until late in the night, no news of interest to me appeared. While I waited, I surfed the other news channels too, just in case.

Tuesday, 30 March.

When I woke up, I felt a little weak and had a deep craving for a cup of tea. If I requested Suleiman, he would fetch me tea and biscuits or even other food. I had deliberately avoided him for the last two days. If he were in the habit of reading newspapers, he may have come across my photo. The more my interaction with him, the more the chances of his recognizing me, so I kept away from him. Even when he brought in the jugs of water, I kept my face averted. The published photo had me wearing thick-rimmed glasses. Whenever Suleiman came, I made sure I received him without my glasses, although my eyesight was poor. I would also wrap a towel around my head or neck to minimize the chances of being recognized.

Today we should have a decision on the bail. After having survived for so long, I didn't want to throw it all away by yielding to the temptation for tea. I drowned my craving in a glass of water.

At 11 a.m., I was ready and waiting in front of the TV, but there was no news about me for the first half hour. Then a knock on the door startled me—I expected it to be the police. Instinctively, I removed my spectacles and draped a towel casually over my head, before answering the door. It was the cleaning lady. I sent her away, saying she needn't sweep the room as I had allergies and the dust would only make it worse.

I went back to the news, which was breathless about a murder suspect dying in police custody. Since it had happened in Palakkad, I felt I was relatively safe from police incursions as they had their hands full. I remained glued to the TV until 4 p.m., but I didn't figure in the news.

Normally, the court dispersed by that time unless the hearing stretched on for some reason, which was unlikely in the case of a bail application. It was clear that the issue of my bail application hadn't been taken up.

I pondered over my next move. What was the point in being cooped up in this fashion? I hadn't read the newspaper over the past three to four days. There were no fresh revelations on the news channels after the release of the lookout notice. In any case, until the accused was arrested, there wouldn't be anything sensational to report?

I decided to call Joy Mathew. Not wanting to repeat a mistake twice, I decided to travel to a place at least a couple of hours away. I slipped my glasses into my shirt pocket and changed my hairstyle from swept back to a side parting.

I felt a little unsteady as I stepped out, but the feeling passed. I hadn't eaten any solid food for two days. I had a dosa with sambar at Indian Coffee House, at first without my glasses, and then with my glasses on, impelled by the fear that, purblind, if the sambar contained some gecko or cockroach remnants, I would ingest those too.

As I headed for the KSRTC bus station, I saw a private bus with destination Ottapalam, almost as if it were waiting for me. I decided to climb aboard although I had never been to that area before and had only read about it in books. I had left my mobile phone in the hotel. Thoughts of a thief breaking into the room and switching it on, and the police discovering my location and homing in on me kept me worried throughout the journey. I consoled myself with John Greenleaf Whittier's words:

For of all sad words of tongue or pen,
the saddest are these: 'It might have been!'

I alighted at the private bus terminal at Ottapalam. A dirt path ahead was teeming with pedestrians. Upon enquiry, I discovered that the lane led to the railway station which was less than a kilometre away.

It made sense to make the call from the railway station, because it could lead the police to suppose that it had been made in the middle of a train journey. The station, not a stop for express trains, was smaller than the one in my imagination. It showed signs of life only when one of the trains that had a stop there was due to arrive.

There was a lone phone booth from which I dialled Bindu's number, which I had memorized by then. It was switched off. I decided to try after a while. A train came and as soon as the hubbub of the alighting and boarding passengers was over, I went to the booth again. Her phone was still switched off. I felt peeved at being told to call only the one number and that number being kept switched off while I was at a loose end.

The optimist in me then rationalized that someone as clued in as Joy Mathew wouldn't have done so without adequate reason. I decided to wait another day, assuming that they were under police surveillance and had found it safer to keep the phone switched off. But if that were the case, the police wouldn't have allowed them to switch it off either. In all probability, the bail application would be taken up the next day. As soon as it was in place, phone calls wouldn't be monitored and there would be no reason to fear the police.

I was back in my room by 9.30 p.m. And hit the sack immediately after a bath.

Wednesday, 31 March.

A knock on the door and the usual panic. It was Suleiman.

'Sir, would you like some tea? I shall get it for you.'

Why did he suddenly ask me this?

'If you are going out, then get me one.' I tried to look nonchalant.

'Aren't you eating anything at all, sir? I don't see you going out either.'

Was this suspicion or compassion?

I said with a forced smile, 'Can anyone survive without food? I'm having food outside; it's just that I don't leave my key at the reception counter when I go out.'

He may have been convinced. 'Shall I get you some biscuits?'

'No biscuits. But if you find small plantains, get me half a kilo,' I said to allay his disappointment, handing over a fifty-rupee note.

I switched on the TV. There was a flash news. The Idukki district president of one of the splinter groups of the Kerala Congress had announced that he was going on an indefinite hunger strike in protest against my non-arrest.

Although I felt a twinge of regret that a faithful Christian's Easter celebration—which was around the corner—was going to be disrupted solely on my account, when I later heard that he was to commence the hunger strike very strategically and thoughtfully only after two weeks, I was relieved.

After a while, Suleiman returned, and placed the packet of bananas, and the balance amount on the teapoy. He washed out a glass tumbler and poured tea into it from a flask, before asking me, 'Why are you staying here? Where do you work?'

Since I had been expecting the question, I replied evenly, 'I have come to write a novel.'

'So, you are a writer. No wonder you have locked yourself up in the room.'

The ingenuous Suleiman had swallowed my story. When he had left, I asked myself, 'What'll be the climax of this story?'

Energized by the tea, I continued my vigil in front of the TV from 11 a.m. I had a banana occasionally and topped it with water. The bananas got over, but the news I was waiting for didn't come.

I decided to call Joy Mathew. I would do it from Ottapalam railway station. This time I carried my mobile phone. I only had a cup of tea at Indian Coffee House before boarding the bus. Dusk was falling when I reached the station. The telephone-booth operator was missing. Enquiries revealed that he had gone into town and was expected back soon. He surfaced after half an hour.

I dialled the number and waited expectantly. The phone rang; but the person at the other end cut the call. I was stunned. I dialled again after a few minutes. This time the phone was switched off. I felt a void inside me. Like a sleepwalker, I walked to one of the concrete benches on the platform and sat down. As soon as reason returned to her throne, a question spread its hood and swayed menacingly in front of me—what now?

The platform juddered as a long-distance express train rushed by. When its din had subsided, my mind stirred. Should I end it all? I only had to wait for the next train.

My mind spat at me. *Phthoo* . . .

Then what should I do? Who was there to advise me? Like Arjuna on the chariot floor, I sat listlessly on that cement bench, disillusioned.

After a while, Shri Krishna, who had counselled Arjuna through *Geethopadesam*, came to my side and touched me with the words

Even if the whole world were to turn against you, don't turn against yourself.

I felt reinvigorated.

Then I had another vision. Jesus Christ, the Son of Man, was approaching me with his unshod feet, bleeding from the nails driven into them. Jesus's hands with their passion wounds touched my heart.

Do not fret over tomorrow. Tomorrow by itself shall fret over itself. Bear only each day's sorrow.

Together, Jesus and Krishna helped me off that cold bench, propping me up on either side. I was battle-ready.

9

Joseph Mathew of Kattappana

I paced the platform, brooding over what to do next.

I could no longer depend on Joy Mathew. Nor was there any point in parking myself in front of the TV waiting for news of my bail.

The first thing to do was to find out whether my bail application had been filed in any court. If not, immediate steps should be taken to do so. It made no sense to remain incognito any longer.

Whether I continued to remain underground or emerged and appointed a lawyer to represent me, I needed funds. I had only about Rs 1000 with me. If I had a gold chain or a ring on my person, it would have come in handy now. But I was dead set against men wearing jewellery. That principle was proving unfavourable to me.

Should I call a friend who was not likely to be under police surveillance? However, all their numbers were in the mobile, and I couldn't switch it on for fear of being traced.

If I removed the SIM card, would I be able to switch it on? My previous mobile didn't work that way. The present one was about two years old, and I had never tried it without the SIM card.

I extracted the SIM card. I could switch it on. The call register also continued to have a record of the calls. Joseph Mathew's name jumped out at me.

He was my BEd classmate at NSS Training College and currently a teacher at Government Tribal Higher Secondary School, Kattappana.

His wife, Latha, taught at the same school and his children, Janma and Jeevith, were students there. We had visited each other's homes.

He answered the phone himself.

'I am T.J. Joseph,' I said without preamble.

'Where are you now?'

'That can wait. You must've heard the news. What's the latest?'

'You're a goner,' he was blunt to the point of rudeness. 'You may have done nothing on purpose, but because you absconded, everyone assumes that you are guilty. You should have been available to present your case. That is a mistake you made.'

'I didn't go to the college because the management asked me not to come. The manager even advised me to stay away from my home,' I explained.

'They've washed their hands of you after putting all the blame on you. Instead of explaining things and saving you, they issued a public apology which only made matters worse for you. They effectively sold you out.'

I didn't lose my equanimity. 'What's the situation in Thodupuzha now?'

'Prohibitory orders haven't been withdrawn. The police are frantically searching for you.'

'Let them.' I then broached the subject that I had called for. 'Will you be able to send me some money?'

'That can be done. But what is your plan? Do you intend to remain underground? Can't you surrender? Wouldn't that be better? Or take anticipatory bail?'

'I had arranged for someone to apply for bail. I don't know why, but he is not even taking my calls.'

Joseph Mathew replied, 'Achhoyi had called. He knows a few lawyers in Ernakulam. He said if you are okay with it, he can arrange for the bail.'

Achhoyi was the pet name for K.J. Joseph, a common friend. He was a social worker with a wide network of contacts.

'Let's find out about the bail application at Thodupuzha. I'll give you two telephone numbers. Please call and find out what has happened.'

I gave him the contact numbers for Joy Mathew and Prof. Thampi Varghese, another friend of mine.

'I'm leaving the place that I am in now. I will reach another place in two hours. Try to get the information out of them by then. Tell them that you are a friend, nothing more. Don't mention that we talked.'

He agreed.

I looked at the time as I got out of the booth, 8 p.m. As soon as I reached Palakkad, I called Joseph Mathew.

'Joy Mathew picked up the call after a few attempts. He seemed to be afraid to say anything. Then I called Thampi Varghese. He also spoke as if he had no idea about anything. When I specifically asked about the anticipatory bail, he spoke as if there had been no such move.'

'They may have thought it was the police who was calling,' I said.

'I specifically said I was Joseph Mathew, friend of T.J. Joseph, but they may not have believed me.'

'Shall we go by Achhoyi's suggestion?'

Joseph Mathew suggested something different, 'Instead of anticipatory bail, why not surrender to the court and then move a bail application?'

'I must reach Ernakulam to surrender to the court. Will I be able to do it avoiding the police?'

'Why are you afraid of the police?'

That question struck me. Why was I fearful of the police indeed? 'Should I come to Kattappana and surrender at the police station there?' I thought that would be the easiest way.

'That also can be done. I know the Janamaithri police here.'

'When should I come to Kattappana?'

'Tomorrow is Maundy Thursday,' he said, 'by late afternoon, there won't be many people in town. It'll be good if you come at that time.'

'I'll see you tomorrow then.' I glanced at my watch—10 p.m.

A multitude of novel experiences lay ahead of me—arrest, lock-up, court, jail. One must prepare oneself in advance.

First of all, I must buy myself a shirt because I had brought only one with me. The one I was wearing was cotton and needed starching and ironing. Although I had washed it, it was creased.

I decided to buy a dark-coloured shirt, given that, once in custody, I wouldn't be able to change my clothes, which meant that I needed one that would not show the ill effects of continuous use. I bought it from a makeshift stall that kept late hours beside the KSRTC terminal.

As soon as I decided to surrender, my financial worries disappeared. I had Rs 900 left with me and was prepared to spend Rs 500 on the shirt. Nevertheless, I procured it for only Rs 250. I reached Indian Coffee House just as it was about to close. Although I was not hungry, I ate a couple of chapattis.

I returned to the lodge, had a bath, and tried to get some sleep as on the morrow I had to leave early. However, nightmares about police torture and third-degree methods kept me awake. Scenes in movies flashed before me: a lock-up room with shadows of the bars on its door; trussed up under a blinding light in some unknown interrogation centre. Would inebriated policemen on night duty take out their aggression on me? The brutal custody death of Sampath at the hands of the Palakkad police only two days ago weighed on my mind. Thoughts about torments to come were more painful than the memories of torments already undergone.

Unable to withstand my self-inflicted mental torture any longer, I decided to check out. It was 12.30 a.m. I got dressed and went down. The receptionist and Suleiman were present. I paid up, tipped Suleiman, and despite the risk of being seen walking with a bag at the dead of night and being taken for a burglar, I hurried to the KSRTC terminal. At the terminal was a police aid post. I kept under the radar in their vicinity and managed to find out that the next bus heading south was at 2.30 a.m. I had a cup of tea and then sat behind a pillar, avoiding the gaze of the police.

After 2 a.m., I started checking the arriving buses to read their destination boards; it was dark and with my spectacles safely tucked into my trouser pocket, I was unable to read the boards even at close quarters and had to ask the other people milling around in the bus stop. There were no buses headed towards Kottayam; only to the mofussil areas of Palakkad district. It was past 3 a.m. by now.

Another bus drove in. I asked its destination from a man standing nearby.

He berated me in Tamil, 'What's the matter with you? Can't you read? It's written up there in Malayalam. Don't you understand Malayalam?' He jeered at me, 'Eyy, are you illiterate?'

A Malayali asking a Tamilian to read out a board in Malayalam!
I felt humiliated that he should think that this Malayalam professor
was uneducated. It is an insult to Kerala which is vain about its high
literacy rate. I moved away from him quickly.

I stopped asking people. As each bus roared in, I stood inconspicuously
in a corner, slipped on my spectacles, became literate, read the board, and
discreetly slid the glasses back into my pocket.

A traffic block at the Walayar check-post, the border between Tamil
Nadu and Kerala, had caused an hour's delay for buses from the south.
At long last, a bus each for Ernakulam and Kottayam arrived almost
together and the entire group of waiting passengers swarmed around
them. I managed to squirm my way into the Kottayam bus. It was packed
like a can of sardines, and I had hardly enough space to keep both my
feet on the floor. I hung on to the overhead bar, placing one foot on top
of the other.

The bus was full of students from the engineering and nursing
colleges in Tamil Nadu returning home for the Easter holidays. By the
time the bus left the station, I felt suffocated in the crush. Standing on
one leg, I deplored my idiocy in boarding this bus.

How foolish could I be? All I had to do was to reveal my identity
at the police aid post. A jeep would have arrived in a trice, taken me to
the local station first, and thence to Thodupuzha. I could have travelled
in comfort and saved my bus fare too. Instead, did I have to lurk in the
shadows, be at the receiving end of the Tamilian's taunts, and travel in
utter misery like this?

The bus would take me to Perumbavoor; from there to
Kothamangalam and then on to Kattappana. My ticket had the origin,
time, date, and destination; I kept it safely. I might need it to prove
Joseph Mathew's innocence. The police could suspect him of harbouring
a fugitive in his house because I would be surrendering at Kattappana.

By the time I reached Kothamangalam via Perumbavoor, the day
had dawned. As there was the possibility of running into acquaintances
here, I did my utmost to keep my face hidden. Even in the private bus to
Kattappana, I kept my head down, pretending to be asleep. I raised my
head only once, to buy the ticket.

I reached Kattappana at 10 a.m. and immediately took an
autorickshaw to Joseph Mathew's house. The door was opened by his
wife, Latha.

'It's an absconder,' I tried to crack a joke. She didn't seem to relish it. She put a finger on her lips and after a quick glance around, gestured me to go inside. She bolted the door behind me.

As I entered their living room, an anxious Joseph Mathew asked me, 'Did anyone see you come in?'

'Other than the auto driver who brought me here, I don't think so,' I said, wondering if there was much to be afraid about.

Their children were present in the room. Latha warned them, 'No one should speak of sir coming here.' They nodded, seeming to know the gravity of the situation.

'I was expecting you to get here much later, in the afternoon,' Joseph Mathew said.

'I thought it was better to be early.'

'Come.' He picked up my bag and went into another room. 'Have you eaten anything?'

'Please let me have a bath and freshen up; I'll eat after that,' I replied.

The doorbell rang at that moment.

'Wait here, I'll go and see who it is,' he whispered.

I could hear the sounds of indistinct conversation. The visitor seemed to have entered the drawing room. The voice seemed familiar.

Was it Joy Mathew? I listened intently. Yes! It was he. However, I couldn't make out what they were discussing.

After about ten minutes, Joseph Mathew came into the room and said, 'It's Joy Mathew sir.'

'Have you told him I am here?'

'No, should I?'

'Why has he come?'

'I had called him a couple of times yesterday. He wanted to find out if I had any news of you.'

'Is there anyone with him?'

'No.'

'Then let him come in.'

As soon as he saw me, Joy Mathew started to sob and embraced me. I felt miserable.

10

A Police Station Sans Merci

From the show of emotion by Joy Mathew, I inferred that things had taken a turn for the worse—much worse than I had bargained for. He took a deep breath and seemed to recover his composure.

'Why didn't you answer the calls I made to Bindu's phone?' I snapped, making no effort to disguise my displeasure. 'Giving me a contact number only to keep it switched off . . . what kind of behaviour is that?'

'The police were checking the calls to that mobile,' he said despondently. I had assumed that was the case. He continued, 'The bail application didn't happen as we had planned. The lawyer's opinion is that anticipatory bail is not easy.'

'Has the application been submitted in the court?' I asked.

'No. The lawyer has advised that it's better to surrender to the police and then apply for bail.'

Either the lawyer was not interested in taking my case, or he had buckled under police pressure.

'Where should I surrender?'

'To the Thodupuzha DySP. I was told it's equivalent to surrendering to the IG.'

'Who said that?'

'IG B. Sandhya told advocate Kiran.'

'Who is advocate Kiran?'

'The son of advocate N.M. Mathew whom we had approached to file the anticipatory bail.'

I wondered whether the police had tried to hinder my anticipatory bail. An accused evading arrest by obtaining anticipatory bail reflects poorly on the investigating officer. Advocate N.M. Mathew was a leading criminal lawyer of Thodupuzha. He would have good connections with the police. I wondered whether I would have been better off had I engaged a lawyer from Ernakulam.

'Does advocate Kiran know that you have come here?'

'No.'

At the very instant, his mobile rang. He looked at the screen and whispered to us, 'It's Kiran vakil.'[1]

I remained silent as Joy Mathew kept anxiously interjecting questions: 'When', 'Why', etc. He was growing progressively more distressed as the conversation continued. Joseph Mathew came into the room; seeing a telephone conversation in progress, he remained silent. After the call was over, Joy Mathew asked Joseph for a glass of water.

'What is the problem?' I asked.

'The police have said that they are going to arrest Bindu. They've gone to my house,' Joy Mathew stammered.

'For what? What kind of justice is this?'

'It's their brand of justice. They believe that we know of your whereabouts. It's just pressure tactics.' After drinking a glass of water, he continued with more self-control, 'It's merely police tactics . . . nothing to be fazed by. They are not going to take her to the station and lock her up.'

Joseph Mathew and I stood by, unsure of what was to be done.

'I must leave now,' said Joy Mathew, 'What do you say about surrendering? Or don't you want to do it for the time being?'

'I had come here with the intention of surrendering at Kattappana police station. But if you think it should be at Thodupuzha, that can also be arranged.'

'Then I'll inform Kiran vakil. He'll inform the DySP. If he asks for a time, what should I say?'

'Tell them around 4 p.m.'

Joy Mathew called Kiran, but the call didn't go through. After a few attempts, Joy Mathew said, 'I think there is no range; the signal keeps disappearing.'

'Is that a BSNL number? It's like this here—sometimes there is no signal at all, sometimes we have good signal.'

'Should I use another phone?' asked Joy Mathew.

'That should be okay. In any case I'm going to surrender,' I said.

Joy Mathew used Latha's phone and informed Kiran vakil of my decision to surrender at 4 p.m. at Thodupuzha. He also agreed that the police could be informed.

'Let me go, then,' said Joy Mathew, handing over the phone. We shook hands. He left on his motorbike.

I had a bath and a breakfast of appam and vegetable curry. Latha did my laundry and hung up my clothes to dry. Joseph Mathew started to make arrangements for my 'police station march'.

At exactly 1 p.m., a white Indigo taxi arrived; the young driver was known to Joseph Mathew who told him that the passenger was no ordinary person, but also assured him that there would be no trouble. Should there be any fallout, he, Joseph Mathew, would take care of it. The driver seemed to have implicit trust in him.

Although Latha insisted that I have lunch before leaving, I declined. She had ironed my clothes by this time. I wore the shirt purchased the previous day. Joseph Mathew was to accompany me. I said my goodbyes. Joseph Mathew's son, Jeevith, was worried that I would be beaten up by the police; Joseph and I reassured him that only petty thieves were given a thrashing.

Two others joined us at Kattappana town—Latha's sister's husband and his friend. Both were local leaders and social workers. We had not yet decided on the route to take to Thodupuzha.

Although the Kerala police are smart, they have a penchant for displaying the traits of Ettukaali Mammoonj—a character created by Vaikom Muhammad Basheer—who goes around claiming every illicit pregnancy as his own with a now legendary 'athu njammala' (I'm the one). Irrespective of whether the accused had surrendered voluntarily or had been chased down by the general public and handed over, the police version would be that they had captured him in a display of extraordinary daring.

I had an inkling that this would happen in my case as well and told the others of my apprehension: 'It's not going to be easy to reach Thodupuzha and surrender. They will catch us long before we get there;

only then will they get the credit. If we take the shortest route, which is via Idukki, we'll be captured before we reach Thodupuzha, so let's take the Vagamon route. From Erattupetta, we'll take an internal road to Thodupuzha. The police could be stationed there as well, but let's take that route anyway; if they capture us, so be it.'

The others neither supported nor objected to my suggestion. I asked Joseph Mathew to switch off his mobile. He asked the driver whether he was nervous, but he was quite coolheaded about it. Thereafter, no one spoke for a while. We drove past hills and valleys filled with tea gardens. After about half-an-hour's drive, a call came on Latha's brother-in-law's phone. It was Latha; Joseph Mathew spoke to her.

'There are problems in Thodupuzha. We could be attacked there. The DySP's office called and informed her,' Joseph Mathew explained.

'How did they get Latha's number?'

'Didn't Joy Mathew sir call Kiran vakil from her number?'

'When we ourselves are headed there, why do they need to call my house and intimidate her?' asked Joseph Mathew.

'Let's carry on,' I said. Latha called after fifteen minutes. The message was the same. Mobs were building up at various locations. We had to be careful. I understood how the police's mind was working.

'Please switch off that mobile. They are tracking it and seem to know our route,' I said.

'That is not possible. How could they possibly know this number?' Joseph Mathew protested.

As we approached Vagamon, the phone rang again. Joseph Mathew answered the call and after he had hung up, he said to us, 'Latha is also frightened now. They have been calling repeatedly. The news has spread that you'll be surrendering at 4 p.m., which is why the Muslims are gathering in big numbers.'

'Stop the car,' I said harshly, 'Switch off that mobile! They must be tracking Latha's outgoing calls. They will know exactly where we are now.'

Joseph Mathew said nothing and switched off the phone.

I felt rebellious—the police could not have it their way. I said, 'Turn the car around. Let them not seek glory by making fools of us. I'll surrender at the Kattappana police station. Let that police station get the credit for arresting me.'

'If, after informing them that you'll surrender in Thodupuzha, you go to Kattappana, what if they take it out on you later?' Joseph Mathew asked.

'It doesn't matter,' I said, 'we can always tell them that we returned to Kattappana because they themselves had called home and intimidated us.'

'Then let's do that. I know the Kattappana circle inspector too,' said Joseph Mathew. We reached Kattappana police station by 3 p.m. Accompanied by my three best men, I walked into the station—like an expectant, nervous, and rather shy bridegroom entering the church—to get arrested.

My friend asked a policeman who was standing outside, 'Is the CI here?'

'He's having his lunch. Why? What's the matter?' Was it possible that he didn't recognize me?

Nodding towards me, my friend said, 'He is the accused in the question-paper case. He has come to surrender.' I looked at the policeman keenly to observe his expression.

He said with no particular change in his mien, 'He's on the other side. You may go and meet him there.'

Joseph Mathew and his companions went to meet the CI, leaving me alone. I scanned the pictures of fugitives on the station's notice board to see if I featured amongst them; I wasn't. I tried to peek into the inner office to check out the lock-up room in which I would be installed after my arrest. I failed in that endeavour as well. The policeman asked me to sit down in one of the chairs. My eyes strayed to the calendar on the wall. 1 April —Maundy Thursday and All Fools' Day. Not a bad choice as the day of my surrender.

The three of them returned and Joseph Mathew gave me the disappointing news, 'He says you can't surrender here. If the arrest is recorded here, it'll only mean a lot of paperwork for the policemen here. They will have to do a lot of writing. At Thodupuzha, they would have got the documentation ready. All they need is the accused. For the department too, your surrendering here will become an issue. In the CI's opinion, all things considered, Thodupuzha is the better option.'

I was peeved. An accused, one who had been on the run and for whom a lookout notice had been issued, was surrendering of his own volition, and here was a police station mercilessly spurning him!

'Now what? Will they arrange for me to be taken to Thodupuzha?'

'He says we should make our own arrangements.'

As an accused, I felt like an orphan, bereaved and alone. As we were leaving, I turned back and looked once more at the heartless police station.

11

All Fools' Day

We walked to the car. 'Now what shall we do?' asked Joseph Mathew, sounding rather helpless,

What could possibly be done? All our calculations had gone awry. I admitted defeat, ready to let fate take over.

'Let's just do as the police say,' I said, 'and get in touch with the Thodupuzha DySP. Joy Mathew should have his number.'

'Let me try another way,' said Joseph Mathew. As a teacher, he often visited the district education deputy director's Thodupuzha office. The incumbent deputy director was Thodupuzha DySP K.G. Simon's wife. He got his number from her and called him.

After a week's frustrating search, K.G. Simon and Idukki Crime Detachment DySP V.U. Kuriakose—given special charge of my case—were relieved that I was ready to surrender. From what I could gather, they were in the middle of making arrangements for a dramatic arrest by waylaying us en route to Thodupuzha, using their cyber cell's advanced tracking and triangulation equipment. And then, for the last couple of hours, we had dropped off the radar, adding to their frustration. Like summer rain on parched land, Joseph Mathew's call reached him. He had discovered by then that Joseph Mathew had a role in my surrender.

'Where are you? And what took you so long?' demanded Simon.

'While we were on our way here, via Vagamon, there were many calls to my home from the DySP's office with warnings that we could be attacked by Muslim mobs. We were frightened and so we went back to Kattappana. When he tried to surrender at the police station there, the CI refused to take him in, insisting that the surrender should take place at Thodupuzha, otherwise there would be departmental issues. Now what should we do?'

'Where are you now?'

'Right beside the Kattappana police station.'

'Come to Thodupuzha. What make is your car?'

'Tata Indigo.'

'Colour?'

'White.'

'Number?'

Joseph Mathew read out the number.

'Which route are you taking?'

'Which route should we take?'

'Come via Idukki. We'll be waiting for you on the way.'

'Okay.'

In my disappointment at losing the battle, I muttered to myself, 'I know why you'll be waiting.' I consoled myself with the thought that it was better to give in than to be defeated.

We took the route recommended by Simon. The entire journey was completed largely in silence.

Now that the knots of my fate had started to unravel by themselves, I felt light-hearted. My fears and worries dissipated and were replaced by hunger and thirst. We stopped on the way to buy some water.

I switched on my mobile, called Mithun and told him that I was on my way to surrender. He told me only that he was suffering from tiredness and being treated as an in-patient in a hospital near my wife's ancestral house. Since my wife was by his side, I asked him give the phone to her.

All I could hear was a piteous wail from the other end. I kept repeating, 'Hello . . . hello . . .' but the weeping continued.

After a little while, Mithun came back on the line. 'Where is Amy?'

'At Vimalagiri, in Solly aunty's home.'

'Tell Saju uncle that I am going to surrender. The rest, I suppose, you can watch on TV.'

He didn't reply. I hung up.

Frequent calls from Simon were coming in to ascertain our location and Joseph was updating him, providing a clear picture of our journey.

When we reached the forest area ahead of the Idukki Collectorate, we could see a police jeep waiting. We parked by its side. There was the sound of an approaching vehicle.

Simon's call came on Joseph Mathew's mobile: 'Don't get out of the car now. Get out only when I tell you to. And keep the phone switched on.' This was to prevent any third party witnessing my surrender. We waited for over a minute. In between, a bus and a jeep went past us.

The call came then: 'Okay, you can get out of the car now.'

Clutching my bag, I got off first; the others followed. We went up to the jeep.

The left rear door opened, a tall, heavy-set man emerged and told me to get in.

I climbed into the vehicle. To my right was a DySP; in the front passenger seat was another one. Both the officers were in uniform, as was the driver. It was only much later that I discovered that the one in the front was Kuriakose, and the one beside me was Simon. The titan, who was the only one in mufti, squeezed into the vehicle on my other side.

I assumed he was a high-ranking police officer. Simon told Joseph Mathew and the others to go back and they immediately left without even saying goodbye to me.

Our vehicle moved forward; I was squashed between two police officers. None of them spoke to me initially. All three were busy on their mobiles letting the world know that I was in custody.

'We've caught the accused in the question-paper case.'

'The professor has been found. The question-paper accused.'

'We have picked him up . . . the teacher . . . the guy in the question-paper case.'

'We nabbed him just a little while ago . . . we'll be in Thodupuzha shortly.'

'Close to Idukki . . .'

'Yeah . . . snagged him very tactically.'

As I sat listening to them, I could only marvel at these modern-day Ettukaali Mammoonjs as they communicated with their superiors and the media. The titan was the only one who referred to me in a demeaning manner.

After they had enlightened their tiny world, they turned to me. I was given a bottle of water; I drank only two gulps. Then, Simon started the interrogation.

'Tell us, where were you? Where were you holed up?'

'Palakkad.'

'Tell us everything from the beginning.' The titan started the voice recorder app in his phone and shoved it in front of my face.

I narrated the incidents from the time I left home. In my fraught state, it was not easy to remember the sequence and they kept egging me on with '. . . and then . . .' every time I paused to marshal my thoughts. Seated in a speeding vehicle and talking non-stop in the April heat made my throat parched and my voice hoarse. They made me drink water every time this happened.

I am quite familiar with the Idukki-Thodupuzha route and was keeping a watch for landmarks despite my narration. However, after Kulamavu Dam, I thought we had taken a detour and the roads began to look unfamiliar.

The murder accused Sampath had been killed by police officers in the Irrigation Department's riverside cottage near Malampuzha Dam only a few days ago. Suddenly, I began to wonder whether my story would also end in some halfway house—that put an abrupt end to my storytelling, like a tap that had been turned off.

'What is it? Do you need water?'

After a gulp of water, I regained my composure and carried on with my narrative. Was it just my imagination or had we made a detour? Now the road looked familiar again.

The Kulamav police station was by the side of the road. When we got there, Kuriakose ordered the driver to pull over. He told one the sentries to fetch a pair of handcuffs from the station. He returned with one but was sent back with instructions to get the 'new type'. That was brought and given to Kuriakose.

The vehicle started to move and so did my story. By the time we reached Muttam, I, in my story, had reached Kattappana. I showed them my bus ticket from Palakkad to Kattappana.

The police officers told me not to reveal to anyone that, at the time of taking me into custody, there were others in the car apart from the driver. One needed to be wet behind the ears to miss that the purpose of this elaborate exercise was to eliminate witnesses of my surrender.

We were six or seven kilometres away from Thodupuzha when Simon took the handcuffs from Kuriakose and said, 'This is for use on burglars and murderers. I regret having to put it on a teacher, but I don't have an option.' He then snapped the cuff on to my right wrist.

The titan, showing alarming enthusiasm, grabbed my left hand and said, 'And I'm doing with this great pride and happiness.' He snapped the other cuff on to my left wrist.

I sat there savouring the new experience of having a wrist ornament that bound my hands together. A wry smile appeared on my lips.

'Are you mad?' Simon asked, observing me closely. To the world, this was All Fools' Day. I felt like laughing out aloud at this ludicrousness.

However, I suppressed my laughter and behaved like a model prisoner.

I heard Simon tell someone on the phone, 'We'll be there shortly.' He then adjusted his peaked cap, pulled out a dainty comb and brushed his moustache. The other officers also tried to spruce themselves up and look alert.

When we entered Thodupuzha town, the usual crowd was missing, perhaps because it was Maundy Thursday. With my arrest, celebrated on TV channels, the prohibitory orders had been withdrawn.

The jeep shuddered as it came to a halt in the front yard of the police station where the cameras of TV channels were focused. The police officers leapt down nimbly from the vehicle; hampered by the handcuffs, I had difficulty in alighting and was pulled out. I caught a glimpse of cameramen running to get close to us. Simon grabbed my arm and towed me along; unable to keep up with his punishing pace, I stumbled and would have fallen had it not been for the fact that Simon hadn't loosened his grip on me.

12

The Diviner of Vindhya Mountains

I was taken to the DySP's office on the first floor. N.N. Prasad, the Thodupuzha CI, Shinto P. Kurian, the sub-inspector, and a few others casually dropped by to gawk at me. Kuriakose sat me down on a chair, pulled another one close, and started to berate me for being inconsiderate towards my wife and children and not calling them while I was on the run. I didn't allow this to affect me. I kept looking at my handcuffed hands with studied indifference.

Suddenly, they re-organized the arrangement of the chairs in the room. Kuriakose told me that K.P. Philip, the superintendent of police, Idukki district, would arrive soon. He also asked me to explain the background of the question paper.

My handcuffs were removed. Philip eventually arrived and first conferred with the DySPs. And then it was my turn. He asked me the relevance of the impugned question. I explained its innocuous background. Philip smiled. I could make out from his expression that he had realized the truth.

Tea was brought in along with *cherupazham*, a variety of banana. I limited myself to taking one banana.

Next came the meeting with the media. Kuriakose had asked me to make a statement that the question hadn't been constructed with any ulterior motives, and I apologized if I had inadvertently hurt anyone's feelings. I thought that this was a sensible thing to do.

Perhaps because a recent press-meet by Deputy Inspector General Wilson M. Paul—on the progress of the murder investigation of Muthoot George—had turned controversial, Philip opened with, 'I don't know whether it's proper for the police to hold a press meet, so nobody should think of this as a press meet. It's a chance for you to ask your questions and we'll be answering them.'

He explained to the gathering that there was only a sense of humour behind the controversial question and no hidden agenda. There was no prejudice or conspiracy behind it, and it wasn't instigated by anyone. He also announced that the accused had been on his way to surrender, when he was taken into custody lest he should have a change of heart.

'Why didn't you take the driver and the car into custody?' someone asked.

Philip responded: 'Why should the poor taxi driver be taken into custody? He had been merely engaged for the trip. We got our accused. Isn't that enough?'

The press dispersed after they had tea. I wasn't given an opportunity to speak.

After Philip left, I was brought down to the lock-up room on the ground floor.

'Not that it's necessary with you, but this is safer for you,' said CI Prasad. He summoned four or five policemen by their names and charged them with my protection. Then he came to the door and whispered, 'Don't eat anything other than that which is given to you by the two DySPs and me—even if the person giving it is a policeman.'

'All right,' I said, realizing the import of his words.

'Don't let anyone talk to the professor,' he gave strict instructions to my sentries.

I had read about lock-up rooms in books and seen them in movies. Even the one I was in felt fictional. And I, the creation of some author's imagination.

The policemen who came to see the 'controversy man' after the CI left jolted me back to reality.

'Sir, you have taught my son.'

'Just think this is fate.'

'Don't worry about anything, sir. We are with you.' From the other side of cell's door, they did their best to comfort me with their words.

'Sir, do you need tea? Anything to eat?' they asked kindly. I realized that they were not privy to what the CI had told me.

'I had tea and a banana upstairs. I don't need anything now.'

'Don't hesitate to let us know if you need anything.' They left, and I returned to the solitude of my cell. The cell was dirty. Scraps of newspaper, burnt matches and beedi butts lay strewn around on the dusty floor. It appeared as if it had had no inmate for a long time.

Outside was a large table and some benches used by the policemen. I wondered how they ignored the filth around them. In one corner of the cell, I saw a broom and grass mat, propped up against the wall. Probably it was the convention for the inmate himself to keep his cell tidy.

The toilet was in another corner, which couldn't be seen from the door. It had a tap and a large mug, but no bucket. At least eight to ten mugs of water would be required to clean the place. My predecessor had been lazy on this score. The stench of stale urine was overpowering.

Luckily, there was water. I tried to get rid of the stench by pouring six or seven mugs of water down the commode and around it. Then I swept the room a couple of times to remove as much dust as was possible. I shook out the accumulated dust from the grass mat, spread it on the floor and sat on it in the lotus position—like a yogi.

I remembered the story of a yogi who had lived in one of the peaks of the Vindhyas. Although he led a solitary life, at times he would descend into the valley, cross the river, and stay with the villagers for a few days. One day, while meditating, he had an epiphany—on the first day of Shraavana, the fifth month of the Hindu calendar, the river water would get poisoned. Those drinking its water would become abnormal. But as soon as the month of Bhadra started, the water would become pure again.

He hurried down the mountain to warn the villagers. He exhorted: 'Before the start of Shraavana, collect and store enough water for a month. As soon as the month of Bhadra starts, it will be all clear. If you don't do this, it could lead to a lot of problems because whoever drinks the poisoned water will lose his mind.'

The villagers scorned his dire warnings.

The ascetic went back to his abode after collecting enough water for a month for himself. A week after the start of the Shraavana month, the yogi descended from the mountain to check on the villagers. He realized that the revelation had come true; the villagers had indeed gone mad. However, he noticed one thing: There was no dissonance among them. In their view, he was abnormal.

There was nothing else to do. The yogi stepped into the river, drank a handful of water, and became 'normal'.

The majority of the population in the nation had become abnormal after drinking the poisoned water of blind faith and intolerance. To fit in, even the society's overlords were quaffing the poisoned waters. The ruling class was singing hosannas to them to prevent leakages in the vote banks.

I was brought back from my reverie by the sound of a baton banging against the steel bars. It was Shinto P. Kurian, SI, resembling a mainmast with its sails that had caught the wind, his bulging muscles threatening to burst out of his uniform. In his other hand was a wireless transceiver.

He beckoned me to the cell door. I went forward with some amount of trepidation. He demanded, 'Where were you, man?'

'Palakkad.'

'That isn't enough. I want you to describe everything after you left your home.'

I started my narration. In between, he would go away to attend to something or the other. I would go back and sit on my grass mat. He would return to hear the rest of my story.

During such intermissions, I thought of my family. A big family gathering had been planned in my house in Muvattupuzha between Maundy Thursday and Easter Sunday. My sisters, along with my brothers-in-law and my nieces, had been invited. This was the time when we would be cutting the unleavened Passover bread, the one we call pesaha appam in our community. My role, as the eldest of the family, was to be the host. And here I was, incarcerated.

My mother, wife, and children were either in hospital or staying at relatives' homes. Our Muvattupuzha home was deserted, dark, and silent. Suddenly, I felt a blast of heat rising inside me. To counter it, I got up and pressed my face against the cold steel bars of my cell door.

After obtaining permission from the DySP, some of my relatives and friends came to meet me—my cousin, my wife's two cousins and a teacher from Nirmala College. Although I was allowed out of the cell, they were not allowed to come close, or speak to me. They observed me from a distance as they would a corpse. There was a funereal formality on their faces which I found unbearable. I wanted to shout out to them that I wasn't dead yet.

13

Kamlesh Kumar Chowdhury

After my relatives and friends had left, I was not herded back into the lock-up but was asked to sit on a chair outside. At around 10.30 p.m., Shinto Kurian asked me to get into a police jeep.

Why? I wondered with apprehension.

Would they take me to some isolated spot and beat me up?

I decided that I should tell them that I was a hernia patient before they started the assault. I didn't want both of us to get into trouble if, unaware of this fact, they were to kick me in my lower abdomen.

I was made to sit in the rear seat. Four or five policemen also climbed in. The SI sat in the front and commanded, 'Taluk hospital.'

I realized the purpose of the visit. It is mandatory for all the people under arrest to undergo a medical examination. The taluk hospital was about a kilometre and half away, and my college was on the way. As we drove past it in the night, the huge building appeared to be looking at me in mute, helpless commiseration.

Although there were very few people in the hospital yard, I was allowed to alight only after the police cleared the area. I was examined by a lady doctor who looked about thirty-five years old. She asked me if I had any bruises or wounds, examined me with a stethoscope, and read my blood pressure.

I asked her, 'How's my BP?'

'Normal,' she replied. My doctor had recommended that I keep tabs on my blood pressure. I was mildly hypertensive.

When we came out, the SI bellowed at a young man who was loitering around, 'What are you doing here? Scram!'

The SI was the gnome guarding me, the treasure.

The young man whom the SI had rudely barked at had brought in his mother, complaining of chest pain, and was waiting anxiously in front of the casualty. He asked the SI who would attend to his mother's needs if he were to go away. Such questions don't discomfit people such as Shinto Kurian. I shall desist from reporting his expletive-laden response.

When we returned to the police station, Kuriakose had arrived. To celebrate my 'capture', he had bought biryani for everyone. He handed over a packet to me as well; it was vegetable biryani. Despite my protests that I wouldn't be able to eat even half of it, he pressed it on me. Perhaps a week's starvation diet had shrunk my stomach. Although I hated wasting food, I had to throw away more than one-fourth of it.

After dinner, I was returned to my cell. I was feeling sleepy, especially because of the previous night's sleep deficit. However, as soon as I lay down, a policeman told me that Kuriakose wanted to meet me. I was taken to his office on the first floor.

Kuriakose sat me down beside him and told me affably, 'Tomorrow you will be produced in court and you will be remanded. Don't try to take bail immediately. In a couple of weeks, things will quieten down. It's better that you remain in custody until then.'

The leaders in power and the police as peacekeepers have to mollify the fanatics before they attend to anyone else. As a disciplined citizen, I nodded my head in acquiescence.

'When you were underground, we had taken your passport and bank account passbooks from your home. The passport will be deposited in court. After you are granted bail, you will have to receive it from the court. The passbooks, however, we can hand over to your son if you ask him to contact us.'

I nodded again.

'Except for that question you set, whomever we asked about you in your background check, had only good things to say about you,' he said in conclusion.

When I was returned to my cell, someone was seated on the grass mat! A roommate! Well, I thought, at least I had someone to chat with.

'What is your name?' I asked as I sat down beside him.

He seemed to have heard me but didn't respond. Is the guy a mute? I wondered.

I asked again, 'What is your name?'

'Malayalam *nahi maloom.*' Although I had studied Hindi up to the tenth standard, I didn't know much more than its alphabet. So, I repeated the question in English.

He replied, 'Kamlesh Kumar Chowdhury.'

As I was not used to speaking in English, my speech was stilted; his was worse. His pronunciation didn't make for easy comprehension. Nonetheless, I managed to learn what had gotten him into the lock-up.

He was an Ayurvedic doctor from Kanpur married to a Christian nurse from Thodupuzha, working in the same hospital. They had a child. A few days ago, after an argument, his wife had gone off in a huff to her maternal home. He went to see her, and they had started to fight again. The wife had complained to police, who charged him with domestic violence and had arrested him on the spot.

'Did you hurt your wife?'

'I hit her once . . . just once.' And then he started to sob uncontrollably.

I wondered about the state of that wife who—on this Maundy Thursday evening—had gotten the father of her child thrown into prison. Maybe she was also weeping.

Marital life is a kind of war. An extraordinary war that lasts a lifetime. In a normal war, the one who defeats the opponent wins the war. In a marriage, the one who defeats the other will also lose. Therefore, marriage is a war where one must win without defeating the significant other.

Kamlesh Kumar Chowdhury and the Malayali nurse were living with their Pyrrhic victories.

Just then, I got called out again. My interlocutor was the police writer, Assistant Sub-inspector M.B. Kamaladharan, who sat across me to record my statement. He introduced himself and told me that his son was a first-year BCom student in Newman College. As he had opted for Hindi as an additional language, he wasn't my student and, therefore, didn't take my examination.

I had to again explain the background behind the question. He wrote down everything I narrated; in between, he took smoking breaks. Assuming that the statement would have an important bearing on my case, I drifted into the literary allusions of the dialogue, but he remarked that this was turning into an essay, and I needed to give him only a précis. As it was late, I assumed that it was sleepiness which had made him say that. Under the firm belief that my fate lay entirely in the contents of the statement, I didn't hold back and waxed eloquent on my defence. Driving away his sleep with whorls of smoke around him, he kept writing. By 3 a.m., he completed it.

He then handed me a sheaf of papers with carbon papers inserted in between them, saying, 'You must've made students write impositions in the past. Just take this as a punishment for that.' He gave me a copy of my question paper and told me to make sixteen original sets of that. When I asked what they were for, he said it was for the forensics department—a mere statement from me affirming that I had made the question paper would not be enough, it had to be proved scientifically. Or, when the case was eventually tried in the court, what if the accused changed his statement and got acquitted?

Occasionally, Kamaladharan came over to check on my progress. Taking advantage of the acquaintance developed over that night, I asked him, 'What's the college authorities' attitude towards me?'

'I'll not tell you.'

I didn't ask him anything more. It was well past dawn by the time my imposition ended.

Baby, my elder sister's husband who had arrived the previous night, was sent to me after my writing assignment was over. He arrived bearing a cup of tea. I was allowed to use the bathroom reserved for the policemen and took out my toothbrush and toothpaste from my bag.

As I sat on the chair outside the lock-up, policemen in uniform and mufti and some others came to gawk at the accused in the question-paper case. I stood up each time to pay my respects to them like a tame culprit. Titan came in, still in his civvies. He took out my things from my bag and made a list. He made me take off my wristwatch, added that to his list as well and placed it all in the bag. He checked to make sure I wasn't wearing any jewellery. He did a physical examination and recorded two identification marks.

My brother-in-law arrived with breakfast. Possibly due to two consecutive sleepless nights, I had lost my appetite. I opened the food packet only because Baby insisted. When I placed the dosa soaked in sambar in my mouth, I felt nauseated and pushed away the packet.

That made the titan cackle, 'Look at the arrogance! Someone's trying to keep him from starving and what does he do?'

'Did I ask to be fed? Did I ask for anything?' I retorted. I had guessed by now that, despite his attitude, he was but a lowly constable. My outburst was the expression of my anger at his behaviour and the way he had spoken to me from the time of my arrest.

The titan leapt to his feet. 'Despite all that has happened, look at his arrogance!' he snapped, and grabbed my arms. 'Don't imagine that you can sit here and poke fun at people. Your place is in the lock-up.' He shoved me in. My brother-in-law who witnessed this was alarmed.

This was a blessing in disguise because I actually felt more relaxed inside the lock-up. Outside, I had to stand up obsequiously every time a policeman approached me, and their irrelevant and inane questions had to be answered with as much patience as I could muster. I was heartily sick of it all.

When he saw me, Kamlesh Chowdhury sat up on the grass mat.

I said, 'Good morning.'

He yawned in reply and sat there gloomily. Allowing him to wallow in his private sorrows, I got busy with my own. After a little while, my brother-in-law arrived with Kiran vakil. I signed over the power-of-attorney and Kiran said that I would be produced before a magistrate at his residence in Kattappana, as the courts were closed for Good Friday. After this, I would be duly remanded and moved to Muvattupuzha sub-jail. I told them that I didn't need the bail right away and that they should apply for it only when I asked them to do so.

After they left, two special branch policemen in mufti arrived. They asked me if I had any complaints and I said I had none. I understood from their conversation that Kamlesh Kumar Chowdhury was also going to be taken along with me to the magistrate. No one had come to plead or negotiate on his behalf. Someone from the police station would call his wife and if she did not withdraw the complaint, he would also be remanded and transferred to the sub-jail.

When the police called her and suggested she withdraw the complaint, she was not ready to make a compromise. When Chowdhury was told that he was to be sent to jail, he started to sob. I tried to cheer him up. Up until then he hadn't asked me who I was or what crime I had committed. He may have assumed that a man who sits in the lock-up with such equanimity was a habitual offender for whom gaol was a second home.

The titan came and took me out of the cell. I wondered: where now? I had heard of the accused being given a final roughing up before they are taken to the court. I accompanied him with my heart in my mouth. He made me stand against the wall in an empty room. I stood there stiffly, expecting his knee to crash into my underbelly and to be winded completely.

I was wrong. The titan took out a ruler from his pocket and placed it flat on my head.

'Your height has to be recorded. Your job in the college is as good as gone. We're trying to see if you can be employed in the police force.' He said this with a straight face!

It took me a while to get my breath back. As we left the room, I glanced at the wall—the heights of many had been recorded there.

14

Good Friday and Calvary Mount

Armed policemen from the police camp, in their marine blue bus and a pilot jeep, had arrived to escort us to the magistrate. Chowdhury and I were given tea in the presence of the CI, following which we were handcuffed. I considered it a special ornament for special occasions; but Chowdhury broke down and wept upon looking at his handcuffs.

There was an array of media people with their probing eyes and zoomed-in cameras. Simon and Shinto Kurian marched me out, but they didn't get into the bus. The bus, which had gained notoriety in Kerala as '*idivandi*' (mobile torture cell), contained about thirty armed policemen in uniform. There were another four special branch policemen in civvies. I was seated by the window and one policeman sat beside me. We followed the white police jeep carrying the DySP and others. It was a mini motorcade.

In a wedding procession, the bridegroom is the star; in a funeral cortège, it's the corpse. I was the star of this one; all this elaborate security and bandobast was for my sake. And my sake alone. I looked at my handcuffed hands with smug vainglory.

During the journey, one of the special branch policemen switched places with the uniformed one seated beside me. He had come earlier to check on my wellbeing. I suddenly wanted to know the titan's details—he had been behaving like a boor from the time I had been taken into custody. I described him and asked about him.

'He's a policeman in the team assigned to the question-paper case,' he replied. I asked what his name was. It was a Muslim name. Then I understood where all his animosity was coming from. I felt annoyed with the DySPs who had given him a free hand to abuse me.

'Why? Was there a problem?' the special branch man asked me.

'No, nothing.'

Our two vehicles negotiated the hairpin bends of Natukanimala and entered the cooler clime of the high-range. Complete silence reigned inside the bus. Most of the policemen were asleep. I glanced behind me. Chowdhury was sleeping like a baby, his mouth slightly agape. My eyelids also grew heavy, and I slipped into the void of sleep.

When I woke up, the bus was wheezing up the climb that starts from below the Idukki arch dam. From certain points, one could see the extremities of the dam that had completely tied down the Periyar river. There was a time when the Periyar gushed forth, free and unbound. However, today, man has sentenced it to life imprisonment.

After the ascent, when we reached Vazhavara, to the right I could see Calvary Mount—the highest point of the Kalyanathandu Hills that stretch from Idukki to Kattappana. Beyond the hill is Idukki's catchment area, the best view of which is from the Mount. I have climbed the hill numerous times on study trips with my students.

Being Good Friday, I could see a small group of people making their way towards the crucifix at the foot of the mountain. One of them was bearing a decent-sized wooden cross. The young men were trying to channel the sufferings which Jesus Christ had undergone to absolve mankind of its sins.

It was pure coincidence that I was also arrested on a Maundy Thursday. As in Jesus's case, I too was accused of blasphemy and defying God. After holding my trial yesterday, the henchmen of the state—the police Caiaphas—had declared to the media that I was innocent. Yet, the state hadn't ruled 'not guilty'. With a first information report composed of blather and a dubious case diary, they were hauling me into the presence of some magistrate in Kattappana, just as Jesus was brought before Pontius Pilate. Would he be just and equitable? Or would he, like Pilate, wash his hands of me?

The vehicles entered an untarred path off the main road. After some distance, they stopped and the policemen alighted. I was asked to alight as well. We had to go some distance on foot to reach the magistrate's house.

Rows of houses flanked the path. Women and children stood behind the fences to watch the procession of two handcuffed men and a small army of policemen. They had perhaps never seen a prisoner with such an impressive security bandobast.

The magistrate lived on the first floor. The court is wherever the magistrate sits. Before we entered the apartment, our handcuffs were removed. The police officers went in first; Chowdhury, our guards and I were left standing outside. We were asked to enter after a little while. Clad in a lungi, a man of about forty-five years was seated on a sofa, riffling through the sheaf of papers given to him by the police. He didn't even raise his head to look at the accused.

I looked around the room. Among the many English and Malayalam books, *Gurusagaram* by O.V. Vijayan caught my attention—a book I had taught my students that year. It was about transition from the battlefield of life's struggles to a state of serenity through the blessings of one's guru. I assumed that if he read books such *Gurusagaram*, he would be an aesthete and bibliophile, have the nous to understand the triviality of the charge sheet and would ask me some questions about the controversial question.

Not only did he not ask any, he didn't even raise his head to look at me. He signed on the remand petition and issued the order to send me to jail. After handing over the paper, he sat there with his head bowed.

Kamlesh Kumar was also remanded. As soon as we were led out of the house, the handcuffs went back on. It was close to 2 p.m. when we reached the vehicles. The armed policemen were muttering about being hungry. Hunger had abandoned me for the past week. Perhaps it was loath to enter someone with a troubled mind.

It was decided that on the way to Muvattupuzha sub-jail, we would stop for lunch at Cheruthoni, which we reached at 3 p.m. Being Good Friday, the restaurants were closed. The policemen had to make do with water and nenthran bananas bought from a roadside kiosk. I only had water.

By the time we reached Muvattupuzha, it was nearly 6 p.m. As a resident of Muvattupuzha for over seventeen years, I knew where the sub-jail was. Located on a hillock, its high compound wall was visible from various points in the town. I have seen many undertrials, in handcuffs and without, being taken to and from the jail. When I reached the portals of a world, which, although just two kilometres away from my home, was until then as inaccessible to me as it was alien, my armoured journey ended.

Four policemen stepped out of the vehicle with Kamlesh and me. One of them rang the calling bell beside the gate. A small window in the gate opened and a warden peered out.

'There is an admission,' announced the policeman. The iron door squealed open. A little away from the gate was a building each to the left and right side of the gate. The one on the left was the jail superintendent's office; to the right, the admission office. We were led there, and our handcuffs taken off.

The jail officials entered our details in their register from the papers submitted by the policemen. My mental state was like that of a new student enrolling for a higher course.

After our 'admissions' were done, the policemen left. The warden who admitted me appeared to be an iron statue which moved and spoke. The molten lead of revulsion had been poured into his face.

He asked me to take off my belt to conduct a physical examination and as I did so, my trousers slipped down. One week of starvation had taken its toll on my body.

The warden deposited my belt in a wooden crate and said, 'Remember to collect it when you leave.'

I hadn't known until then that, at the time of arrest, all clothes except those worn on the body are taken away. In the sub-jail, inmates are not given uniforms. Everything I needed was a couple of kilometres away, at my home. However, that was no longer a home. No one was there; it was locked up.

If only I could call one of my friends in Muvattupuzha, I could ask someone to bring over some essentials such as a mundu, toothbrush, toothpaste, towel, etc. I suddenly recalled my friend, Kurien's landline number.

I asked the warden with marked humility, 'Can you please make a phone call on my behalf?' hoping that, despite his hard features, he could be expected to help a new inmate.

With an expression in which arrogance and scorn were present in equal measure, he replied, 'This is not that kind of place.'

I was mortified. This was jail—a place where all your rights are extinguished.

Everything is banned, prohibited, proscribed. Except thoughts. Small mercies! The thought processes of most of the people outside prison is trammelled. In reality, I was freer than them, I consoled myself.

Kamlesh and I were allotted different cells. The *meisthiri* or 'foreman' arrived to take me to my cell. Meisthiri is a designation given by the jailers to a trustworthy prisoner when they elevate him to supervisory duties.

This meisthiri seemed to be made of sterner stuff than the jailer I had met earlier. He didn't say a word as I followed him. He seemed oddly familiar, but I couldn't place him. He unlocked Cell No. 4 for me. When I entered the room, he muttered something to the prisoners seated near the door. Those who heard him didn't respond and only glanced at me.

The meisthiri locked the cell door behind me and tugged at the padlock to make sure it was secure.

15

New Friends

I looked around the cell. It was only slightly bigger than my bedroom at home. Fourteen people were either sitting on the bare floor or lying on grass mats.

When I entered, those who were lying down sat up. They all looked at me as if I were the prodigal son returning to the bosom of the family after a long absence. I too was filled with a strange feeling of homecoming.

One of them made space for me on his mat and invited me to sit down. When I sat down in their midst in the lotus position, I felt light-hearted and relieved. Noticing my drawn and desiccated appearance, one of them offered me a steel glass of *kanji* or rice water. I gulped it down and chewed on the few grains of boiled rice that came with it.

'Have one more glass. Get rid of your fatigue.' When I drank that as well, I felt my withered body starting to cool down and come alive again.

Had anyone ever tried to quench my thirst quite so generously? I could think of none, not even my own dear ones. Then what made these strangers do it? Everyone who arrives here passes through fraught states such as life as a fugitive, and surviving the police station, lock-up, courts, etc. Therefore, they all know the piteous state of anyone who enters the cell.

'Supper is served at 5 p.m. After that, we get food only the next day,' said the *mooppan*, acknowledged as the leader of the cell. Seated by the cell door, he looked about twenty-five years old. 'But don't imagine that you'll have to starve. Most of us eat only by 8 p.m. We store it; we'll give you from that.'

I stayed silent. I saw steel plates lying around covering something beneath them. A handsome thirty-year-old man who was sitting beside the mooppan came over to sit beside me.

'You are that professor in Thodupuzha college?' I nodded. 'When I read the newspaper report in the morning, I guessed that you would be coming here.' He smiled, revealing dimples; it was the first time I had ever seen such exquisite dimples on a man.

'Would the others here know who I am?' I asked him softly.

'All those who have read the newspaper know. Every paper carried your photo.' The dimples appeared again.

An electric bell rang suddenly.

'It's time to take the "file"; the bell is for that,' said dimpled cheeks.

'The file? What is that?'

'You take attendance in schools and colleges. It's the same thing. Here it is called file,' he explained.

Seated on the floor, we formed two lines facing the cell door. A warden, holding a clipboard with a list, stood at the door. Behind him was another warden. They could see all of us from that angle. At a nod from the warden, the inmates started the count. The roll call started with one, and ended with fifteen, with each prisoner saying his number. In the midst of it, I too said a number and became part of the first roll call or 'file' after my admission. The second warden was scribbling something on the small blackboard outside the cell. I assumed he was replacing '14' with '15'.

'Sir . . . sir . . .'

The wardens turned around at our mooppan's calls.

'Sir, we've got a new admission. We're yet to get the mat and the kanji vessel.'

'There is no stock of mats and vessels in the store. Manage with what you've got . . .' retorted one of the wardens.

'Okay, we can manage without the vessel, but without the mat, it's not possible. However much we adjust, it won't work,' the mooppan tried to reason.

'Today you manage with what you have. We'll see tomorrow.' And they moved onto the next cell. Their refusal to provide a mat and a vessel didn't cause me any great sorrow.

'They're doing it on purpose. Looks like they have something against you,' said dimpled cheeks.

'By tomorrow, we'll get you a mat,' promised the mooppan. 'What you need immediately is a lungi to change into.'

'I'll stay in trousers tonight,' I said. 'I'll find a way to get a mundu from home tomorrow.'

'Even if it's for a day you'll need a mundu. The toilet has only half a door. Whether you are peeing or defecating, you'll need to squat. It won't be easy with the trousers . . . Sumesh, give him a mundu,' said the mooppan.

Sumesh was a dark-skinned man who looked to be around thirty with very little facial hair. Although he didn't protest, his face reflected his reluctance to give away a lungi. He undid his bundle and handed over a faded, chequered lungi.

The toilet had a tiled floor, looked clean, and was directly in front of the cell door. The tap was outside in the cell, with a drain hole under it. A towel, wrapped around the spigot, acted as a filter, preventing water from splashing on to the floor, and dampened the sound of falling water.

They explained the protocols of toilet usage. There was a small steel pot for carrying water—only one pot for peeing and two for defecating were allowed, a discipline imposed by the inmates themselves.

Bath time was in the morning. Bathing in the toilet was not allowed, but those with emergent needs could take mini baths, unseen by the wardens. They would need someone to pass them water from the outside.

After I changed into the lungi, a cellmate gave me a towel and yet another handed me the water, a potful at a time. The mini bath washed away some of my gloom as well. Then it was time for dinner.

Three of the men had eaten only half their quota of rice at 5 p.m. The balance was set aside to be eaten at 8 p.m. Plates appeared from various corners of the cell and from the windowsill on the left side of the cell; the window was always kept shut.

The mooppan washed a plate, served half of the rice and curry from his plate using his hand, and handed it to me.

Truth be told, after I had left home following the question-paper controversy, this was the first time that I relished my meal—white rice and jail 'puzhukku' made famous by books and movies.

I finished my share quickly. The mooppan asked whether I would like to have some more; I told him honestly that I had had my fill.

After dinner, the floor was swept clean. I understood that this was done by turns.

As we sat around, dimpled cheeks asked, 'Although we read about the question-paper controversy in the newspaper, we didn't really understand what it was about. What was the issue, really?'

Most of my cellmates turned around to hear my answer. I told them the truth without leaving anything out.

One of the listeners mused, 'If people start creating problems like this, how can stories be written and movies be made?' This was Jabbar, a Muslim who had dropped out of school after his second standard. I have always felt, then and now, that my question was proper and beyond reproach for any person with reasonable sense and intellect; even the near-illiterate Jabbar could understand the essence of the question.

I was introduced to each one of them. Jabbar was a pickpocket. There was one more Muslim, Pareeth—a wiry man of about sixty who, with the Dutch courage provided by alcohol, had assaulted one of the local leaders of a political party. Mooppan was Anish,[1] who had been introduced to the art of burglary at a rather young age and was no stranger to jail. But this time, he had been incarcerated in connection with his wife's death. Word on the street was that she had committed suicide.

The hunk was Santhosh. Though he also was a thief, he was reluctant to admit it. Sumesh, who had lent me the lungi, specialized in robbing tubers and harvested tapioca, elephant yam, colocasia, and such agricultural produce that belonged to others. Dimpled cheeks was Krishnanunni. He mentioned in passing that his was a stabbing case, without going into details.

Middle-aged Rajaram, a strict vegetarian, was a watchmaker. According to him, he was completely innocent. All he had done was ask a girl who was wearing a watch what the time was. Shortly after, a police van drew up and the rest was history. The girl's father was a policeman which is what had cooked his goose, claimed Rajaram. No one in the cell believed this story.

The elder of the cell was Philippose, addressed affectionately as Peelippappan. He was past seventy, but he was irascible and had a mean temper. His two daughters had been married off, and his son was working in the Gulf. The son, who had come down on his annual leave, had had an argument with his father. Peelippappan had swung a chopper at him.

The blow, which had struck the bridge of his son's nose, had, luckily, not been fatal. The son was rushed to hospital; the father, to jail. This had been a month ago. There was no one to arrange bail for him.

The rest were a mix of hooch-sellers and hired killers, the latter notorious in Kerala as 'quotation gang'. Two out-of-staters were also present—a Tamilian and an Andhraite. The former had been 'admitted' on that same day for a case of cheating. The Andhraite looked like a beggar and had been arrested under suspicious circumstances.

Lights-off was at 9 p.m. Pareethbhai gave me space. He spread a bedsheet beside his mat and gave me half of the area. Although the light in the jail cell was switched off, the bulb in the corridor was not, so it was not completely dark in the room.

After lights-off, the prisoners were not allowed to talk. Therefore, conversations, if any, were in whispers.

The people around me appeared to have fallen asleep, but sleep evaded me. I didn't dare to move or turn over, lest my limbs inadvertently brushed against someone and disturbed their sleep. After a while, I could feel the cold from the cement floor seep through the mat and the cotton sheet and enter my body. After a bout of rheumatic fever in the past, sleeping on the floor was difficult for me. Even if I lay on a proper mattress, I felt stiff when I woke up in the morning. However, those were problems for the morning. What I required just then was a deep sleep to get over the present discomforts.

As I lay there, two or three mosquitoes—singing in a high falsetto—started to hover over my face. Mosquitoes have always been partial to me. I have never understood why they couldn't fly in quietly, suck blood, and leave. It was the incessant buzzing that drove me to distraction.

All around me were accomplished thieves. When people like Jabbar picked a pocket, even the pockets would not realize they had been picked. Why couldn't the mosquitoes be professional like that?

16

The Sixth Holy Wound

The bell for the file woke me up. The attendance is taken twice a day, at 6 a.m. and 6 p.m. As I sat in the lotus position for the roll call, I could feel my rheumatism tormenting my joints. Probably because that April day was warm, it didn't get worse.

After the wardens left, I borrowed a dab of toothpaste from Pareethbhai and brushed my teeth using my finger. I felt like drinking something. Tea is served only with breakfast at 8 a.m. I had to make do with a glass of water from the tap. I started to feel an itching sensation in my throat, which was usual with me if I drank anything cold.

At 7.30 a.m., the meisthiri unlocked our cell door. That day, the inmates of our cell had the first turn at the baths. The next day, we would be pushed to the bottom of the queue. And so on.

The water tanks were located at the far end of the compound along the wall. A narrow flight of steps by the side of the superintendent's room led to this area. Before the prisoners arrived for their ablutions, a warden would check the tanks and its surroundings. This was to make sure that no acquaintances of the prisoners had dropped hashish or any other drugs, mobile phones, weapons, etc., over the wall.

Two or three wardens stood sentinel along the route to the tanks. The prisoners walked down, each of them carrying their own towel, soap and a mug to scoop out water from the water tanks. I had none of these. Each inmate was given five minutes to bathe. I borrowed the towel and mug from the first to finish his bath, grabbed the first bar of soap which I saw lying there, poured a couple of mugs of water hurriedly over my head and soaped myself. By this time, the inmates of the next cell had already arrived. I hurriedly poured another couple of mugs of water over myself, somehow towelled myself dry, wrapped my lungi around myself and almost ran to catch up with the others.

One of the wardens standing by the superintendent's office spoke to me as I hurried past him, 'It was probably your brother-in-law—but someone has brought in clothes and other stuff for you. Collect these from the office.'

'Sir, I didn't get a mat to sleep on,' I said meekly.

'Tell the meisthiri, he'll get one for you.'

When I opened the bag after reaching the cell, I was happy to see that it contained two cotton lungis, two bedsheets, a towel, a toothbrush, a toothpaste and some soap. He had brought it the previous evening, from hundreds of kilometres away in Murickassery, and had given it to the warden. If only they had been given to me yesterday evening or at least this morning, I thought with a tinge of sadness.

Breakfast starts only after all inmates have finished their bath. The meisthiri opened the cell door and we formed a queue outside, plate and glass in hand. The prisoners who are deployed as cooks in the kitchen act as servers too. Two wardens keep watch over us.

I was served two thick chapattis and chickpea curry, which was mostly gravy. The tea was piping hot. For many years, breakfast in Kerala's jails was always boiled wheat rolled into balls and coconut and green chilli chutney, so much so that it had become a metaphor for going to jail. I had missed the notorious wheat balls by a mere week or so, when Muvattupuzha jail had switched to chapattis. We returned to the cell with the food. The meisthiri locked the door and went to the next cell.

We sat in a circle as we ate; this allowed us to pass on whatever we could spare to those who wanted more. Some of the elders gave away a chapatti and made do with the previous day's rice, which had been preserved by adding water. They had a cache of yoghurt that they added to the gruel. The young men preferred chapattis and ate four or five each. They ate less rice during lunch and supper and remained lean. Perhaps their profession demanded such a physique.

I didn't share the two chapattis that I was served. This was the first meal given to me after my arrival in the jail, fully paid for from the government treasury. I polished it all off.

The floor was swept after food; there was no compromise on that practice. How could there be? There was not more than 180 square feet floor space to accommodate fifteen men. Some of the youngsters turned to reading—the cell had a small library of weeklies and film magazines. These are usually bought by undertrials who have to go to court. Some played board games such as Ludo, Snakes and Ladders, and chess. A carrom board was available, but we had to request the meisthiri for it. Playing cards was banned.

As I watched a chess game in progress, Krishnanunni nudged me, 'There goes the meisthiri. Tell him you're still to get your mat and that the warden had said that the meisthiri would give it to you.'

I had gathered from the others that the meisthiri's name was Mohanan.

I went up to the cell door and called out respectfully, 'Mohananchetta . . .' and added deferentially, 'I didn't get my mat yet. The warden said it'll be given . . .'

He gave me a sympathetic look and asked, 'Did the warden say that it'll be given?'

'Yes,' I said, hope rising in my heart.

'Then the warden will give it to you.' He sailed past me.

Krishnanunni had overheard our conversation. When I went back inside, he said, 'The meisthiri is very angry.'

'Why?' I asked anxiously.

'He hasn't understood this question-paper case. He thinks that the students' futures have been affected because of you.'

'"Students' futures have been affected"? How?'

'That's what he says.'

'Also, he knows you from before.'

'How? From where?' That piqued me. I had also gotten the impression that I had seen him before.

'He didn't say how or from where. Only that he knows you from before.' I thought that was possible.

'Yesterday, when he opened the cell and let me in, what did he whisper to you?'

'Ayy . . . nothing . . .' he tried to avert his face.

'Is it something that I mustn't be told?'

'Not that. It's just that . . . I don't know how to tell you.'

'Don't worry. Tell me.'

'He asked me to welcome you with a *natayati*.' Krishnanunni sounded embarrassed.

I had guessed that that was what had been said; but, when I heard it now, I felt a little twinge in my heart.

I knew what natayati was from prisoners' stories. It's a rite of passage, in a manner of speaking, where a newcomer is given a thrashing by a group of people, all simultaneously, and he wouldn't even recognize the people beating him up.

'Then why didn't you do as he had instructed?'

'You are a professor. Not only that, you are not here because you committed some crime.'

'But you realized that only after I explained it to you.'

'The exact story, yes. But from all the news stories we had read, we felt it was only an unintentional mistake on your part.'

'Is this still a practice?'

Krishnanunni explained, 'People involved in murder and sexual abuse cases are welcomed with natayati. The ones who are thrashed the most are the ones involved in sexual violence against women, and it is not confined to a thrashing. If the prisoner complains to the wardens, he is transferred to another cell. When he goes there, it's back to square one again. The wardens largely turn a blind eye to this assault.'

I marvelled at the fact that Malayalis at all levels—even prisoners—were invested in the other's morality more than in one's own. They are so vigilant that even in the case of mating dogs they make no exception and throw a stone at them.

I wonder whether any other community has so much intolerance towards sex and sexuality as Malayali men. I have always thought this sham morality of the Malayali men—who, given the least opportunity, will ogle at the opposite sex, or turn into peeping toms and have no qualms about invading people's privacy—is the revolting manifestation of their own repressed sexuality.

'Until he gets convicted, the accused in peddling spurious liquor, pickpocketing and similar cases can escape *natayati*; but in order to get accepted among the cellmates, there are certain rituals. When a new admission comes, depending on their imagination, the seniors in the cell try to make the scene as dramatic as possible. As planned, everyone ignores the new entrant altogether. The atmosphere is more solemn than that in a courtroom. As the man remains helpless in that lifeless cell, the mooppan will point to the farthest corner and order him, with all the gravitas of a judge, to sit there. As soon as he is seated there, from this corner, the mooppan will start to grill him dramatically.

'"What is your name?"

'He has to answer loudly for everyone in the room to hear. If he doesn't, he'll be made to.

'"Where's your place?"

'"What's your crime?"

'He must reply very humbly. If he doesn't then things will get serious.

'"Okay, come here," the mooppan will command.

'When the man approaches him, the mooppan will show him a matchstick and ask him, "Do you know what this is?"

'"A matchstick."

'"Reply only to the question," the mooppan's tone will become severe.

'"Do you know what this is?"

'"Yes, I know."

'"What is it?"

'"It's a matchstick."

'"No, it's a measuring stick. Now use this to measure the perimeter of this room."

'Till the perimeter is measured using that 'ruler' no one will utter a word. Sometimes, two steel tumblers will be kept a foot apart, mimicking goal posts. A piece of paper will be crumpled and made into a ball by the mooppan who'll throw it on the floor at the other end of the room. The new guy must get on his knees, blow air from his mouth, and score a goal with it. Usually, it's the young prisoners who are made to do this.'

Not everyone who comes to jail is subjected to such ragging. Some of the men are beaten up so badly by the so-called peacekeepers that, by the time they arrive at the jail, they lack even the strength to stand up. The hapless men arrested in forest cases are often half-dead.

Those who come to the cell after experiencing such physical trauma— except sexual predators—are not only spared the ritual ragging but are

cared for—their wounds are tended to, their bruises are anointed with
balm, and a healing fomentation is given using hot rice bound in a towel.

I understood from the other prisoners that the forest officers were
the most brutal and ruthless. According to the prisoners, compared to
their savagery, what the state police did was nothing.

Around 10.30 a.m., the meisthiri asked me to report to the
superintendent's office. The previous day, when I had been brought in, he
had not been present. Today, when he reported for duty, he must have
felt the desire to meet the extraordinary prisoner who had been jailed
for something as innocuous as setting a question paper for an internal
examination.

At his office, I greeted the uniformed superintendent by placing my
hand over my heart and bowing my head. He must have noticed that I
was clad in a simple lungi. He gestured towards a chair and asked me to
sit down.

'Which department of the college are you from?' he had a friendly
expression.

'Malayalam.'

'The problems started with a question paper, isn't it? What really
happened?'

I looked at the name tag on his shirt. His name indicated that, while
he was not of my religion, neither was he of the one which I had allegedly
insulted. It was only natural that he wanted to hear the story from the
horse's mouth.

I began my narrative in a relaxed manner, as one professional to
another, a college professor to a state government employee, on equal
terms. However, he didn't have the patience to listen to my story.

'When I was in Thrissur,' he interrupted me, 'some guy wrote a play
called *Kristhuvinte Aaram Thirumurivu* . . . (The Sixth Holy Wound of
Christ)'.

'P.M. Antony,' I interjected automatically. As a professor of literature,
I knew of the playwright and his dramatic activities. *Spartacus*, which his
drama troupe had performed—before the controversial *Kristhuvinte
Aaram Thirumurivu*—was very famous. *The Sixth Holy Wound* became a
legal case. Caught up in its tentacles, his drama practice ground to a halt.
His dramatic genius throttled by 'literate' Kerala, the poor man was now
eking out a living by rearing cows and selling milk.

'Ah-yeah . . . some Antony,' the superintendent continued, '*Sixth Holy Wound*[1] . . . it's the other thing . . . sex. A group of believers led by a bishop protested against the staging of the play, but the drama troupe, along with some intellectuals, insisted that the play would go on, claiming their constitutional right to freedom of expression . . . religious sentiment getting hurt—isn't that the most incendiary spark? Oh, what a hullabaloo . . .'

He was talking in a loud voice. After his declamation as a first-hand witness, he concluded, 'Therefore, when you do such things, you should be doubly careful, otherwise you could end up inside.'

I responded with a smile, 'Well, I am inside.'

That caused him to smile too. He gestured to me that I could leave.

'Sir, I haven't yet got a mat to sleep on.' I didn't forget to press my only demand.

'You'll get all that,' he replied dismissively.

17

A Song in the Jail

When I returned to the cell, I felt there was a marked diminution in its population. However, the only two missing were the ones who had been commandeered to assist in the kitchen for the next day's Easter feast. The kitchen needed extra hands for two days to prepare for the feast for the prisoners. Preparation of pickles and side dishes had started already.

Had I been at home, I would have been busy too. We would shop until noon; cooking would start after that. Traditionally, on special occasions, meat dishes were cooked by men. However, my Easter this year was in this government 'guest house'—no expenses; no toil. All I had to do was wash my hands and sit at the table. A special feast with a family of uncommon brothers.

The meisthiri asked me to accompany him. Apparently, I had a visitor. The inveterate smokers in the cell asked me to get the visitor to buy a packet of Jyothiman beedis.

My first visitor at the jail was Prof. George Justin. He had retired the previous year from the English department of Nirmala College. Our friendship went back to the time when I had started my teaching career at Pavanatma College. He asked if I needed any monetary or legal help. I told him that I would let him know and, in my heart, bowed to his generosity. However, as an immediate request, I asked him to buy some packets of beedis and leave them at the office with instructions to deliver them to Cell No. 4.

Around noon, a newspaper was delivered to our cell. The pages were distributed among the inmates. Others tried to read over their shoulders, or the reverse side, all showing an avid curiosity about the outside world, the world that had rejected them. Jabbar, though illiterate, eagerly got someone to read his sheet out aloud. From their reactions, I could make out that the news about cheating, burglary, and defrauding were the ones that thrilled them.

My eccentricities precluded my being a part of the cooperative reading culture of the jail. I was particular that every page of the newspaper which I was reading should be in its place. When I was reading the daily, if someone were to ask for a sheet, I would either refuse to give it altogether, or hand over the whole newspaper. To me, many people sharing a newspaper was as abhorrent as many men ravishing one woman at the same time. I resented it even if someone peeped into the paper which I was reading.

'There's news about you today.' Krishnanunni read out the piece to me, the gist of which was that I had been sent to Muvattupuzha sub-jail.

The meisthiri came to let us out for lunch. Jabbar picked up his plate chortling, 'Oh boy, it's mutton today!' I had heard that mutton was served once a week in jails. Unfortunately for me, I had an inattentive server who didn't really care whether or not what he served actually landed on the plate. Consequently, my portion of the mutton fry remained stuck to the ladle, and all I got was two or three fragments of bone.

The prisoner-cooks dished out mouth-watering food. The potato stew made to complement the mutton was delectable. Even the meagre amount of masala adhering to the bits of bones on my plate tickled the palate. Being a mutton-special day, vegetable curry and yoghurt had been cancelled. By the time I finished half my rice, the potato stew was over. As I licked the bone pieces clean to accompany the remainder of the rice on my plate, I glanced across at the vegetarian, Rajaram's plate. He had been given aviyal in place of mutton. Just for a moment there, I wished I were a vegetarian.

After our 3 p.m. black tea service, the meisthiri came with my mat and a small bundle of beedis. Apparently, Justin had left a parcel for me containing twenty beedi packets. Only half of that eventually reached me. Anish divided the beedis equally between the thirteen smokers in the cell. Rajaram and I were the exceptions. After a meal, the smokers invariably

lighted up; without a breeze or proper ventilation, the cell quickly filled up
with beedi smoke. Gasping for air, Rajaram and I would stand near the cell
door, our faces squeezed between the bars. While Rajaram didn't have any
qualms about showing his displeasure, I did. As I had been a heavy smoker
for a longish time before I quit, I didn't feel quite the same level of discomfort
that he did.

It was while I was incarcerated in the confines of the prison cell that
I realized that, if a person wanted to walk to exercise, he didn't need acres
of park or a long stretch of road. It was fascinating to watch men walking
for about an hour or more in a room that housed fifteen adults. Only
three of four people walked at a time, in a line, one behind the other and
without bumping into one another. All the others flattened themselves
against the wall, affording the walkers as much room as possible.

As I watched my cellmates walk in that fashion, it dawned on me
that dogs running in circles in their kennels and squirrels doing looping
runs in their spinning cages were all efforts to keep themselves fit.

Jabbar would walk chanting an Arabic prayer. Although he didn't
know its meaning, he said it was to avert dangers. I joined his walk of
worship.

That evening, I noticed Peelippappan whisper something in
Krishnanunni's ear. Since the old man's expression was conspiratorial,
I asked Krishnanunni what he had said. Krishnanunni looked at
Peelippappan and laughed out loud as he said, 'Peelippappan didn't know
what your crime was, sir. Last night when he asked me, I told him that
you and your wife had had an argument, and that, in a rage, you had shot
her with your gun. Ever since then, Peelippappan wants to slap you. As
he cannot do it by himself, he wanted us to do it. He was reminding me
that. You had shot your own wife, and Pappan cannot stomach that.'

Krishnanunni looked at Peelippappan and grinned mischievously.
Peelippappan squirmed, now that his 'good intentions' had been exposed.
What a specimen! He was the one who had slashed at his own son's
neck—it's another matter that his son didn't die—but when it comes to
others, he wants summary justice to be meted out. All men are the same.
Blind to the plank in their own eye, they will pay attention to the speck
of sawdust in the other man's eye.

'Let it be, Pappa,' Krishnanunni consoled him, 'at least it was his
own wife . . . not someone else's wife.' Pappan didn't say anything.

Didn't the old man understand that Krishnanunni was only pulling his leg? I don't know!

Krishnanunni's[1] innocent looks, smile, and way of talking were enough to attract anyone. How could he be an accused in a case of stabbing? When I asked him, he smiled, once more revealing his dimples. 'Yesterday, I said it was a stabbing case just for a lark . . . but mine is a case of theft,' he confided.

'This Sumesh guy is also a thief. However, his swag is petty, trifling stuff—elephant yam, colocasia, tapioca, latex . . . he can't even think beyond them. Ours is a few grades higher—but whether you call it cheating, robbery, or whatever else, in effect, they're all the same.

'We have a home-nurse supply company as our front with a posh office in the town with computers and stuff. We even have a lady staff member; no one would dream of suspecting us. Among the home-nurses whom we deploy to the various households, we have "our own" girls. We send them into the homes of rich women who live alone. These confidence tricksters look after the old ladies—deprived of the care and company of their own children and grandchildren—like their own mothers or grandmothers and win their complete trust. They will behave demurely and humbly with the children or relatives who visit or call once in a while. After a while, they start to build a sob story of a dead father, terminally ailing mother and money-grubbing relatives.

'One of them may claim that as she is worried that her bullying brother, a drunkard and a gambler, will forcibly take her money away, she would like to hand back her salary to the old lady for "safekeeping". Another nurse may give Rs 20,000 or Rs 50,000 to the gullible old woman, again for safekeeping, claiming that she had bid and won a chit-fund auction. She will say that it is for her wedding and that she's asking for help because she is afraid her brother will take it away. It's human nature to trust those who trust us. To support the scam, we would send these amounts from our office to be handed over as chit-fund money.

'Within a couple of months, the girl will become the old woman's confidante and be trusted more than her own children. The girl will eventually inveigle her way to become a member of the household, handling not only her employer's bank deposits but also taking care of the gullible old lady's ornaments kept both at home and in the bank locker, etc.

'Then, on the day when the maximum number of valuables and amount of money can be looted from the house, she will mix sedatives in the old lady's tea or food, as directed by us. The victim will lose consciousness for five to six hours and within that time, we get there in a car and carry away the money and valuables along with the home-nurse. It's only after she wakes up from her drugged sleep that the old lady realizes who her home-nurse really was.'

'Where do you get the sedatives from?' I interrupted him.

'There are doctors we know who will arrange all that, and also tell us the correct dosage.'

'Do they suspect just the home-nurse? Don't they come to your office?'

'They do come. When they do, we give them the girl's address and other details. When they investigate, they discover that it's all phoney.'

'Doesn't it become a problem for you as it was you who had sent her?'

'We are able to show the ID proof given by the fraudster. They will think that we too have been duped.'

'Then how did you get caught?'

'The chances of getting caught were slim,' Krishnanunni continued, 'because usually neither the lady nor her folks will complain to the police. The children are usually not interested. They are prepared to forget what they lost. They are the ones who don't have the time to look after their mother. In most cases, the people didn't complain. One party came to know that another lady had been duped in the exact same fashion that they had been. When they found out that in both cases the girl had been sent by us, they complained to the police. The police very cleverly grabbed us.'

'Who all?'

'My partner and me. Also the woman in the office. Everybody is here.'

'Isn't that woman innocent? Isn't it awful that she has to pay for your crimes?'

'She knew what was going on and was paid a share of the booty.' Krishnanunni had no regrets about her being punished.

'However, the police have not been able to capture the girls who went in as home-nurses. Although we were hung upside down and bird's-eye chilli paste was applied to our eyes, neither my partner nor I have told the police about their whereabouts. As long as the girls cannot be traced, the case will be dismissed. We've already spent Rs 1.5 lakh now; another Rs 2.5 lakh will have to be spent on lawyer fees and all that. We've set that money aside.'

'How did you spend all the money that you looted?'

'All that has been secured using proxies.'

'What are your plans after you get out? Will you run the same scam again?'

'No, now I won't do it again. I'll do something else. I was first caught by the police in a currency doubling scam. The home-nurse scheme rose in my mind while I was serving the jail sentence for that. Every jail sentence is an opportunity to dream up schemes and discover new ones, and not a time to regret and cry over getting caught.'

'Good sportsman spirit,' I said, involuntarily. Krishnanunni smiled, and his dimples bloomed.

Easter breakfast was idli and sambar, a change from the usual chapatti and chickpeas curry. I had a stream of visitors until noon. One of the visitors was a bakery owner who whimpered as he embraced me. I used to copy edit their notices and advertisements for Onam and Christmas.

We were seated in a row in the corridor in front of the cell for the feast in the traditional style, with food served on plantain leaves. Apart from the vegetarian dishes of the traditional Kerala *sadya* or feast, the main dish was a well-made beef curry.

Sunday was movie day—the jail had a TV in the reading room. However, with the wardens being preoccupied with Easter celebrations, on that day we didn't get to watch a movie. The prayers groups would also come on Sundays to provide solace to prisoners and to try to convert or reform them. However, as they were probably too busy celebrating the Resurrection to think of the sinners that day, they didn't show up. The prisoners got bored, so they started to sing. Jabbar kept the beat; Sumesh and Santhosh were good singers. Krishnanunni provided percussion accompaniment inasmuch as he could.

When the soirée ended, Jabbar came over to me. 'You are the one who teaches songs and stories; I need your help.'

'What kind of help?'

'I've written a song. Please correct the errors in that.'

I got hold of a sheet of paper and pen and wrote it down. This was a song composed by a semi-illiterate man. After changing some words and adding a few, I made it:

O peacock, you dance to the beat of thappu,
O cuckoo, your heart fills with ragas;
We are rocked in this boat of life,
And our hearts meander with the waves.

'Sing the rest of it,' I said, as I got ready to transcribe.

'That is all. You have to write the rest.' Jabbar then sang the revised version with a pleasing tempo.

Krishnanunni suggested, 'You are sitting idle, anyway, so let this be an assignment for you.'

I decided to make an attempt. I have been approached by various people for filling in application forms, writing petitions, speeches, slogans, notices and to even ghost-write poems published in school and college magazines and the like. I have never disappointed anyone by turning them away. I always considered it my responsibility to fulfil all such literary needs.

I did my graduation and post-graduation from government-aided colleges where I paid no tuition or examination fees. Therefore, right from my college days, it became ingrained in my psyche that it was my duty and responsibility to fulfil the need of the common man. When my short poems were published under others' names, I felt more gratified than if they had appeared under my name.

I applied my mind to Jabbar's song. Love and sorrow were the leitmotifs. I added a smidgen of the pangs of separation from my side. I channelled Changampuzha into my soul and wrote the additional lines:

Your sole memories are
The rock candies of my heart;
Heaven will descend on this earth
The day we become one.
Bathed in tears of happiness
We hummed the nightjar's melodies;
The constellation of stars
Danced in glee to our rhymes.

There's a story behind these lines, which shall be told in good time.

I copied this down neatly on another sheet of paper and handed it over to Jabbar. I retained the first draft with me. Jabbar and company experimented with many tunes and kept singing this repeatedly.

Later, Jabbar told me, 'I must make my daughter sing this and make an album.'

'How old is your daughter?'

'Twelve.' Jabbar seemed to be an indulgent father.

The next day also brought me a number of visitors. Many of them met me in the presence of the jail superintendent. He spoke to all of them, showing sympathy towards me. He said that he had even considered shifting me to the hospital block but had decided against it because of the security issues.

'Why the hospital?' I asked.

'There you'll have a cot,' he said.

'So, how is it here?' asked one of my friends curiously.

Probably amused by my friend's ignorance about the conditions in a jail, the superintendent smiled and said, 'Here, he must sleep on the floor.' My friend looked at me with sadness.

'So what if they have to sleep on the floor, there are no other issues. We had a fantastic feast yesterday for Easter,' the superintendent spoke with the dignity of a paterfamilias, and turned to me and asked, 'How was the feast?'

'It was good,' I replied.

'You are a man of language and literature. I guess you'll be writing about your life here. And people like me will figure in that as characters, won't we?'

'Assuredly,' I said, but to myself.

In between, the superintendent lowered his voice and spoke to me, 'Don't forget that all your cellmates are hardened criminals. In the midst of a conversation, in the heat of the moment, do not inadvertently reveal your telephone number or the location of your house. You won't know how or when you'll get screwed.'

I nodded distractedly.

I had revealed all these details in my cell long ago. Fear gripped me. Would something untoward happen?

As soon as I was back in the cell, lunch was served. The day's special was fish curry.

Muvattupuzha jail served fish on Mondays and Wednesdays. Although it is usually fresh fish, on that day it was dried fish, because fresh fish had become very expensive.

I waited with a steel plate in each hand for the rice and the fish. The first server dumped some rice on to the plate in my left hand; the second server placed a piece of fried shark on the other plate. The third server poured a piping-hot, tamarind-and-chilly curry into the second plate almost immediately. The four fingers of my right hand which had been supporting the plate from beneath felt like they had been scalded. Unable to withstand the burn, I begged the server to hold the plate, but he ignored me. Quick thinking made me place the plate on top of the other. In my pain and distress, I didn't catch something that the server muttered while refusing to help me.

As I sat down in the cell to eat, my fingers were smarting. Small blisters had already started to appear on all of my four fingers. When he caught me examining my fingers, Krishnanunni asked, 'What happened?'

'Usually we roast fish, but in the jail, the fish roasted me.' With that, I started to pick at my fish with my blistered fingers.

18

Who Wants Freedom?

The barber's day in the jail is Tuesday although all barbershops in the state are closed on Tuesdays. So, although the rate given by the jail is lower, the barbers get to earn an extra bit working on a holiday.

I only needed a shave. This was the first time in my life that I was getting this service for free. I had poor facial hair growth, which had caused me some sorrow during my youth. However, that turned to relief when I saw the struggles of people wanting to get rid of their stiff stubbles.

It was when I went to the Philippines in 2004 to attend a seminar that I reigned as a moustache king for a while. I felt proud when I overheard people referring to it as thick and lush, although it was a case of the one-eyed man being king in the land of the blind. Being mainly of Mongoloid race, the Filipino men's upper lips had a few hairs at the corners at best.

Very few racial types in India can match Sikhs in hirsutism. Sikhs were among the early migrants to the Philippines and have been settled there for generations. Traditionally, they have been moneylenders and are dubbed as 'Bombaywallahs'. Their hirsutism is beyond the aesthetics of Filipinos. If *kaattumaakaan* or the wild cat was the bogeyman used by Malayali mothers and grandmothers to intimidate their intractable wards into eating their food, the Bombaywallah was the bogeyman used to frighten children in Philippines.

Although we were prisoners, a new blade was being used for each shave. As he took a new safety razor blade, snapped it in two, and fitted one half into the slot in his straight razor, he asked me in a friendly manner, 'Where's your house in Maradi?'

'It's not in Maradi. It's in Muvattupuzha.'

'Oh . . .' one swipe of the razor.

'The newspaper said Maradi.'

'They got it wrong.'

'Oh . . .' another swipe of the razor.

A couple more questions and answers and the rasping razor had done its job.

After returning to the cell, the inmates admired their beauty in the sliver of a broken mirror, Jabbar's prized possession. I was also given my turn. I laughed when I saw my reflection in the mirror, hardly the size of a human eye. Patches of my sparse beard could be seen in various spots on my face, unshaven.

In the evening, Mithun and Saju, my brother-in-law, came to see me. They were on the way back from the court in Thodupuzha. They had expected my bail to come through, but the judge had put off the hearing to the next day. They seemed disheartened. Strangely, I was unaffected.

In the night, before lights-off, Peelippappan started to feel a discomfort in his chest. He started to moan holding his chest. The inmates started to massage his chest and pat his abdomen like they were his sons. Jabbar and the others heated a glass of water by burning a piece of paper and an old plastic toothbrush. After drinking that, he let out a few burps and belches and smiled in relief.

'He has filled his tummy with gas, smoking so many beedis. Don't give the old man any more beedis from now on,' said Pareeth. It was true—if he saw anyone smoking, he too would want one. If they said they didn't have any, he would beg for the stub.

I know professors who desisted from carrying their own smokes, not wanting to share their cigarette or beedi packets, and preferring to cadge from others. Our cell didn't have such selfish people. However, considering the state of his health, everyone decided to limit the beedis they gave Pappan.

Of all the communities I have come across in this world, the one place where I saw fraternity and equality practised the most was in Cell No. 4. Even if they were criminals, I witnessed more love for their fellowmen than among the people roaming free outside. Jabbar would wash Peelippappan's clothes like a son—for a man who had been incarcerated for trying to murder his own son.

When I woke up the next morning, the sun hadn't risen. Mohanan was sweeping the jail. If he could hold down a job outside with the same diligence, he would have risen in his career. Why then was he going around burgling the collection boxes of churches and temples, which, I had been told by others, was his metier? It was some strange kind of fate, I thought.

I sat watching him sweep out the yard. Suddenly some of his previous exploits flashed through my mind.

During my college days, there was a family that tended to our paddy field in Murickassery. The tilling and the maintenance of the ridge were done by the menfolk in the family; gathering and re-planting the seedlings, weeding, harvesting, etc., were done by the womenfolk. They lived about half a kilometre from our house. They were fed rice at our house, twice a day, in the morning and afternoon. During the days that I spent at home, I would join them in the field and serve them food.

Mohanan was related to that family. Sometimes he would accompany his uncle to work in the field. That three-decade-old acquaintance had been lying buried among the detritus of our memories. Mohanan ended up as a meisthiri in the sub-jail. I was a student then and had now ended up as an inmate in Cell No. 4 in the same sub-jail.

The same comrade, with whom I had stood shoulder-to-shoulder in the muddy field, had given instructions to my cellmates to welcome me with *natayati*. I felt sad. Apparently, he had not recognized me. I decided to let it remain that way.

That day's newspaper had an item on me: 'Question-paper controversy—Prof. T.J. Joseph's bail application hearing today.' The case was to be tried in the Chief Judicial Magistrate's court at Thodupuzha. If I were to be granted bail, I could return to the bosom of my family, ending my stay at this wellness resort. I suddenly felt swamped by a feeling of homesickness which I had been spared of ever since I had left home.

Although I was anxious to know the outcome of the hearing, I wasn't taking any chances and saved half of the fish curry from my lunch for my supper. At around 5 p.m., the meisthiri asked me to go to the superintendent's office. My friend, Kurien, was there.

'Professor, your bail has been granted. Please get dressed and come back.' I was clad in only a lungi. As I walked back, I felt as if a huge load had lifted off me.

'You've got bail, haven't you?' Jabbar asked.

They had taken for granted that my bail would come through and had even divvied up amongst themselves my cache of oil, washing soap and other jail supplies. I took back only my lungi because I wanted to donate the rest to Anish, who had shared his dinner with me on my first night here and also because he had requested for it. He was yet to return from the court, where he had to appear for his hearing.

I gave it to them announcing that it had to be given to Anish. The lungi I had worn until then, I gave to Sumesh, who had given me his lungi on the first day. The rest of the things remained with whoever had laid a claim to them.

I was helped by the inmates to get dressed. After putting on my shirt and trousers, I tried to gather up my papers. I couldn't find the piece on which I had written the ditty. As I searched for it, Jabbar asked, 'What are you looking for?'

'That paper on which I wrote the song.'

Opening his left fist halfway, he revealed a slightly crumpled piece of paper. 'Why are you taking it with you?' he scowled.

I replied disarmingly, 'Just like that.'

'You don't get to take this,' he said with an air of finality.

For a moment, I was filled with helpless anger and sadness. I had composed those lines with serious mental effort. I wanted it only as a holy relic of my stay in the jail. Jabbar, planning to release an album with his daughter, probably didn't trust me. He may have suspected that I may use the song before he got it released. However, was it right on his part to take it away from its creator with such arrogance and impunity?

I suddenly recalled the lines of my childhood—the poet's view that the greatest wealth is instruction of knowledge:

No robber can plunder
The more you give, the more it grows.

Only after the lines were written in my mind, were they transferred on to the paper now in Jabbar's hands. Which thief can steal that first edition?

With the smile of a victor, I looked at Jabbar, and then bid goodbye to all the others.

As I was leaving, Pareethbhai caught hold of my hand and said, 'In our community, some have extreme views. You should be careful.' He had shared his mat with me on the first day of my stay. I could see his eyes brimming with affection.

As I walked to the superintendent's office, I turned around for a last look at Cell No. 4. The barred door and the souls inside looked like a sketch.

After comparing the identification marks on my body with the ones in the bail order, the superintendent read out one of the conditions of the bail: I should not enter Thodupuzha taluk. The college I was teaching in was in that taluk. Since I was under suspension, there was no immediate need to go Thodupuzha.

After he made me sign on the bail bond and other papers, the superintendent stood up and told me, 'Now you are free.'

I recalled the scene in Vaikom Muhammad Basheer's *Mathilukal* (Walls) in which the protagonist is being released from jail. When the jailer says, 'You can go Mr Basheer. You are free,' the protagonist asks him, 'Why should I be free . . . who wants freedom?'

Basheer was saying: Free man! Free world! Whose free world? To get into a bigger jail? Who needs this freedom?

'Yes, boss,' I said to myself, out of the superintendent's earshot. 'But I don't have an option.'

The superintendent extended his hand; I shook it and went to the warden's room. I asked for my belt stored in the wooden crate, and walked out to Kurien.

'Sir . . .' I turned around on hearing the call. One of the wardens was hurrying towards me.

'Are you leaving without giving us a "treat"?' he asked in an undeservedly amiable tone.

The same worthy had told me with overweening disdain, 'This is not the place,' when I, untutored in jail regulations, had requested him with all humility to make a call to the very same Kurien, who stood by watching, so that he could bring me a change of clothes.

'Soman sir is transferred to Viyyur Jail. We want to have a party before that . . . you *have* to get us two full bottles . . .' He was pleading.

Hiding my scorn and anger, I said sweetly, 'I don't have any money on me.'

'You can get him to buy them,' he gestured towards Kurien. I was at a loss for words.

'If you have a problem with buying it, it's all right if you just give the money instead.' He was reduced to begging.

I said nothing. Reading my expression, he said disappointedly, 'If it's such a problem for you, it's okay, forget it.' I found the wretched look on his face repulsive. He let me go only because he wasn't getting anywhere with me.

Only when I emerged from the jail did I notice the others who had come to take me home—my brother-in-law, Saju, his friend, and my sister's husband, Baby, were also in the car.

'What were you discussing with that warden? He didn't seem too pleased,' Kurien asked me as we walked to the car.

'He wants two bottles of liquor,' I said without enthusiasm.

'Should we? If you want, I'll arrange it,' Kurien said earnestly.

'There's no need,' I said, as I got into the car.

Saju started the car with the observation, 'Most of the jail wardens are bigger crooks and extortionists than its inmates.'

'After you were remanded, I called a friend in Muvattupuzha and asked him to go to the sub-jail. The jail authorities demanded Rs 50,000 to provide you with the amenities allowed in the jail. If we had paid that, you would have been put in a room near the kitchen and not in the cell with the criminals. He asked me what was to be done. I told him to come away from there. When we came there at around 8 p.m. with the lungis and other stuff, they said we would need to pay if we wished to ensure that the stuff actually reached you, and extracted Rs 2,000 from us.'

'After taking that money, they still didn't send me the things. They didn't even give me a mat to sleep on,' I interrupted him.

'They were getting back at you for not landing that Rs 50,000. They must have assumed that, as a college professor, you would automatically pay up.'

I realized that the superintendent's truculence during our first meeting stemmed from this.

'The wardens extorted either money or liquor from almost everyone who came to meet you.'

I felt deeply mortified to hear this. I said, 'They will demand, but that doesn't mean you all have to give.'

'Everyone gives fearing that if they were to refuse, you would be beaten up or harassed.'

'That I'll be beaten up! They all become like this and worse because people like you get scared and give in, giving them money and liquor.'

'Don't get upset,' Baby tried to calm me down. 'This is the way things work in all the jails in our state.'

I was being taken to my in-laws' house in Murickassery, where she and my children were billeted. Kurien got off at Muvattupuzha town. It was a three-hour drive. I kept nursing the memories of my sojourn in the jail. I felt like a man returning to his family after serving a life-sentence.

19

Peacekeepers' Sorrows

We reached my wife's house by 9 p.m., after dropping Baby on the way at Kambilikandam. Apart from my immediate family, my wife's uncle and some younger relatives were present. I could make out that no one seemed to be in celebratory mood. Salomi started to sob. Mithun looked lost and numb, although Amy looked happy to meet me. All of them seemed to be suffering from the unexpected psychological blow. It was a funereal atmosphere, enough to drain my zest at having fought valiantly and returned home to tell the tale.

I hadn't imagined that my craven flight from home to escape unknown persons and undefined threats would mark the beginning of a chapter of miseries for my family.

As soon as Mithun returned after dropping me at the bus station, a posse of policemen from the local police station had arrived. To their questions about my whereabouts, he told them the truth. They didn't believe him and stood guard at both entrances of my house. They kept peeping in through the windows to keep watch on my family's movements and to listen in on any telephone calls.

Mithun switched on the TV but after he saw the channels trying to outdo each other in covering the question-paper controversy, he switched it off in disgust. Mother and son felt stifled by the hovering policemen. Not wanting to tangle with the police, none of the prudent neighbours or locally important persons came to lend their moral or physical support.

In the afternoon, despite her distress, Salomi made lunch and summoned Mithun. He was so distraught that he didn't even hear her.

Another group of policemen from Thodupuzha arrived in the afternoon. They had come to arrest me under non-bailable charges of trying to cause religious enmity. This group also behaved rudely with Salomi and Mithun. They entered the house and searched every nook and cranny. They questioned Mithun and Salomi repeatedly and aggressively. Mithun told them that he had dropped me off at the bus station and that I hadn't told him where I was headed.

The policemen threatened to take away the son if the father couldn't be found. That really scared Salomi, who clutched Mithun close to her. In her bid to prove her husband's innocence, Salomi dug out *Thirakathayute Reethisastram* that contained the dialogue reproduced in the question paper and showed it to the policemen. In their thrill of laying their hands on the 'weapon' used in the crime, the policemen examined it minutely, passing it around from one policeman to the other. When they eventually went away, they took the lethal weapon with them. After the Thodupuzha posse left, the Muvattupuzha posse continued their vigil.

Monsignor Thomas Malekudi, the manager of Newman College, called on our landline. He told Mithun that it was advisable that I surrender to the police, and that Monsignor could come with me when I surrendered to Inspector General of Police B. Sandhya. Although Mithun had misgivings about the monsignor's advice, as my phone was switched off by then, he couldn't convey the message.

At around 5 p.m. T.A. Joy arrived to take Salomi and Mithun with him, as I had requested. They took our car, leaving the police to guard the empty house.

Salomi's brother, Saju, arrived by 10 p.m. and took them from Joy's house to Murickassery. Saju's house was adjacent to the local police station. Early the next morning, a policeman came to say that Saju and Mithun were to report to the police station. When they went there, the sub-inspector was away and they were made to wait for an hour for his return.

He questioned them and took their mobiles to check their call registers. He called the Thodupuzha police station and reported that the absconding professor's son and brother-in-law were in his custody.

He was instructed to take them to Thodupuzha. He asked Mithun to carry our house key, as they wanted to search the house.

At 11 a.m., in the company of the SI and another policeman, they left for Thodupuzha. They had reported to the police station as soon as they had woken up, and were starving by now. To top it all, on the way, Saju was forced by the policemen to pay Rs 1000 for diesel for the jeep.

They reached Thodupuzha police station by 2 p.m. The DySP Simon questioned them both separately and jointly.

From 27 March until the morning of 30 March, Mithun was in police custody. For three days and nights, my son was detained unlawfully, held in custody and tortured. I, as a father, am not able to describe the depravities he had to undergo, which he narrated to me. I felt, and to this day feel, devastated and powerless.

The police had thought that they would be able to track me down easily. However, when they couldn't, they came under tremendous pressure. They were questioned by higher-ups: why, when they could arrest top criminals, was there such tardiness in finding a bumbling pedagogue. The political parties that vied with one another to hold candles to fundamentalist ghouls filled the scene with statements and challenges. The government lacked the spine and integrity to withdraw the prohibitory order issued in Thodupuzha without arresting me.

The Thodupuzha DySP office was the nodal point of the four squads formed to arrest me. Mithun, whose only crime was that he was my son, asserted before the State Human Rights Commission that he was dragged along the ground, bumping over the steps of the staircase, by Shinto Kurian and constables to the first-floor offices of U.V. Kuriakose and K.G. Simon, the DySPs in charge of the investigation.[1] Whether it was their failure to track me down, or innate viciousness, Kuriakose's behaviour towards Mithun was particularly brutal and he was wont to fly into rages. Mithun alleged that he was held by the collar and shaken and thumped on the chest, which made him fall, among other things.

Although he was not a member of the investigation team, the SHO Shinto Kurian questioned Mithun many times in the absence of the DySPs. He didn't lose his temper like Kuriakose. Mithun stated that he used torture, all the familiar third-degree methods practised by the police, with great equanimity and deliberation.

Shinto Kurian had no compunction in abusing my innocent, twenty-two-year-old engineering graduate son, whose detention was never recorded and who was kept in custody unlawfully. He has complained that he was made to sit on the floor and beaten mercilessly on the soles of his feet with a cane by Shinto Kurian, screaming at him to reveal his father's whereabouts.

In another fraught moment of questioning, Mithun alleged, this sorry specimen of a human being made him kneel down, gripped his head between his thighs, bent him over, and smashed his elbow repeatedly into his back, displaying his prowess in third-degree methods.

During the day, hauling Mithun along with them, the police went to the homes of my teacher friends. Many of them who led righteous and ethical lives were subjected to threats and abuses simply because they were my friends. Many were summoned to Thodupuzha police station and on many occasions detained for the whole day without warrant or arrest.

The two people I met last before I went underground—Joycy and Philip—were detained for two whole days. Since he was a well-known writer, and he told them whatever he knew in elaborate detail, Joycy escaped threats and abuses. Philip, on the other hand, went through hell.

One night, Kuriakose and his gang reached Muvattupuzha and got Mithun to open the house for them. They broke open table drawers and almirahs and took away my passport, bank records, appointment letter, official letters, and service papers. Some of the artefacts and objets d'art also disappeared as the result of this visit.

Whether he was inside the police station or taken on rounds outside, the policemen didn't give Mithun a glass of water. Whatever little food a worried Saju—who hovered around the police station, unable to go home without his nephew—bought for him, the policemen didn't allow him to eat in peace.

More than the abuses and physical violence, what scared Mithun was Kuriakose's loaded and lewdly delivered statement that if I were not found, his mother and sister would be taken into custody and that their method of interrogation would be different from his own. Mithun couldn't imagine how low Kuriakose—already a volatile man, unbalanced further by his failure to smoke me out—would sink in his desperation. In our great democracy, peacekeepers are given a free rein and are a law unto themselves.

Amy, my daughter, was a nursing student and a resident in the college hostel in Muthalakodam near Thodupuzha. Mithun asked Saju to secrete her away during her Easter holidays to my sister-in-law, Solly's place in Vimalagiri.

In between the officers' interrogations, whenever Mithun was brought back to the lock-up, every passing constable found in him an easy prey and harassed him, possibly with an eye to glory—what if it was their questioning that broke him finally? In the few hours that he was left alone, the other tormentors-on-night-duty—mosquitoes—didn't allow him any repose.

On the second day of his unlawful custody (to call it arrest would be a misnomer), he was transferred to the nearby Karimkunnam police station because the police wanted to hide him away from some state minister expected to be in Thodupuzha that day. Those were the few hours he was treated humanely during those days of relentless torment. Not only did the policemen there not assault him, they even bought him food.

The police tried to feed Mithun many made-up stories. They tried to make him believe that I was holed up in an interior village of Idukki with a woman with whom I had had relations in the past. Then they tried to cite features of unclaimed corpses and allege similarities with me. After weaving such macabre stories, their average police intelligence couldn't go beyond observing his reactions and listening in on his telephone calls.

Perhaps Mithun wanted an end to the wild surmises about my disappearance. He felt that it would better that either the police find me or I surrender to them myself. As the maximum number of calls I had made from Philip's house was to Joy Mathew and he was the one trying to arrange my bail, the police had kept his number under observation. In his limited world view, to bring things to a closure, Mithun suggested to Kuriakose that they could look at Joy Mathew's wife, Bindu's phone. When the police looked at Bindu's phone, they found the call lists had been deleted. This was the reason for the needle of suspicion to swivel to Bindu.

An absconding accused in a crime, surrendering before a court or obtaining an anticipatory bail, reflects poorly on police and their efficiency. Therefore, my aspirant captors also kept trying to stymie both from happening as much as they could.

The lawyer, whom Joy Mathew had approached for making my anticipatory bail, backed out. They hounded Joy Mathew and didn't allow him the space or time to find another lawyer. Instead of taking him into custody, they dragooned him into accompanying them on their forays in search of me. The excuse was that he was the spotter—the one who could recognize me. Joy Mathew pleaded to the officers that there were thousands of others who could recognize Prof. T.J. Joseph. He appealed to be spared, that hunting me down was police work and not his.

He also told them categorically that, as a friend, he would never betray me. They then threatened to take his wife, Bindu, into custody. Aware that Mithun was still in police custody, that threat really threw him. He knew that his wife, Bindu, was too soft a person and would never be able to withstand the police's crude, minatory behaviour and perhaps even physical torture. When he was told that the police were going to look for me in Pota Ashram and Muringoor Divine Retreat Centre, he agreed to accompany them, certain that a person like me would never step into such places, even if it meant going to prison.

Based on Joycy's statement, the police raided all the lodges in Thiruvananthapuram and Thrippunithura. They frequented my relatives' houses. They questioned everyone in my friends' circle.

One of my pre-degree classmates, based in Parathode in the high ranges of Idukki, had to flee at 4 a.m. in his sleepwear after being warned by his relative next door that the police were coming for him. By the time he escaped through the back door, the police had rung his doorbell. His family had to search for him and found him cowering in the coffee plantation behind his house, at around 10 a.m. Following our meeting after thirty years, his number had been saved in Salomi's mobile—the only basis for the police to track him down. When he finally reported at the Thodupuzha police station in the company of a local political leader, that hapless, blameless schoolmaster friend of mine was made to stand a whole day, suffering their threats and vile abuses.

When Mithun's detention stretched into the third day, the family decided to file a habeas corpus petition in the high court. My brother-in-law, Baby, and others went to Ernakulam to meet a senior lawyer. The police somehow got wind of it and expressed their willingness to release him.

The police party, which left on 29 March with him, went to many of our relatives' houses on the way. Shinto Kurian led them.

By 2 a.m., they reached my elder sister, Mary's house in Poothali, near Parathode. Her husband, Baby, who had gone to Ernakulam hadn't returned yet. Only my sister and her daughter-in-law, Prabha, were at home. They were woken up and Shinto Kurian started to interrogate them. Again, as with many things connected to these policemen, such words are misnomers. Showering two helpless women with dire threats and vilest of abuses doesn't classify as 'interrogation' by any definition. The civil and courteous sub-inspector of Kerala Police stomped out of the place after pointing to the image of the Holy Heart on the patio wall and warning my elder sister that very soon her brother's framed photo will have to be hung there and adorned with a flower garland—which, in Kerala, is a mark of posthumous honour.

Finally, at 5 a.m., Mithun and Saju were dropped off at Murickassery after more visits to my relatives' houses. Shinto Kurian proceeded to grill my wife—who was distraught as she had had no news from my side—with irrelevant questions and finally bounded out of the house screaming that she would see my corpse covered with a shroud. His wrath still not assuaged, he walked up to the jeep that was parked thirty metres away and in a voice that would put a loudspeaker to shame, screamed obscenities to no one in particular. The people around my wife's house woke up to a *poorappatu*[2] that put to shame the lewd, bawdy songs sung during the Bharani festival at the Kodungallur temple.

Mithun was admitted the same day to a local private hospital, as he was a physical and mental wreck from starvation and the abuse he had received at Thodupuzha police station, and exhausted from the extensive travels when he was not at the receiving end at the station. On the day I surrendered, he was shifted to the District Hospital at Painavu. He was discharged only five days later, the day after Easter. On the day I got my bail, my daughter was brought home from Vimalagiri.

None of my relatives, except my wife's uncle, blamed me for anything. He took my hands in his and said, 'Although you are educated and sensible, how could you do such a thing?'

I stayed silent. However, his rebuke remained in my heart like a piece of glowing coal.

20

The Justice of Caiaphas

After my release, a few of my relatives and friends from in and around Murickassery came to meet me. There were also calls from various parts of Kerala from strangers wanting to know the truth behind the controversy. A good number of them were rationalists.

A TV news channel also came looking for me. In the interview, I explained the essence and thought behind the question paper and tendered my apologies to my Muslim brethren who had misunderstood the intent of my question, and to the government and college management for the troubles they faced following the controversy. Whether by design or because of time constraint, only my apology was telecast.

Two days later, Amy went back to her hostel. Usually I take her there; but as my entry into the taluk was banned, Saju and Mithun dropped her. She whimpered as she said her goodbyes; my eyes too became moist.

My friends in Muvattupuzha advised me over the phone to stay away. Some of the Muslim fanatics had planned to attack my house and set it on fire on 26 March evening. However, a group of my friends and police congregated before the house and prevented such mishaps.

After 26 March, except for that one brief visit by Mithun, none of us had set foot in our home. We wanted to get back home badly. How long could we stay in my wife's maternal home? Before the start of this ordeal, we had dug up the plot to plant elephant yam and other tubers.

The summer rains had come and gone and we had overshot the time to plant. Therefore, we decided to make a visit to Muvattupuzha.

Salomi, Mithun, Saju and I reached Muvattupuzha at around 11 a.m. After cutting up the elephant yam seedlings, I went to our neighbour, M.C. Joseph's house, to remain safe from any surprise attacks. Saju and Mithun did the planting while Salomi cooked our lunch.

As we were having lunch, the doorbell rang. For a moment, we froze on our seats. Saju and Mithun looked out from behind the curtain. It was the postman; there was a registered letter for me. I received it myself— it was from the college extending my suspension period. I was also prohibited from entering the campus during the suspension.

We returned to Murickassery before nightfall. I chafed and felt rather ashamed at having to stay there out of fear. I decided to move back to Muvattupuzha. My rationale was that as I had taught thousands of students, a large number of whom were Muslims, even if some misguided elements wanted to harm me, wouldn't they first ask my students, and wouldn't my students stand up for me and disabuse them of their wrong notions about me?

Although I was wary of going out, the very next day after reaching Muvattupuzha, I went to Bishop House in Kothamangalam. The first person I met with in the visitor's room was Vicar-General Monsignor Thomas Malekudi, also the manager of our college. I wished him with folded palms before kneeling to touch his feet, and said, 'I did nothing intentionally. This is a controversy that has arisen because I attempted to do my job with diligence. I regret the inconvenience that I inadvertently caused to the college and its management.'

Until I stopped speaking, he didn't move. After he stepped back slowly, I got to my feet. I asked if I could be allowed to meet Bishop George Punnakottil and he directed me to the bishop's parlour.

I greeted the bishop with my palms together. I kissed his ring when he extended his hand to me, genuflected and then touched his feet.

'I've done no wrong knowingly. Please forgive me.'

'Please rise,' said the bishop. As I stood up, a tear fell to the ground from my welling eyes.

He asked me to sit down and then spoke to me for about ten minutes. At the time the trouble broke out in Thodupuzha, he was attending an event in Vazhakulam. When the news reached him, he hurried back to

Bishop House. Police protection had been arranged here as well. Finally, he granted me leave to go.

I also met Monsignor Francis Alappatt, the corporate educational secretary, Father Kuriakose Kodakallil and Father Koyithanathu and explained to them my non-culpability in the question-paper matter. I felt like a heavy burden had been lifted off my shoulders when I started back for home.

During the initial days, none of our neighbours or acquaintances visited us and they kept their gazes averted every time they passed by our house. One day, the doorbell rang, and the sight of two strangers in our yard made me nervous.

'I am Ravi Muvattupuzha.'

'I am Binil.'

Both were rationalists from the Muvattupuzha area. They had come to offer any help that they could provide. I assumed that they had taken me for a fellow-rationalist, who had been charged with blasphemy.

'I am not a rationalist.'

Ravi said, 'It doesn't matter to us whether you are a believer, or an atheist, or a rationalist. We only see you as a human being who is being hounded by religion, the media, and the government. It's only our humanity that has made us look you up.'

I liked that sentiment; they were also the first people who had approached me offering help. They left their phone numbers with me. A few teachers from Newman College and Nirmala College close to me also visited me. I learnt from them about the steps taken by the college authorities in my absence.

While things were being explained to the protestors on 26 March, the decision came from the higher-ups in the management to give up all defence and throw me to the wolves. A press release that I had been suspended was issued. The college principal, Dr T.M. Joseph, held a press conference in which he apologized to the Muslim community for wounding their religious sensibilities. That was tantamount to pouring oil on the fire—protestors turned into rioters.

If the college authorities had been steadfast and honest enough, the controversy would have died down in a day or so. However, they joined the protestors, became their mouthpiece, and showed remarkable alacrity to abuse me. They ensured the case was filed solely in my name and worked to create evidence against me. The handwritten copy of the question paper was retrieved from the wastepaper basket of the Malayalam department and handed over to the police by Father Raju Jacob Pichalakkat, my ex-student, colleague, and the college bursar. The next day, in his speech in the college church, Father Pichalakkat also announced that finding that paper had saved his skin.

Half of the questions in that paper had been set by Father Pichalakkat. Now imagine if that particular question had also been set by Father Pichalakkat. Would Father Pichalakkat have had the integrity to admit that although the handwriting in the manuscript wasn't his own, the question was his? I can only hope so.

I had always been on good terms with the college management. The manager used to interact with me like a friend. On the first day after this issue flared up, he had advised me to stay away from home on the basis of that friendship.

However, as soon as the management decided to adopt Caiaphas's justice, he was ready to tell even outright lies. In his statement to the police, he declared that I was unhappy with the management and that was why I had tried to cause them problems by setting such a controversial question.

I had believed that my ex-student and colleague, Father Pichalakkat, would be my sturdiest defender in my absence, holding up my honesty of purpose. However, he proclaimed everywhere that my question did hurt Muslim sentiments.

To my utter surprise and consternation, the following categorical statement was made by Reverend Dr Thomas Periyapuram, in the college's managing board meeting following the controversy:

> T.J. Joseph has insulted not only Islam and Prophet Mohammad with his controversial question. He has done that to our Holy Trinity as well. The poser 'how many pieces will there be if a mackerel is sliced up' and its answer as three pieces was written down on purpose to blaspheme the Holy Trinity comprising the Father, the Son and the Holy Spirit.[1]

We need to take into account that the reverend is a doctorate-holder in Malayalam language and literature, a guide to research students, ex-principal of Nirmala College and the Vicar of the Kothamangalam Cathedral. It was amazing how, in his pursuit of the impetus for the controversial question, his research instincts smashed through the bounds of literature and landed in the hallowed precincts of Christian theology.

This éminence grise and maven conveniently overlooked the documented fact that the dialogue was in P.T. Kunju Muhammed's article just so he, the reverend, could stir dissension and animus in the hearts of Catholic board members.

While I was in jail, in a contrived op-ed piece on secularism in the *Deepika* daily, the revered Archbishop Mar Joseph Powathil wrote:

> This deed of a teacher should have never come from a Christian name-bearer.

When I read that piece, I lamented that the light from the pellucid Biblical proscription 'Judge not, and you shall not be judged,' had not touched the reverend's heart. Monsignor Thomas Malekudi was the chairman of *Deepika*, owned by the Catholic Church. I had no idea at that time that this op-ed piece was part of the intrigue to ostracize me.

One day, DySP Kuriakose called and asked me to meet him at Painavu or Thodupuzha. I reminded him that both places were in Thodupuzha Taluk, my entry to which was banned. The enforcer of law said that I shouldn't mind those things. When it was clear that I had no intention to transgress the court order, he agreed to come to Muvattupuzha PWD Guest House the next day at 3 p.m.

As I couldn't second guess his intention, I had taken Saju with me. The driver of the police jeep, which was parked outside, took me into Kuriakose's room. Another assistant sub-inspector from the investigation team was also present. He returned my bank passbooks and deposit slips. One of them was a receipt for Rs 50,000 deposited in Newman College Employees Cooperative Society.

When he handed that one over, he remarked, 'You have deposits, eh?'

Getting his drift, I quickly replied, 'That was money set aside for my son's MBA admission. However, for taking bail and lawyer fees I have already spent Rs 50,000. I had to pawn my wife's gold chain to meet those expenses. Now I must use the society deposit to redeem the chain.' Although I said it as an anticipatory block against monetary demands, it was also the truth.

'People believe that we have received a lot of money from you, professor. Not only did we get nothing, in reality we are out of pocket for buying you food.' He was hinting at the vegetable biryani bought for me on the day I surrendered. I didn't reply and remained deadpan.

As I walked back to the car, the ASI called out to me from behind and said softly, 'I don't need anything, but you must pay the DySP something. The final report is yet to be written.'

'I don't have any money with me,' I said swiftly.

'It needn't be immediately. You can send it to him.'

When I got back home, I was still wondering what to do. Could a DySP be paid Rs 500 or even Rs 1000? It had to be a decent sum. The police writer too would have to be paid some amount. However, where did I have the money for all this now that I had been suspended from my job as well? I had no clue on how to pay bribes. If I didn't pay, would they cook my goose? After all my cogitation, I decided that I would pay no one. If for that reason, they decided to embellish the charge sheet with false charges, let them do it.

After meeting the bishop and other college management priests, I had assumed that, convinced of my innocence, my suspension would be withdrawn. Therefore, on 19 April, when I received a memo of charges through speed post, I was perplexed. However, the manager called and assured me, 'Don't get upset with the memo of charges. That is the procedure; you send a written reply.'

21

Memo of Charges

When I sat down to prepare my reply to the memo of charges, I realized it had been prepared by a lawyer. The charges laid against me frightened as well as saddened me.

The first charge was that I had added question number eleven in the Malayalam question paper prepared for the second-semester, BCom, internal examination. The second was that it wounded the religious sensibilities of followers of all religions, especially of Islam. Thereafter, every charge laid the responsibility and culpability for all the unlawful and violent protests by some people in the name of that question at my door.

There can be no guilt without a guilty mind is one of the well-known principles of criminal law. If I, as a teacher, should have committed a crime, I should also have a guilty mind. Here the crime was blasphemy. One third of the memo was dedicated to painting me as a blasphemer.

The essence of those charges was:

I was someone who would, at every given opportunity, speak out against and mock faith, religious beliefs and practices, and believers, in an insulting way. I abused my position as a teacher to inject heresy into the students. I had been given a punishment transfer from Nirmala College, Muvattupuzha, to Newman College, Thodupuzha, due to dereliction of duty and unsound character. However, I showed no improvement—I continued to be recalcitrant with authorities and arrogant with colleagues. As a man who habitually sowed discord and disunity in every institution I had been part of, I had set question number eleven with premeditation and an ulterior motive of fomenting enmity, hatred, and hostility among the various religious communities.

Every teacher should be a model citizen who abides by the laws of the country. However, I had absconded for six days to frustrate the rule of law, its implementation and to avoid arrest. I had been arrested after sustained search and efforts of the police. I, therefore, possessed a grave character flaw.

At this point, I said to myself: I trust no one has been told that it was on the manager's express advice that I went underground.

On 26 March, after he became nervous when he saw the police in the college premises, Father Pichalakkat called and asked me to stay away. My reassuring statement to him that since there was no fault on our side, we needn't worry and that the police were there for our protection was given a diabolic twist and found its place as a charge in the memo—that I had told Father Pichalakkat that I had no worry about the consequences of my action. This was deemed as adequate evidence that I had included that question with an ulterior motive. If the lawyer could distort what I had told my ex-student and colleague, Father Pichalakkat, and include it in the memo of charges, it could have happened only after Father Pichalakkat had told him this. I felt gutted when I considered that. I could only find solace in the thought that, even in the case of the greatest teacher of them all, Jesus Christ, he had disciples who thought differently.

Although the manager had assured me that all they needed was a reply, I was worried by the perverse thinking that had gone into drawing up the memo of charges. I sought advice from two non-ecclesiastical members of the college's management board, both ex-principals. They maintained that there would be no punitive action from the management's side. I was relieved by their assurances and advice that I could draft the reply to the memo myself and need not spend money engaging a lawyer to do so.

In order to reply to the malicious memo with adequate proof, when I looked for my service records in the almirah, I was shocked—all my official papers had vanished.

Mithun told me that when Kuriakose and his gang had raided my house, they had taken away a lot of papers. Why then, when he had returned the bank passbooks and receipts, had he retained those official papers?

I spoke to a friend of mine, a DySP in Special Branch at Thiruvananthapuram, about the missing documents. One of his friends was a DySP at Painavu. My friend got him to talk to Kuriakose and told him to return my official papers and service records. Kuriakose gave non-committal responses. Following the instructions from Thiruvananthapuram, the DySP from Painavu asked him to state categorically whether he would return my documents or not. Only then did Kuriakose concede that he would. One of my wife's relatives was sent to Painavu collect the documents. One of the underlings in Kuriakose's office handed them over. On that occasion as well, this peacekeeper could not refrain from griping about not receiving any gratification from my side.

On 5 May 2010, I submitted my carefully prepared rejoinder to the memo of charges to the manager, only after getting it vetted by the two sagacious ex-principals. Its relevant portions read as below:

Dear Respected Father,

[Sub: Reply to the Memo of Charges Ref No. D.A.2/2010/ NCT/1 dt.19/04/2010]

I am respectfully submitting below my sworn reply to the Memo of Charges tendered by you.

I was in charge of the internal assessment of the thirty-two students who were enrolled for the Model 1 Malayalam Additional Language in the second-semester BCom course, started in December 2009 in Newman College, Thodupuzha. As per the Credit & Semester programme initiated by the Mahatma Gandhi University at the Degree Courses level from 2009–10, internal examination is defined as the test paper set by a teacher in the subject taught by him or her for the students in his or her class.

As a part of the continual assessment of the students, the responsibility for setting the question paper for Model 1 Malayalam Additional Language test on 23 March 2010 for second-semester

BCom course and evaluating and marking the answer sheets was mine. The textbooks prescribed by the university for prose and composition course are *Navakam* and *Ezhuththola*. *Navakam* was taught by Father Raju Jacob and *Ezhuththola* by myself. The questions for the test on 23 March 2010 were based on the portions from these two books.

Ezhuththola is a remedial text for improving and perfecting written language. In the said text, chapter three, titled 'Punctuation', discusses the usage of punctuation marks such as period (full stop), semi colon, comma, colon, double quote marks, hyphen, exclamation mark, interrogation mark, brackets, and so on.

Question number eleven has been prepared based on this chapter. What had to be provided was a passage that gave the opportunity of using the maximum number of appropriate punctuation marks. For such passages, either extracts are taken from other books, or a passage is created by the question-paper setter. For question number eleven, I had adopted a dialogue from *Methodology of Screenplay*, a Kerala Bhasha Institute publication, collated and edited by Shri P.N. Binukumar.

The said book is the recommended reference text for the paper 'Theatre and Cinema' in the fourth semester of the Malayalam MA degree course of MG University, and for the complementary course 'Methodology of Learning Malayalam' of second-semester BA degree Malayalam programme. A piece of dialogue from an article entitled 'Screenplay: Discoveries of a Believer', written by P.T. Kunju Muhammed—script-writer, director, and ex-member of the state legislative assembly—contained in the said book was adopted by me for question number eleven.

When I extracted that piece of dialogue from the said book, I thought it was germane to give the character, referred to in it as 'mad man', a name, and, since it is Muslims who generally address God as *padachchone* (creator), it should be a Muslim name. As it had been excerpted from P.T. Kunju Muhammed's article, I used only the Muhammed in his name for the character. Muhammed/ Mohammad is the most common name among Muslims. Accustomed as I was to hearing names such as Muhammad Basheer, K. T. Muhammed, Mohammed Rafi plentifully, when

I wrote Muhammed, the thought never crossed my mind that anyone would misunderstand it as Prophet Muhammad.

At the university level, studying Malayalam entails the study of language and literature. The study of language and of literature is treated as complementary in Malayalam classes. As a Malayalam language teacher, I had a salutary aim in including that metaphorical discourse between God and a character named 'Muhammed' in question number eleven. Muhammed, the character engaged in a conversation with God—represents the entire human race—a symbol of inconsequential and helpless humans.

Hunted by tribulations and endless doubts, man always seeks refuge in God. He takes God's name a few times in every instant: 'O Creator, O Creator.'

God, engaged in the preservation of the whole universe, hears man's call and responds to it, despite his overwhelming roster of duties: 'What's it?'

God is displeased at being called upon at every instance, which is why He uses the harsh 'sonofabitch' to address the man in His response. And to the God who answers his call always, what has man to ask, but a trivial question: a mackerel, if it is sliced, will give how many pieces? He has asked God this question many times before. And every time God has given him the one right answer. Even when the question is repeated, God doesn't refuse an answer. How many times have I told you it's three, you dawg! The ennui of giving the same answer causes harshness to blend into His words.

Humankind's sorrows and apprehensions are revealed in this discourse with God. God turns out to be the only sanctuary of the insignificant and powerless man. By answering to his calls every time and remaining committed to responding to man's even trivial questions, God's consideration and mercy towards mankind is revealed. This piece of dialogue which reveals the pathetic state of humanity and God's greatness through His infinite mercy is a prime example of the sublime humour described by the famous humourist and thinker, Stephen Leacock, in his book *Humor: Its Theory and Technique*, published in 1935.

As the person in charge of the internal assessment, evaluating the answer papers of the abovesaid test was also my responsibility.

All the while, I have followed a practice of distributing the marked papers to the students in the class and discussing each question and the right answers to it. I had included the piece of dialogue with the intention of not only discussing the appropriate punctuation marks, but also the metaphors in the dialogue and, in citing them, the methodology of sublime humour—to enhance the students' knowledge of literature, its aesthetics and appreciation.

The dialogue used in question number eleven has been excerpted from a book recommended as reference text by MG University. Therefore, charging me with the phraseology used in it or its inappropriateness is highly unwarranted.

I never meant to detract from religious faith or inflame communal feelings through question number eleven. All that I intended to do and have done is—as a teacher of language and literature and an examiner of student's comprehension levels—try to elevate the performance of my duties to the best and highest level possible.

The abovesaid question paper has been prepared for only the thirty-two students of Model I Additional Language Malayalam in the second-semester, BCom course in Newman College, Thodupuzha. To the best of my knowledge, neither the students who took the test on 23 March 2010 nor their guardians have complained about the question paper or raised any objections against it to me as the department head or to the class tutor or to the college principal. To the best of my knowledge, nor has any student who has appeared for the abovesaid test complained to or filed any objections with the departmental grievance redress cell, college-level grievance redress cell, or university-level grievance redress cell (formed to address the students' complaints on the various examinations) on the impugned question number eleven.

To my understanding, prohibitory orders (under Section 144 of CrPC) had to be declared in Thodupuzha only because some people who have no direct/overt or indirect/covert connection to the abovesaid test managed to procure a copy of the impugned question paper, misinterpreted and misrepresented question number eleven in it with mala fide, malicious, and devious intent to start riots and civil disturbances. I humbly submit that to charge me with the onus for the attacks and rioting unleashed by such social miscreants and the consequent breakdown in law and order is not in keeping with the truth and against all canons of justice.

I am a believer and a member of the Catholic Church. I honour and respect other religions and faiths and consider them at par with my own. As a teacher, I have always conveyed to my students the message that the quintessence and purpose of every religion is the same. The papers I have prepared for Value Education classes are examples of these. I have portrayed Jesus Christ and Prophet Muhammad as paragons of love and non-violence in these articles.

My only aim while setting question number eleven was enhancement of the linguistic and literary knowledge of my students. Blasphemy or religious conflicts were never among my aims. To this day, I have never abused the glorious vocation of teaching.

I regret that external forces used question number eleven to misinterpret it and cause civil disturbances whereby the students of Newman College, their parents, my colleagues, my superiors, and the public had to undergo many inconveniences.

Newman College, established with the mission of academic excellence, spiritual vitality, and social concern through its decades-long sterling service, is a reputed institution in the educational space. I believe that the noble reputation earned by the college by working for inculcation of spiritual and moral values in all communities without discrimination of caste, creed, religion or other considerations, cannot be destroyed by the momentary vilification by a small group of mischief-makers and protestors.

I express my unconditional regret and offer my sincere apologies for the anxieties and mental anguish caused to the college management by the question-paper controversy. To this day, I have not harboured any subversive thoughts or conducted myself in any manner that contravene the values being upheld by the Newman College and the college management and that are contrary to public good and welfare.

22

Signs of Terror

On 5 May 2010, I reached Bishop House bearing my response to the memo of charges. As soon as I was sighted, the manager came into the parlour and asked me to take a seat.

He started by saying that he had been receiving calls from many Muslim organizations. They wanted to know what the Church and the college management's stance was towards me, and what action would be taken against me. He told me that he had told them that action would be taken as per the rules.

I handed over my reply to the memo. Without betraying any expression, he said, 'Let's examine your reply. We'll let you know after that.'

On my way back from Bishop House, the manager's words kept haunting me. My worry was not what action would be taken against me by the management; it was the keenness of the Muslim organizations to learn of the management's stance towards me. Could they be extremist groups? Didn't the manager's statement that action would be taken as per rules in effect disown me? Wouldn't the extremists take it as a licence to attack me?

There were other reasons which exacerbated such anxieties. From the time I got out of jail, I had feared that fanatics among the Muslims may attack me. We remained in Murickassery for a few days because of this fear. Even when we returned to Muvattupuzha, this dread persisted although, with the suspension order getting extended and the memo of charges being served, my mind was preoccupied with these more immediate worries.

A few friends had overheard Muslim brethren making overt threats such as, 'We won't leave him alive on the face of this earth' and 'We'll chop off his limbs' and reported them to me. I had discounted them as fleeting emotional outbursts and consoled myself. Now the manager's words seemed to herald new terrors.

After returning to Muvattupuzha, I had stepped out of the house only twice—both times to go to Bishop House. I used to have my friends come over if I wanted to meet them. On 6 May, the day after I went to Bishop House, accompanied by my brother-in-law, Baby, I went to my friend, Prof. T.A. Joy's house around 5 p.m. to borrow some money. Only my mother, wife, and my elder sister, Sister Marie Stella—who had come from New Zealand on holiday—were at home.

About half an hour after both of us left, a group of six people arrived at my home. They all carried shoulder bags and claimed to be students from some college. They said they wanted me to write my memoirs for their college magazine. Sister Marie Stella believed them and told them I had gone out and invited them to wait inside. They left, saying they would meet me outside.

I had misgivings about strangers, especially ones carrying shoulder bags, suddenly turning up without an appointment. But as I didn't want to scare my family, I didn't mention my fears. When no one turned up later asking for my memoirs, my doubts strengthened.

On 17 May, around 5 p.m., my nephew, Joby, his wife, Prabha, and I were at home. The doorbell sounded and Joby opened the door. When I heard a man say he had come to meet sir, I went to the sit-out and stood behind Joby. There were five men; the one who stood near the doorbell was wearing kurta-pyjamas; the others were in shirts and trousers. All of them were carrying shoulder bags; two had prayer caps on. Three were standing to the side, near the car porch.

On seeing my questioning look, the man in kurta-pyjama gestured towards the guy with a stubble standing beside him and said, 'His daughter is under treatment for kidney disease. We have come to ask for financial help . . .'

That person's face showed no anguish; all I could see on it was a cruel, indifferent expression. I also saw a resemblance to one of my old students.

'I know you,' I said. He seemed taken aback when I said that.

I edged closer to the front door from where I could see all five of them.

'Thomas sir has sent a letter,' saying thus, the man in the kurta-pyjamas handed an envelope to Joby.

'Which Thomas sir?' I asked as I took the envelope from Joby.

'Thomas sir who's doing pineapple business in Vazhakulam.'

That set off alarm bells inside me, for I knew no such Thomas.

I took two steps back and got back into the house. I glanced at the envelope. 'Professor Joseph, Muvattupuzha' was all that was written on it. A cold shiver ran through my body. A nameless fear that the envelope contained something that could harm me stopped me from opening it. I thought it contained a bomb that could detonate at any moment.

I said we had no donation to give and handed the letter to Joby, asking him to return it. I slammed the door shut and bolted it.

Although Joby didn't understand what was happening, he did as he was told. To see the expressions on the men's faces when the letter was given back, I peeped out from behind the curtains. I saw them walk out of the gate, their faces impassive.

We got more information about the donation-seekers when Salomi—who had gone for a walk on the road that went around our house—returned. They had come on bikes wearing full-face helmets. They had parked the bikes at the junction near our house and walked to the house. A sixth person waited by the bikes. Salomi had watched them entering our gate, and standing in our yard talking to us. I was certain they had come to attack me.

Trembling, I called my neighbour and ex-principal, M.C. Joseph, and told him what had just happened. His advice was to shift out immediately. Where could I go at this hour with my old mother and the rest? My nephew and his wife had come for their first visit after their wedding. I started to panic.

When I called a friend in Muvattupuzha, he invited us over to his place. I told him that we would come only after dinner and asked everyone to get ready. I suddenly had this thought that I should inform the police. I knew only DySP Kuriakose's number. I called him and told him of my fears. Although he didn't forget to pass a loaded comment, 'Don't forget when there is a situation like this, only we are there,' by 8 p.m. a police team headed by an SI arrived from Muvattupuzha.

They took down the details from us and helped us speak to the CI. He assured me that there would be night patrols and asked me not to worry. I asked the policemen whether we should stay elsewhere. According to them, everyone's haven was their own home and they asked me where else would I find complete safety? Their words echoed my own thoughts on the matter. I called my friend and thanked him for his generosity, and told him that we had decided to stay at home after all.

Sister Marie Stella suggested a pilgrimage to Velankanni to be spared of the dangers we were facing. I had also been planning a trip along with my family for quite some time, but it kept getting put off for one reason or the other. This time, the decision to go was made quickly. There were tourist buses to the shrine that left on Friday evening and returned on Sunday morning. We booked seven seats for 28 May. The day coincided with my mother, Elikutty's and my daughter's birthdays.

My sister, Mary, whose house was in the hills, arrived early. Mithun and Sister Marie Stella collected Amy from her nursing college and brought her home by around 2.30 p.m. While they were having lunch, I stepped out to tell M.C. Joseph of our forthcoming trip and to ask him to keep an eye on our car while we were away. Although I hadn't told anyone, Salomi, happening to look out through the rear window, saw me going out.

In about half a minute of my leaving the house, someone rang the doorbell. The front door was open; Mithun who had been having his lunch went out to see who had come. Two men, carrying shoulder bags and who looked like officials, told him they were from HDFC Bank and wanted to meet me. When he told them that I had gone out, they didn't believe him. One of them, who introduced himself as Ajith, insisted that I had asked them to come. Mithun told them he would check and came through the house to the rear compound wall and called out to me.

I had only reached my neighbour's front yard. I smelt danger and as I stood arguing with Mithun that I had asked no such person to come, he turned around and darted into the house.

After Mithun went out through the back door, Sister Marie Stella looked up and saw a man standing at the threshold, with another right behind him. The man in front barged into the house. When my sister challenged him for trespassing, he said they were policemen. When asked why they weren't in their uniforms, he said they belonged to the special branch. By this time, he had searched every room of the house. Then he entered the kitchen and went out through the rear door. The second man had also darted in behind him and followed him out though the back door.

The shaken womenfolk went out through the front door. A vicious-looking, third man was standing on the porch. He scowled when he saw the ladies and grunted menacingly. The women were tongue-tied from fear and didn't dare to ask him anything.

The men who had reached the backyard saw Mithun speaking over the compound wall in the direction of our neighbour's house. They probably assumed that Mithun was telling the neighbours of their presence. They circled the house and returned to the front porch. All three men went out to the road. Across the street were three other men waiting for them. Salomi started running towards them and she was joined by Mary.

When the men saw the women pursuing them, they too started to run. When Salomi was almost abreast of them, she demanded to know why they were leaving without telling us what they had come for. One of the men turned around and with an intimidating stare, used the universal sign language for silence—a finger on his lips.

They left on two motorbikes which had been parked at the junction. Salomi was able to note down the registration number of the second motorbike. She had run after them to do that.

Mithun realized the gravity of the situation only when he saw the 'HDFC officers' coming out of the rear door. That was when he cut short our conversation and dashed back into our house. I saw the two men running off to the side. Realizing that they were looking for me, I ran into my neighbour's house. He instantly understood the mortal danger I was in and quickly shut the door behind me, bolted it and asked me to go up to the first floor and wait.

But how could I remain there, when five women, including my daughter, were at home with only Mithun to protect them? I ran downstairs again. Although my hand reached for the bolt, my fear didn't allow me to unlock the door. I ran up the stairs again and tried to see what was happening through the window. I came down again and looked for Joseph sir. However, he was not there. I stood there like a manacled man inside the fortress of helplessness. The only sound that reached my ears was the thumping of my heart.

After a while, I heard the sound of conversation and looked out through the window. It was Joseph sir and Thomas, another neighbour. I went out. They looked aghast. Mine must have been the most terrified face they had seen in their lives.

I was still trembling when I reached home. I immediately prepared a complaint to give to the DySP at Muvattupuzha. In my report, I complained that some unknown persons were trying to harm me and requested that I be provided police protection. I included the registration number of their motorbike. We submitted the complaint to the DySP's office and left for Velankanni.

Three days after our return, two policemen arrived to enquire into my complaint. They gave us the telephone numbers of the police station and officers of the SI, CI, and DySP ranks. There was no further action on my complaint. We wrote down the numbers they gave us in large digits on a paper and stuck it on the wall by the phone.

My family set a security protocol. The doors were always bolted. The gate was locked even during the day. Although our compound wall was low enough to easily climb over, at least we could watch out for such trespassers. I was not allowed to be alone, inside or out. However, I often broke the rule by going out alone. No one could predict what time I would go out, which route I would take, and what time I would return. I made many such solo journeys.

However, it was not possible to attend church or go for a movie. If I was seen entering the church or a movie hall, it would be possible to work out when I would come out. I had been, until then, an avid moviegoer.

I asked a blacksmith near my house if he could make me a weapon for self-protection. He refused, fearing that it would end up as a police case. Therefore, I bought two machete-like choppers used for harvesting pineapples from a shop near the Vazhakulam pineapple market and kept them behind the drawing room window curtain. I told my son that, should the need arise, he should not hesitate to wield it.

23

Enquiry

On 7 May, two days after submitting my response to the memo of charges, I received an order removing me from the post of head of the Malayalam department and appointing Father Raju Jacob Pichalakkat in my place. It caused me no heartburn, for it was an official procedural necessity. Until now, Father Pichalakkat had had to go by my directions; from now on, I would follow his directions. The manager asked me over the telephone to report to Bishop House on 10 May.

I reached there, expecting to receive the order withdrawing my suspension. However, the manager asked if I had anything more to say in the matter of the question paper.

I again told him that I had never spoken, written or acted against any religion, and, as a teacher, I had never shown any discrimination, whether based on religion or caste, while interacting with students, and no student had ever raised any objection to my style of teaching or presentation of ideas or concepts. I expressed my profound regret at the controversy triggered by the question that I had prepared, although there was no premeditation on my part, and I tendered my sincere apology for it.

The manager wrote down all that I stated in English on the Kothamangalam Diocese's letter-pad. Then he asked me to print my name under that and sign it. He added his signature and then sent me away with the promise that I would be informed of their decision in due course.

After two days, I received through speed post a copy of the notice of the appointment of a lawyer as the enquiry officer, as part of the disciplinary action being taken against me. The manager had stated, in the order, that this was an opportunity to prove my innocence.

The manager called me the next day and asked if I had received the order. He said that since this matter was in the public eye, a summary withdrawal of the suspension would not be possible and only after all the formalities were completed could this be done. He also advised me to cooperate with the enquiry officer so that the formalities could be completed by the time the college reopened after the summer holidays.

My first appearance at the enquiry officer's office near the Kerala State High Court in Ernakulam was on 22 May. A person present there, named N.V. Ajayakumar, introduced himself as the management's representative. He was wearing a mundu and shirt, with sandalwood paste mark on his forehead. I asked whether he was a lawyer. Although he denied it at first, later he said he had an LLB degree, but wasn't a practising lawyer. I didn't try to delve into the veracity of his statements.

The enquiry officer referred to Ajayakumar as the 'Presenting Officer' in his notes. I was given the title of 'Delinquent'. He spoke to me in a friendly manner. He told me that the manager had told him about my tendering an apology and that I need not have any worries. Then he explained the procedures of the enquiry. He said that if I felt the need, I could appoint a lawyer. Since I had implicit faith in the management of which I was also a part, albeit minor, and I had the confidence that I could adequately counter the false charges against me, I said I didn't need a lawyer.

In the next hearing on 24 May, the enquiry officer read out the charges against me. I accepted the first charge that question number eleven was prepared by me. All the other charges I denied. In the next hearing on 31 May, the presenting officer submitted the list of witnesses from the side of the management and their testimonials.

On 2 June, Dr T.M. Joseph, principal of Newman College, Father Raju Jacob Pichalakkat, tutor and bursar, and Father T.M. George Thanathuparambil, ex-principal of Nirmala College, appeared as the management's witnesses. The presenting officer said that Dr Jose George, ex-head of the Malayalam department of Nirmala College, would appear the next day.

Dr Joseph described the skirmishes that happened inside the college campus. He also submitted some of the letters he had received.

The letters said that my days were numbered and that the countdown to my death had started. The fate of Chekannur Moulavi[1] was cited as an example. The Danish cartoonist; Salman Rushdie; Taslima Nasreen— their names were also cited. The senders' addresses were those of some extremist organizations.

Despite him being a doctorate-holder in political science, that Dr Joseph was found wanting in civic sense made me sad. Shouldn't he have handed over such letters threatening physical harm to the police forthwith? Why had he kept the letters, which were received as early as the last week of March, hidden from me? Instead, he produced them as evidence against me in the presence of the enquiry officer!

One of the answer sheets submitted for the test was also included in the document folder of the evidence against me—the one where the girl had crossed off God and Muhammed and renamed them as elder and younger brother.

I had seen Father Pichalakkat conferring with the presenting officer outside the enquiry officer's room. He pretended he hadn't seen me. However, I went up to him and made small talk.

'You didn't call me even once after that call asking me to stay away from the college,' I said.

'I didn't feel like calling,' he said impassively.

He opened his statement introducing himself as the bursar of the college and the only colleague of the 'delinquent' in the Malayalam department. He showed no hesitation in revealing that I was his teacher in Nirmala College. He described the protests following the question-paper controversy. He also parroted the charge in the memo that when he had called me on 26 March morning after seeing the police presence in the college campus, I didn't take it with the seriousness it deserved.

The controversial question paper was prepared by the delinquent. All the problems ensued from that. The question paper was blasphemous. No teacher ought to have prepared such a question paper. These were the points emphasized by him during his statement.

I was given an opportunity to cross-examine him.

'Father Raju Jacob, from the adjunct to your name, it is clear that you are a priest. A priest doubles up as a religious teacher and a religious leader. A person like you could never be secular. You may maintain religious harmony in an attempt at self-preservation. That is the only reason why you are compelled to say that charges laid against me by some unimaginative, misguided fanatics are true.

'Any teacher working in the public education sphere in a secular country as India should be a secular person, especially teachers of literature. Only then will they be able to teach literature by seeing God, devil, devas, asuras, angels, demons and ghouls, as only characters. How can you, wearing the cloth of a religious denomination, be a secularist in the presence of the students? How can you teach literature that is universal and a humanities subject? How will you be able to foster unbounded imagination in your wards and turn them into non-parochial, liberal world citizens?'

I didn't ask Father Pichalakkat any of these questions for I remembered Joan of Arc; I remembered Galileo. I did regret not engaging the services of a lawyer who could have asked all these questions.

Rev. Father Dr T.M. George, the ex-principal of Nirmala College, only submitted some documents. He didn't comment on the question paper. He also said that while he was principal, he hadn't received any complaint against me.

Dr Jose George, the fourth witness, refused to appear before the enquiry officer.

The next day, the presenting officer submitted a supplementary list of witnesses. The DTP operator and the student who had changed the names of God and Muhammed were the new ones.

The DTP operator was from a family with financial liabilities. Her only income was the low salary paid by the college. A few months ago, she needed money for removing a lump in her throat and funds were arranged by the staff of the college.

There were only minor variations between her statement and the reality:

She had done the DTP formatting of the question paper given by me; when she reached question number eleven, reportedly she looked at me. When I said that it was taken from a book, she keyed it in exactly as it was in the manuscript. She said she had smiled at that time because she was not accustomed to seeing such questions.

Despite her wanting to continue her studies in Newman College, the student refused to appear before the enquiry officer and give evidence against her teacher, although the principal and the bursar had insisted that she should.

On 8 June, I submitted my witness list and documents list to the enquiry officer.

I needed some documents to effectively counter the false charges in the memo. One of them was the attendance register of guest lecturers in Nirmala College during 2004–5. Anticipating that the principal would seek the manager's permission to give it to me, I met the latter and requested his permission beforehand. He said that he would inform the principal and that I could go and collect it.

When I reached the college, the principal asked me to give a written request. After submitting it, the vice principal took me to the records room. He unlocked an almirah and told me to take whichever register I needed. All the registers, except that of 2004–5, were available. When I told the principal that I couldn't find the one I wanted, he feigned ignorance.

I had known that in a NAAC-accredited college, not merely records of guest lecturers' attendance, even their appointment letters should be maintained for all times. I noticed that neither the principal nor the vice-principal seemed unduly worried over the missing mandatory register. I assumed that the manager had called the principal in advance and 'educated' him. Why had our priest manager, Monsignor Thomas Malekudi, whom we used to address as 'Most Reverend', done such a thing? I started to have serious doubts about his sincerity, sense of justice, and honesty.

Not that the non-availability of that one register would have dented my defence. I had other documents that would have neutralized the nefarious charges cooked up by the manager.

In order to prove that mine wasn't a punishment transfer from Nirmala College to Newman College, as alleged, I produced my promotion order as the head of the department. When the college management did not follow the criterion of seniority for promotions to the posts of principal or head of the department, here was an order that

was handed over to me in person by the bishop himself after being invited
to Bishop House.

I produced the 2008–9 Newman College calendar-cum-directory to
show that I had been appointed as the director of the value education cell
by the principal upon the recommendation of the college council after
I had taken charge as the Malayalam department head on 2 June 2008.
I alone had been given the responsibility for selecting the subjects and
preparing brief articles for use by other teachers handling value education.
Would anyone give such responsibility to someone who has been sent on
a punishment transfer for bad conduct? An atheist who at every given
opportunity indulged in blasphemy?

I also submitted the 2008–9 annual report to the enquiry officer in
which the principal had clearly noted that, under my leadership, the value
education cell had shown a praiseworthy performance, and the 2009–10
college calendar recording that for 2009–10 too, I was put in charge of
value education.

I submitted a few papers I had prepared for value education classes as
samples of my secularism and egalitarianism. One of them was an article
prepared for a class relating to non-violence centred around Mahatma
Gandhi's birthday. I reproduce the relevant portions here:

> By adding the 'aa' syllable as a prefix that connotes negation to the
> word *himsa* (violence) the word ahimsa is derived. Which is why
> we get the sense 'do not kill' from the word. We treat ahimsa (non-
> violence) as the antonym of himsa.
>
> As per Gandhiji's philosophy, as himsa is a verb, according to
> the rules of grammar, its antonym too must be a verb. Not doing
> something cannot be a verb. Therefore, ahimsa is not not doing
> himsa but it is specific actions as a counter to violent actions. If
> hurting someone is himsa, acting in his benefit is ahimsa. If causing
> sorrow is himsa, causing happiness is ahimsa. If intolerance is himsa,
> tolerance is ahimsa. If the acme of himsa is killing of a human being,
> sacrificing one's life for others is the acme of non-violence. In short,
> causing harm to another is the path of violence and loving another
> human being is the path of non-violence.
>
> While the Vedas and Upanishads touch upon non-violence,
> it turns into a philosophy in the works of Buddha. While

Advaitha philosophy appears in Vedas and Upanishads, as much as Adi Sankara has given it a robust interpretation, Mohandas Karamchand Gandhi gave non-violence the halo of a theory. Having christened love for the human race as non-violence, he had doubts about the extended meaning of such a name. Since love is a word that has many connotations, it didn't appeal to him. More than love, compassion was the word that appealed and spoke to him.

After deep contemplation, he did accept ahimsa or non-violence with interpretational support. As he held steadfast to the theory of non-violence, what the world witnessed was the miracle of liberation of a country and its people. This is why the world has anointed him and respects him as a great soul or mahatma, and 2 October, his date of birth, is celebrated as the International Day of Non-Violence.

The one who was in the vanguard of proponents of non-violence was Jesus Christ. He used the word love in place of non-violence. Driven by his love for mankind, the noble soul sacrificed his own life. Prophet Muhammad also was the prophet of love, destined to enlighten human race.

The essence of every religion is non-violence or love. Every religion exhorts praising God, the manifestation of love. The highest form of divine worship is to love one's fellow beings. Our inability to understand or our tendency to misunderstand this noble truth leads to intolerance, bickering, partisanship, and above all to terrorism.

Now back to the matter on hand.

I had admitted everywhere that question number eleven was my creation. The crux of the matter was whether it amounted to blasphemy. A mere enquiry officer, trained only in law, was insufficient to rule on this; it needed impartial and sagacious teachers of language and literature to give a ruling. The principal and the bursar were the ones alleging that there was blasphemy. Did they have the unprejudiced and unbridled imagination and liberal open-mindedness to rise above vested interests and think independently?

Four professors volunteered and appeared as my witnesses.

Dr A.J. Jose, professor of English, Newman College, stated that it was not an inappropriate question for college-level students. An internal assessment test is part of teaching. Making the process of learning interesting through humour as well as provoking students intellectually were methods of teaching. Questioning the latitude and independence of teachers and taking matters to the street were not desirable. The dialogue used in question number eleven having been adapted from a recommended reference book of the university, it was baseless to allege blasphemy.

Sentences such as 'Rama killed the snake' and 'the snake was killed by Rama' are examples used by teachers in grammar lessons. Would anyone take the Rama in that for Lord Rama? Similarly, if the name Muhammed is used, no one in his or her senses would take it to mean Prophet Muhammad. No one had taken out any copyrights on names.

Prof. T.A. Joy, professor of Malayalam, Nirmala College, also gave his statement that the question paper contained nothing that was taboo, and that many of the textbooks used in language studies would appear to be abominable if viewed with a narrow mind. However, they are included in the university syllabus precisely because they are not.

Prof. Joy Mathew, class teacher of the BCom students who appeared in the test, stated that none of those students had made any complaint whatsoever to him, or the principal, or the university, or any other authority. Among those who appeared for the test, four students were Muslims. From their own words, I am aware that they have only respect and admiration for their Malayalam professor, T.J. Joseph, he said. One of them changing words in the question to elder and younger brother should not be perceived as a complaint.

Prof. Thampi Varghese, head of the zoology department, member of the college council, and director of the students' cell, gave his statement to the enquiry officer that none of the students had any complaints against the controversial question paper. He also said, as a believer and religious person, he didn't find anything blasphemous in the question paper.

The hearing was on 17 June 2010. Only the enquiry officer, the presenting officer, and I were present. What was I to argue in front of these people who were on the management's payroll and probably only too ready to fulfil their wishes?

I did my duty with no desire for its fruits.

My peroration ran, '. . . to foist false charges on a progressive and secular teacher and punish him in order to appease those with vested interests and are blinded by faith, is an unpardonable, heinous sin not only against the community of students and teachers, but even against the future generations.'

After listening to my concluding remarks, Ajayakumar said, 'In this matter, the management ought to have been on your side.'

The enquiry officer let out a long yawn.

Two weeks had passed after the colleges had reopened. I met the manager of our college at Viswajyothi College of Engineering and Technology in Vazhakulam and informed him about the completion of the enquiry proceedings. I requested that my suspension be withdrawn.

'We will punish you. If you want, you can take legal recourse,' he said straight to my face. I was taken aback by this statement made even before he had received the enquiry officer's report.

I assumed that I may be demoted from the post of the department head, or that my increment may be withheld. Let them do what they want, I tried to console myself.

24

Fortifications and Drawbridges

I was always accompanied by my wife or son or sister, or all of them, during my trips to Ernakulam. I later regretted not appointing a lawyer; I could have avoided the repeated trips. I felt it was foolish on my part not to have appointed a lawyer as soon as I started to lose my faith in the manager, in whom at the beginning I had implicit trust.

I was mostly homebound after the enquiry was completed. Only a few friends would come home to meet me. One of the professors from Nirmala College said that people were scared to even discuss my case. There were many rumours. All the signals were that I would be attacked. I didn't bother to dig further or lose sleep over it.

I was fifty-two years old then. Until that time, I had lived a dignified life without having to genuflect in front of any man.

Innocent as I was, if I were to be killed by fanatics, my only regret was that I wouldn't be able to witness the reactions of the denizens of God's Own Country with their hundred per cent literacy.

It's not that I didn't think about the future of my family, wholly dependent on my salary. I was at a stage where I couldn't decide whether my family's future would benefit more if I were alive or if I were dead. Although it seemed a remote possibility, should the management dismiss me from service, the condition of myself and my family would become wretched. What if I was killed? What would happen if someone under suspension died? I reread the Kerala Service

Rules to make doubly sure. If I were to die, the period from the date of suspension until the date of death would be considered as active service for all calculations of benefits. Family pension, that is, forty per cent of my last drawn salary, would be paid regularly to my family. And the family pension would be higher by fifty per cent for the period until the dead employee's retirement date or for seven years, whichever is less.

I thought that would be sufficient. They should be able to live without much trouble on that money. What's more, if I were to be killed, they would miss me too. Wouldn't that be an added bonus?

I had very few liabilities—only a house loan and Amy's educational loan. My gratuity, provident fund, and leave surrender amounts would comfortably cover them. After doing his graduation in engineering, Mithun had taken admission for MBA in SCMS Cochin School of Business in Aluva. We had already submitted an application for an educational loan.

I thought of making a will. I wanted to divide my movable and immovable properties and post-retirement benefits equally between my wife and my children. Since, as per Christian inheritance laws, my wife would inherit one-third of my wealth and my children the balance, I decided that such a will was superfluous.

I kept all the documents—bank passbooks, loan documents, title deeds, etc.— in an envelope and, with the knowledge of my wife and son, locked it up in our almirah. I also reminded them that in financial matters it was better to seek the advice of friends rather than of relatives.

A Hindi professor in Nirmala College, a friend from the days when I worked at Pavanatma College, came to meet me. After telling me of the possibility of my being attacked, he asked me with concern whether I wasn't afraid. Although my answer was, 'What's the use of being afraid?', I consoled him by saying I had taken some precautions.

A few days later, our parish priest, Father George Pottackal, conveyed his desire to meet me through our neighbour M.C. Joseph. I agreed to meet him at 9 a.m. the next day. However, he reached half an hour earlier while I was having my breakfast of boiled tapioca and fish curry. I invited him to join me, and he accepted.

He said he had wanted to meet me because he had heard that a fatwa had been issued against me by some Sharia court. For a moment, I wondered whether we were indeed living in Kerala within the great land of India or in some Muslim nation in the Arabian lands.

The fatwa was to chop off my limbs. He didn't elaborate; nor did I ask him.

People come to meet and compliment those who score a first rank in an examination, win a lottery, or achieve some high position in life. Was a fatwa equivalent to a triumph like any of these? After the priest left, I tried to find some humour in my situation.

The next day, while I was out in the town, I noticed people looking at me in a peculiar way, and many were trying to surreptitiously point me out to their companions. Did their eyes reflect sympathy or dispassion towards someone who had been marked for death? I pretended not to notice and went about my business.

During those days of terror, Sister Marie Stella was a great source of comfort and confidence to all of us. She had extended her leave by two weeks, unable to abandon us in that condition. Even that was coming to an end. She decided that she should meet the bishop of the Kothamangalam Diocese and find some solution to my suspension.

On 2 July, at around 9 a.m., she and I left by car for Bishop House; I was driving. We decided to take the bypass via Chalikadavu bridge. At a place called Randar, some distance ahead of the bridge, in my wing mirror I glimpsed a bike closing in on us. The rider was a swarthy fellow and the pillion rider was a slim man who had his mobile phone glued to his ear. I slowed the car and drew it to the side to let them pass; but they didn't pass me, and started to tail the car.

Growing increasingly suspicious, I speeded up; they followed suit. Fearful that they may be planning to hurl a bomb at the car, I pressed the accelerator down. They were still on our tail. Driving in that fashion, we got on to the national highway and continued for another three or four kilometres. After a while, as I kept checking the rear-view mirror, I saw the bike turn into a lane on the right. I reduced my speed.

My sister, unaware of the bike riders who had chased us, asked me why I had speeded up so much. With my heart still palpitating, I told her. She didn't say anything. I fancied she was saying her prayers.

After dropping her at the gate of Bishop House, I parked a little distance away and waited in the car, not wanting the inmates to know that I had brought her there. I was expecting to be attacked at any time. My sister returned only after an hour. She didn't look happy in the least.

My sister, who had dedicated her life to the service of the Catholic Church, explained my trials and tribulations to Bishop Mar George Punnakottil. She explained that I was the only surviving brother that the sisters had, and that I was the one looking after our mother, who was infirm and had dementia. Both my children were enrolled in professional colleges with high fees. Although she kissed the ring of the most reverend priest and appealed to him in the name of Jesus Christ that my suspension be withdrawn and I be reinstated in my job as I had no other sources of income, the great shepherd remained unmoved.

25

Parashurama's Axe

4 July 2010. Around four or four-thirty in the morning, I was awakened by the rumble of thunder. It was raining heavily. A prolonged thunderclap seemed to shake the house to its foundations. I tried to curl up under the bedcovers and go back to sleep, but sleep evaded me.

It was a Sunday. Although the previous day was St Thomas's Day, I hadn't attended church. Should I go today? I debated with myself. Suddenly I was flooded with a feeling of confidence and energy.

I had decided that trips to church and movie halls presented the greatest risk. However, how long can one live cowering and hiding?

I remembered reading somewhere that if someone was determined to kill a person, the only escape from that is a change of heart in that man. I switched on the light, with prayers that God may bring about a change of heart in those who lay in wait for me. It was 5.30 a.m. The rain was coming down in torrents.

The first mass was at 6.30 a.m. By the time I had bathed and dressed, black coffee had been served. My mother and Sister Marie Stella were also dressed and all set to go to church with me. My wife and children normally attend the 9.30 a.m. mass. Although the church was within walking distance, we decided to go by car as it was raining. As we emerged on to the road, the sight of a stranger walking past holding a plastic packet made me suspicious. I rationalized that it was the fear in my heart or an innate sense of self-preservation causing the anxiety.

By the time the service ended, it was almost 8 a.m. The rain had stopped. I exchanged pleasantries with a few people in the front yard of the church. One of them was a student I had taught in a parallel college where I used to work before taking up the position in a regular college. He was a teacher in a government school. After the question-paper imbroglio, this was our first meeting. When he assured me that I had done nothing wrong, but that I should be cautious nevertheless because, day by day, our society was losing its collective power to think straight, I didn't know how to reply, and could only smile wanly.

We were slowly cruising past the pedestrians who were also returning home after the service. A public school stood between the church and my house. The road ran along a fifteen-foot-high embankment, adjacent to the school grounds. If we turned left at the junction where the school grounds ended, and went a further fifty metres, we would reach our house.

A middle-aged, but fashionable, lady walked towards us on the road. Although she dyed her hair off and on, whenever I saw her, imageries such as 'synonym of whiteness', 'soul of darkness', 'morning twilight', 'midnight and daylight' or 'shadow and moonlight' would flash through my mind. That day, it was 'midnight and daylight' for me as she went past us. We were still joking and laughing about it when a white Maruti van raced towards us from the opposite side, swerved into our lane on the left and screeched to a halt, effectively blocking our way.

I had to perforce stop our car. I initially assumed they had come into the lane to reverse their vehicle. As a mark of my protest at their breaking the traffic rules, I let out a long blast from my horn.

Suddenly the doors opened and six men burst out of the van. Seeing their snarling faces and the speed at which they rushed towards us, I had a sinking feeling in the pit of my stomach. I realized that there was no escape that day. I saw the man in the lead pull out an axe from his shoulder bag even as he ran. A fancy that it resembled Parashurama's axe flashed for an instant through my mind. The axe-bearer reached the driver's door and tried to yank it open. By that time, another man holding a dagger had also reached us and stood behind him.

Almost simultaneously, three men had reached the passenger side where my sister was seated. Two of them held choppers; the third one, a dagger.

A man holding something inside a plastic bag stood in front of the car.

The window glasses were up and the doors, locked from inside. Despite that, my sister and I grabbed the door handles and clung to them.

A smash with the axe and the window glass on my side shattered. Almost simultaneously, a blow from the chopper smashed the glass on the passenger side window. Although the second man with the chopper struck at the windscreen, being laminated glass, it only caved in and sagged, but didn't give way.

Shoving the axe through the now open window, the man started to swing wildly. Both my sister and my mother started to scream for help, pleading for someone to come to our rescue. I focused on shrinking my body as much as possible and withdrawing into the car to escape the axe's blows. I then tried to grab the handle of the axe. Although I did get a grip on it a couple of times, each time it was yanked out of my hands. As my arms were getting slashed repeatedly, soon my hands became powerless as the nerves and muscles were severed. Although my mother, in the backseat, screamed and beat ineffectually at the hand of the axe-wielder with her folding umbrella, it was to no avail, and, in reality, only a weak keening sound was escaping her terrified lips.

When he realized that my hands had lost all their strength, the axe-wielding man put his hand inside the car and unlocked the door. By this time, the chopper-wielders who were on the other side had joined him. The four of them pulled me out of the car and dragged me to the back of the car.

When my sister pushed open the door and tried to come to my help, the dagger-holder grabbed her by her neck with his left hand, and, thrusting the dagger at her face, pinned her against the fence by the roadside.

After I was dragged for some distance from the car, one of the chopper-wielders hacked viciously at my left heel. After that, he hauled me up by that leg, twisted it around, and slashed at the top of my foot for good measure. That was followed by the axe-wielder hacking at the back of my thigh, just below my left buttock. Then he hacked my left leg, above the ankle.

He followed it up with a chop on my foot. My bones shattered wherever the axe hit me. As the blood spurted from my many gaping wounds and gashes, I felt my life ebbing away with it. With my eyes fixed on the raised axe poised to land on me with mortal effect, with an instinctive, animal-like fear of death, I pleaded, 'Don't kill me . . . please, don't kill me . . .'

Then they lifted me bodily off the track and took me further down the road. They lay me down at right angles to the road, my head on the grass verge and my torso and lower body on the macadam.

The axe-wielder lifted my lifeless left hand, and like chopping wood, brought down the axe on it with brute force. It struck my wrist at an angle, slid towards my palm and nearly took off my last three fingers—they hung from my hand as if held by some invisible strings. When the chopper-wielder alerted him that he had chosen the wrong hand for the mayhem, he quickly let go of my left hand and it flopped to the ground.

Suddenly I heard a loud blast; I caught a glimpse of my son Mithun racing towards us through smoke with a chopper in his hand.

In the meanwhile, the second chopper-wielder took my right forearm—covered in gashes—by the elbow and placed it flat on the road. The axe-man swung the axe twice at an angle, hacking my forearm in two places, about two inches apart. The bones were shattered in both places; almost seventy-five per cent of the front end of my forearm was detached from the rest of it. Then they rained a series of blows at my wrist and severed my palm totally from my arm.

Back at home, my wife, Salomi, had been busy trying to set the table for breakfast before we returned from the church. She had heard the prolonged blast of my car horn, followed by the sound of shattering glass and screams for help. Seized by a feeling of terror, she screamed out to my son, who was reading the newspaper, 'Someone must be attacking achchan [father].' He rushed out of the house immediately. Amy, my daughter, who sat studying in the next room, jumped up when she heard this, and along with her mother ran out in the wake of Mithun.

By the time they were halfway down the path, the situation was clear to them. A Maruti van with its doors open; next to it our car with the windscreen smashed in; my sister pinioned to the fence by a man holding a dagger; a group of armed men behind the car; people standing on either side of the road, too terrified to intervene.

Salomi kept running; Mithun and Amy turned and ran back into the house.

Salomi was stopped near the Maruti van by the man holding the plastic bag in one hand and a crude, locally made, coconut-sized bomb in the other hand. She was warned to go no further. As she tried to sidestep him, one of our lady neighbours standing by held her back by force.

Grabbing one of the pineapple choppers from our house, Mithun was back in the next instant. The bomb-man stopped him too. Mithun feinted, dodged him, and ran on. The bomb exploded near his pumping legs. Running through the smoke past the man who had pinned down my sister, he reached us and swung at the back upper torso of the axe-wielder. Perhaps having misjudged the distance, only the tip of the chopper blade sank into his back.

By that time, the two chopper-wielders approached Mithun, swinging their choppers and he took a couple of steps back. The man who had been holding my sister let her go, came from behind, and grabbed both Mithun's hands. In the struggle to free his hands, Mithun dropped the chopper. The bomb-man also reached there and together they pushed Mithun hard enough for him to lose his footing and tumble down the embankment on to the fence that stood in between the embankment and the school ground. He lay almost suspended over the saw-tooth steel plate fixed on top of the steel-pipe fence, like an inverted 'U', his trouser pocket having got caught on it. As he hung there wishing that someone would come and free him, one of the attackers reached him, and toppled him over the fence. Luckily, the fifteen-foot drop to the school ground didn't cause any grievous harm.

By the time Mithun climbed back from the school ground, the Maruti van had driven off. A wailing, flailing Salomi was being held in check by some women. My mother and sister stood frozen. Members of the public were also standing around dazed and stunned in inaction. I lay motionless on the ground, blood still spurting from my multiple wounds. Mithun fell on my body crying.

I regained consciousness to the sobbing sounds of 'Achchaa . . . achchaa . . .' 'Have they all gone?' I asked Mithun. He replied in the affirmative. I asked him to take me to the hospital immediately. That brought my sister back to the here and now. As instructed by Mithun, one of our neighbours reversed our car. As my sister and Mithun tried to manoeuvre me on to its backseat, though still in a daze, one of the neighbours joined in and helped them. I also told them to pick up my severed palm. A quick search ensued, but they couldn't locate it. My sister said that we should leave without wasting any more time. We informed one of our neighbours—a teacher—that my palm was still missing. With that, I lost consciousness.

In less than a minute, I woke up as if from a sleep. I opened my eyes, believing it had all been a bad dream. Seeing the blood-soaked clothes of my sister and my palm-less, severely mutilated right hand which she was holding up to reduce the bleeding, I closed my eyes again, thinking in grief, 'It's all real and happening.'

When I asked for water, it was poured into my mouth from a bottle kept in the car. The water reaching my stomach and the onset of a fiery pain around my navel happened at the same instant. I writhed in agony—it felt as though my lower abdomen had become a molten mass and all the nerves there had exploded in all directions.

I was taken to a private hospital in Muvattupuzha initially. I kept pleading for anaesthesia to put me out of my pain. I heard someone say that if I were rendered unconscious, no one would know if anything happened to me in the meanwhile. After that, they must have administered painkiller shots and there was a modicum of relief from the pain.

My gashed arms were swathed in bandages. My left leg was broken above the ankle. My Achilles tendon and muscles in my calf were severed. Since I had been hacked on the calves and over my feet, my toes had all curled up.

All the visible wounds were bandaged; I was put on an intravenous infusion drip. The general opinion was that my interests would be better served at Specialists' Hospital in Ernakulam, and an ambulance was arranged. I had slipped into a state between consciousness and unconsciousness and was only just aware of what was happening around me, as if I were in a hazy dream.

As soon as she realized that I was under attack, Amy had run back into the house to call the police. Since we had pasted the station number near the phone in huge, bold letters, it didn't take much time. However, the policeman who took the call couldn't hear anything but the screams of a panic-stricken girl. In between her wailing and sobbing, she managed to convey to him that her father was being hacked to pieces and that they should come immediately.

The words 'Newman College professor' registered somehow in her incoherent babble, and they realized the gravity of the situation. They immediately rushed to our place.

After the call, Amy took out the second pineapple chopper and came running to the spot of attack. By that time, the assailants had vanished, and I had been taken to the hospital.

Our neighbour, Joseph sir, kept searching for my severed palm in the bushes along the road. Someone told him that it was lying in a neighbour's yard. When he went and looked, it was true—it lay there like a dried teak leaf on the gravel. He picked it up, shook off the dirt stuck to it and packed it in a plastic bag along with ice. By that time, the police jeep arrived.

The ambulance to take me to Ernakulam was ready. There weren't many people around to accompany us to Ernakulam or to help us. My sister had dispatched Mithun to fetch the small sum of money that was at home.

As I was being loaded onto the ambulance, I heard someone say, 'A lot of people to watch the spectacle, not a single one to help.'

When she realized that there was no else to go with us in the ambulance, my sister appealed to the hospital management to let a nurse accompany us. They agreed. By that time, the police jeep also arrived, and they handed over the plastic bag with my palm to my sister.

Whether it was because I was not strapped in properly, or due to the persistent swerving and careening during the drive, I started to slip off the gurney. My sister was seated at the head of the gurney, clutching the plastic bag like a precious treasure chest in one hand and holding up my severed arm with the other. The nurse was seated at the foot of the gurney, keeping steady the infusion paraphernalia attached to my right leg. She was not strong enough to keep me from slipping off the gurney. Eventually, my sister was compelled to deposit the 'treasure bag' on the floor. It was when she was holding me back that an unbandaged, approximately nine-inch-long gash on my left thigh came to her notice. It was bone deep, and still bleeding profusely.

When I asked for water, she hesitated, probably recalling the previous instance. Instead, she wet my lips and sprinkled water on my face.

Whenever I came to, I would ask, 'Where are we now?'

My sister would reply: Kolenchery, Puthencruz, Vyttila, depending on our progress. We eventually reached Ernakulam in only thirty-four minutes. Even without traffic hold-ups, this is normally a one-and-a-half-hour journey.

Warned in advance, the staff at Specialists' Hospital was ready to receive me. The press was also present in strength. Things were happening as if on the war front. Although I could sense me being taken out of the ambulance, being put on a gurney and wheeled to the casualty section and the general hubbub there, I kept my eyes closed as I didn't feel like opening them.

As the doctors, nurses, and other hospital staff busied themselves around me, I couldn't help marvelling at the paradox of this worldly life. After their long planning and concerted effort, a group of people had mortally harmed me. And here was another group desperately trying to save my life!

The sound of a snipping pair of scissors sliced into my reverie. It was cutting through my clothes to enable them to remove them off my body, piece by piece.

Dr Asha Cyriac, the plastic, cosmetic, and microvascular surgeon who was present there, beckoned my sister, who had been standing outside casualty in her blood-soaked habit, fearful and praying for my life. Dr Asha drew a quick sketch of my smashed-into-smithereens right wrist and explained to her that stitching back the severed palm was a very difficult proposition and, in all likelihood, my right arm would have to be amputated from below the elbow. My sister appealed to her to try their best. The good doctor assured her that would be done. My sister then signed off on the various approval and disclaimer forms.

When I was moved out of casualty to be taken into the operation theatre, I heard the sounds of cameras clicking furiously. I opened my eyes momentarily, and closed them again instantly, but I could sense that the mediapersons were following us along the corridor until we got into the elevator.

After reaching the OT too, I kept my eyes closed. I could sense movement all around me. After a while, as if to assess my wakefulness, the anaesthetist shook me gently and called my name. I only groaned in response. I think he said something like I would be falling asleep. In the same instant, I lost consciousness.

On the way to the hospital, or after reaching there, I was not perturbed by thoughts of my possible death. The reason for my confidence that I would live was the absence of wounds on my torso and head, having been wounded only in my extremities. However, that was far from the truth. In the doctors' opinion, after sustaining such extensive injuries and losing so much blood, it was the accumulated good deeds or benevolence of someone that had kept me alive until I reached the hospital. I was still not out of the woods. In the words of Dr Jayakumar, head of the plastic surgery department, I was half up there and half here on earth.

The primary responsibility of the doctor is to save the patient's life. Everything else comes after that. Dr Jayakumar was on the horns of a dilemma in my case. I had lost so much blood that micro-surgery, spread over many hours, could prove fatal. Re-attaching the palm to the mangled wrist may not be successful. The thing to do in such critical moments was to forsake the severed palm and concentrate on saving my life. However, they decided to take a punt in my case.

Six doctors led by Dr Jayakumar took sixteen hours to sew back my palm and repair my right wrist and arm. They grafted flesh along with blood vessels from my unwounded right thigh on to my right arm to repair it. In between all this, I was clinically dead for a while—my breathing and pulse stopped. Assuming I was dead, they stopped working on me. However, after a minute, the engine of my body restarted. It didn't end there. There were more incidents. After all the patchwork was done, they found that blood was not flowing into the re-attached palm. As he stood wondering whether all their efforts had come to naught, Dr Jayakumar had a brainwave. He tried a new method and the blood started to flow, bringing life back to my palm.

Since surgery had gone beyond the expected time, the broken bones of my left leg and arm were strapped for the time being. Microvascular surgery on them was kept for another day. I was given sixteen bottles of blood infusion on that day.

The eighteen hours I spent lying unconscious were a blank as far as I was concerned. I only felt it as the tiny gap between turning off and turning on of a switch.

I opened my eyes to the sound of my name being called. 'Joseph . . .' It was Dr Jayakumar. 'We have re-attached your palm. Everything looks okay.' Before those words could engender any happiness or even relief in me, I slipped back into sleep.

When my sister got permission to see me at 4.30 a.m. and was brought into the Intensive Care Unit (ICU), the exhausted doctors—after their sleepless, sixteen-hour toil—were slowly leaving my side. I don't remember my sister calling my name and my acknowledging it by opening my eyes. I came into full wakefulness only in the morning when my son came to see me and called out to me. When I saw Mithun gazing at my re-attached palm and other bandages, I told him with a light heart, 'So we have crossed a hurdle, haven't we?'

26

My Religion

My left leg—swathed in cotton wool pads and bandages from my thigh down to my foot—was suspended from a steel stand. So was my left hand, from the elbow to my fingers. My right hand, full of suture marks, was covered in a thin net, immobilized, and placed on a small pillow. To ensure that my re-attached palm received regulated heat, a lit table lamp was placed close to it. On my right thigh—over the wound, nine inches long, five inches wide, and one inch deep, from where flesh, veins and skin had been taken for grafting—the epidermis taken from the other side of the same thigh had been grafted. Both sides of the thigh were also swathed in bandages. Clipped on to my right toes were various leads from multiple monitors and machines.

An intravenous drip was being fed through a vein in my neck. Blood, medicines, painkillers, saline and glucose infusions were flowing into my body. I was voiding my bladder into the urine bag hung to one side through a catheter inserted into my urethra.

I was sharing the small room with a little boy who had been hit by a truck. Since both of us needed intensive care, we had a nurse as our constant companion. The first two days, I was mostly sedated. During snatches of semi wakefulness, I lay still, staring at the white ceiling of the ICU. The faces of the doctors who came in like clockwork to check on me appeared to be floating globes. I felt they were lifesaving demi-gods and had haloes around their heads; the sleepless nurses who were by our bedside twenty-four hours a day were angels to me.

On my third day in the ICU, Dr Sabin Viswanath, one of the directors of the hospital, woke me up from my drowsy state. Although I could not grasp what he told me, the next set of entrants made things clear for me—a lady reporter and cameraman from a prominent Malayalam TV news channel. They had come to record my first response to the attack.

Although drowsy, I did face the camera. I managed to say that I had not blasphemed any religion and I had only tried to excel in my chosen vocation of teaching. I also stated that I had forgiven the people who had harmed me.

It was telecast the same evening as the channel's exclusive report. I watched it on the TV monitor in the ICU. The nurse was considerate enough to raise my head to a Fowler's position so that I could watch the telecast.

Immobile like Jesus Christ nailed to the cross, I lay supine, staring at the white ceiling as these thoughts crossed my mind: Would the public believe that I was innocent? Even if they ignored the fact that I had named the character in the dialogue Muhammed, wouldn't their censure of my including a passage in which God asks 'What's it, sonofabitch?' in an examination taken by impressionable students still persist? While I could defend myself saying that I had only adapted the dialogue from a reference text recommended by the university, would the 'well-meaning' public acknowledge that? I was under no compulsion to use that very same dialogue. If I had no ulterior motive in selecting such an unconventional dialogue, wouldn't the sagacious people feel that I was a little mad or at least eccentric?

Lying on my bed of arrows, I pondered over the rights and wrongs of the controversial question. I remembered an incident from my teaching life.

It was during my BEd student days in NSS Training College. I taught classes twice a week for students in the MA Malayalam class in a parallel college at Palai to alleviate my straitened financial circumstances. Of the twenty students, the majority were girls who, after graduating in science subjects at Alphonsa College, Palai, had chosen to do a post-graduate course in Malayalam. On the other hand, the boys were graduates in Malayalam literature from St Thomas College, Palai.

While providing a preface to the play *Samatvavadi* written by Pulimana Parameswaran Pillai, I asked the students, 'Tell me the names of two leading socialists in the world.' No one responded.

'Two Jews who were socialists?' I gave them a hint; still no answer. Finally, I said, 'One, Karl Marx. Two, Jesus Christ.'

'Good Lord!' the girls shrieked. They lacked the latitude to imagine Jesus Christ as a socialist. They had been brought up in conventional Christian households in the outskirts of Palai.

I had provoked them knowing fully well that they would react in such a manner. Unless I provoked them emotionally and intellectually, and re-oriented their thought processes, they would have been unable to assimilate a play such as *Samatvavadi*, an extraordinary play that analysed a decaying and decadent aristocracy and progressive egalitarianism. There is a reference to Jesus Christ in the play.

If the students had to understand the egalitarian's statement in the play, 'The people were afraid of Jesus Christ because he asked them to love others,' they had to break out of the confining walls of traditional belief.

The mind of a student of literature must be dispassionate. Only in a place where there is no entrenched emotion, can all emotion enter. Only in spaces where no one belief has nested itself, can enlightenment enter and soar.

I became a student and a teacher of literature because of my love for literature. Literature was my religion. All the other religions were included in that one religion. Even atheism.

All religious texts are only works of literature for me. Any verbal expression, irrespective of the speaker, is God's word for me, as long as it serves to further the goodness of humanity. I am an evangelist for the religion of literature. To achieve that, along with conventional means, I may also tread iconoclastic paths. I was also confident that nobody in my class would have raised any complaint that my methods of teaching had hurt either his or her self-respect or religious sensibilities.

A class test is a part of the teaching process. The aim of a class test is completed only after it is conducted, the paper evaluated, and the answers discussed and analysed in the class. Would I become the culprit if some mean-minded, base people intervene and frustrate its fruition by hindering the process? Thirty-two students wrote the test; four of them were Muslims. Only one girl among them displayed some hesitancy. By changing the words into elder brother and younger brother, that smart girl had found a solution to her apprehensions arising from her extreme faith. She had enquired with me whether such a change was inappropriate.

However, her answer paper, which was kept in my almirah after evaluation, was taken out by my own colleague from the bundle of answer papers and handed to the police by the principal. Because of the principal's senseless action, the girl was subjected to police interrogation. Having become a pawn in the game to implicate me, she came under tremendous mental stress and anguish due to feelings of guilt. It was indisputable that the perplexity that she felt while writing the exam wasn't even a tiny fraction of the distress she felt when an innocuous correction she had made in the answer paper had become a cause of misery for her teacher.

I came to know of her torment through her class teacher, Prof. Joy Mathew. I tried to boost her confidence by advising her through the same agency to forget the past and to concentrate on her studies. If the honourable court had not banned my entry into Thodupuzha taluk and the management into the college, I would have conveyed this to her in person.

My sole source of income was my salary and I was well aware that my salary was paid by the public of secular India. I was confident that I had not committed any wrong against the public or the country's Constitution. I had gone beyond the stage of caring whether 'the good citizens and the learned public' realized this truth; I knew it to be the truth.

I used such rationalizations to make peace with myself. However, what about my family who had to go through hell due to my foibles? What misgivings would have been caused in their minds by the statements put out by the college management, embellished news from the media, and the cock-and-bull stories made up by the police? How much pain and fear would Salomi have gone through when the barbarous police took away our son and used third-degree methods on him only because they were incapable of tracking me down?

On the day that I was arrested, my family didn't switch on the TV. They couldn't bear to see me in handcuffs, being dragged through the throng, and being made to stand in front of the officers like a culprit with my head bowed. When I was remanded to the jail, how deeply saddened had they been?

After my release from jail, they would have led a life of constant terror and tension, fearing the imminent attack on my person. And how much would they be grieving now when I am only little better than a corpse for all practical intents and purposes?

A wave of tears smashed against the wall of my heart and roared.

'Sister,' my voice was tremulous.

The nurse came up to me and looked at my face.

'May I cry a little?' My words made her lose her composure. She nodded. Leaving me to cry to my heart's content, she went away.

'Sister,' I called her after a little while.

She came back. 'It's over,' I told her.

That angel brought a towel and swabbed the tears that had flowed down my cheeks and drenched my chest and shoulders.

27

Sunrays on Fingertips

Specialists' Hospital was the first private sector hospital in Kerala to have a plastic surgery department. The founder of this hospital, Dr K.R. Rajappan, was eighty years old at that time. After my reconstructive surgery, he would come every day, feel my palm and check the blood circulation. The micro-vascular surgeons, R. Jayakumar, Asha Cyriac, Senthil Kumar and A.J. Guild, would come by turns and check on my progress. The doctors themselves would apply the medicines and dress my wounds.

As the attack had received wide publicity, there was a crowd at the hospital for a week or so. Many of the ruling front and opposition leaders met my family, either at the hospital or at home. A fact-finding group deployed by the Bharatiya Janata Party from Delhi met my family members in the hospital to gather information.

Teachers from Maharaja's College, St Albert's College, and Sacred Heart College in the city not only conveyed their sympathies and solidarity, but even extended financial help. My colleagues and ex-colleagues from Newman and Nirmala colleges conveyed the funds they had collected to the hospital.

I heard from Sister Marie Stella that a number of my friends and colleagues had broken down after coming to the hospital. Possibly due to such displays of emotion, Dr Asha Cyriac said one day, while she was dressing my wounds, 'People are deeply touched by your case.'

P.V. Paulin, tahsildar, Muvattupuzha came with the Rs 4,00,000 grant from the chief minister's relief fund. They needed either a signature or thumb impression on the receipt. They inked one of the toes on my right foot, trailing the leads from various monitors, and took its impression and went on their way.

Two other worthies who received permission to see me in the ICU were the Communist Party of India–Marxist (CPM) district secretary, Gopi Kottamurikkal, and Father George Panackal from the Potta Ashram, a charismatic renewal centre. The comrade promised me all kinds of support. The priest prayed for me.

When I was underground and the police had gone to Potta Ashram in search of me, Father George Panackal had, after welcoming them and plying them with tea, taken a copy of the question paper from my friend, Prof. Joy Mathew, read through it and queried, 'Where's the blasphemy in this?' Maybe he had been convinced of my innocence at that point itself, which had impelled him to visit me.

When he met Sister Marie Stella, Father Panackal told her that my face had a perceptible radiance. There was some truth in it, although the reasons were all metaphysical and none, spiritual.

The main reason for the 'spiritual' glow was the thought that my trials and tribulations were for a crime that I hadn't committed—whether in thought, word, or deed—for which a few people had hounded me relentlessly and mutilated me in this manner.

I had eschewed visits to the church and movie theatre realizing the risk in going to such places. However, unable to live a craven life for all time, I had decided to go to church, determined that I would face whatever was to happen. I had no regrets whatsoever that if I had been a little more careful, I could have escaped the butchery. On the other hand, even as I lay there swathed like a mummy on that hospital bed, I took a kind of perverse pride that it was only after I had decided to let them get at me, that the numskulls could touch me.

The grant from the government, the generous help from friends, colleagues, and well-wishers, had alleviated my financial worries. The knowledge that the public's sympathies, support, and prayers lay with me gave me great solace and peace of mind.

Dr Philipose Mar Chrysostom, senior metropolitan of Malankara Mar Thoma Syrian Church, sent me a letter conveying that he was praying for my welfare and for an end to my family's sorrows. What medicine can vie with the healing powers of such compliments as 'Your response and demeanour even in the time of a devastating calamity as this one is extremely laudable'?

Although I had gone underground, surrendered to the police, been remanded to police custody and jailed, I suffered no physical abuse. What cut me to the quick was the illegal detention of my son by the police and the torture he had to endure at their hands. My mental anguish was aggravated by the guilt that he suffered a physical trauma as a result of what I did, and yet I had been spared.

His words, though in jest, to others, 'My father created a question to bung in periods and commas, and I was the one who got all the periods' (punning on the vernacular word *kuththu* which can contextually mean period or dot, or poke or stab), truly twisted the knife in my wounded heart. But now, as I lay on the hospital bed, wasted and physically more harmed than he had been, an anguish I had borne on that score for some time diminished somewhat.

I became light-hearted also because I tried to see the humour in my situation. As I lay there like a raiment cut to shreds by rats and then patched back together, I pondered over my state objectively, the way some of the 'stithaprajnas'—men Bhagavad Gita would have us believe are sagacious, equanimous and transcendent—were thinking of me: 'Why did he have to do all this? He could have simply collected a few old question papers and picked and chosen questions from them. Instead of that, he wanted to create one of his own . . . to make it worse, he tried to inject humour into it . . . he deserves this. Very good!'

Sometimes, pain prodded and startled me out of my reverie. At other times, it came like a tsunami and washed over me with a roar. The nurse would give me an anal suppository painkiller and I would gradually slip into a kind of trance.

As soon as I started on solid food, the IV catheters were removed from my neck. The nurses would feed me whatever my family dropped off at the ICU. They would raise the head of the bed into Fowler's position and feed me like a baby. Tea and water were given in that position. I would feel at times that I was an infant and they were my mother.

At times, I would throw tantrums or dig my heels in like a recalcitrant child. One day the nurse was feeding me rice and fish; a de-boned tiny piece of fish after every morsel of rice. As I had had enough of the rice, I asked her to feed me bigger pieces of fish. Feeling that the fish could get over before the rice did, she continued feeding me the tiny bits. I stopped eating. She then suggested that I eat the fish alone and not waste it. I wanted to show her who was the boss. So, I obstinately said I wouldn't eat any more.

Despite using a waterbed, as I had to lie in the same position without moving, after a while, my back would feel as if it were on the top of a stove. I would press down on my hipbone and arch my back to find some relief. Due to poor blood circulation, my body and face would go numb sometimes, causing me great discomfort. The nurse would massage my face and my rib cage. When her hand was in the vicinity on my right armpit, that area would burn as it was an open wound.

Dandruff made me itch all over my head and face. The nurses used a tissue paper to scratch me. However, it was not an unqualified success at all times. By the time the nurse reached the spot following my verbal instructions, the itch would have moved to another location!

After eleven days, I was shifted from the ICU to a room. By that time, I had developed bedsores. By sitting up in Fowler's position and airing my back, the sores were controlled before they could get any worse.

I had Salomi, Sister Marie Stella, and Joby, my nephew, as full-time attendants in the room. Mithun's MBA classes had started the day after I was admitted. I was an asthma patient and the low temperature in the ICU had caused me breathlessness and cough. Surgery on my left arm and left leg had been postponed due to this. As sweat would have hindered the healing of my wounds, we had to keep the AC on, even after moving to the room. My cough persisted and the surgeries on my left arm and leg were done much later than planned. It lasted nearly six hours.

Now both my legs and arms were covered in bandages, raised, and supported by pillows. I looked at my two darling arms with the love of a mother looking at her twin babies swaddled and sleeping on either side of her.

Occasionally, some TV channel reporter would turn up to get a sound bite out of me. Not wanting to disappoint them, I let fly comments such as, 'I am the question that needs to be answered by Kerala's society.' No one, I knew, was there to provide an answer. Present-day culture mavens and leaders are not foolish enough to stick their necks out.

The police had taken statements from Sister Marie Stella and me at the hospital. I was given heavy police protection—armed policemen stood guard at my door twenty-four-seven. Even after I was moved out of the ICU, visitors were screened and only a handful allowed in. Since the doctors didn't want any secondary infection after my surgeries, they also frowned upon too many visitors.

I have read Hellen Keller's autobiography, *The Story of My Life*, in which she has written,

> I have met people so empty of joy, that when I clasped their frosty finger-tips, it seemed as if I were shaking hands with a northeast storm. Others there are whose hands have sunbeams in them, so that their grasp warms my heart. It may be only the clinging touch of a child's hand; but there is as much potential sunshine in it for me as there is in a loving glance for others.

Although we had no previous acquaintance, a young priest belonging to the Latin Catholic denomination would come every morning to my room to pray for me. He was a person with sunbeams in his fingers. I could feel the warmth from his touch flow into my body as positive energy whenever he placed his palm on my head while he prayed.

Our Bishop Mar George Punnakottil from the Kothamangalam Diocese had also come to meet me at the hospital and prayed for me with his hand on my head. However, I could feel only frigidity seeping into me.

The monsoon rains were in full force, lashing at everything. I dearly wanted to see the rain. One day, Salomi, my sister, and the nurse managed to prop me up and somehow take me to the window where I was made to sit on a cane chair. I enjoyed the splendour of the rain to my heart's content.

When the rain stopped, they failed in their attempts to lift me up and take me back to the bed and had to seek the help of the policemen outside. They lifted me like a feather and placed me on the bed. Since one of them had held me around my thigh, the wound on the outside of my right thigh, which had only just started to heal, began to bleed. They were shallow wounds where skin had been lifted to graft over the deep wound from where flesh had been extracted to repair my mangled hand.

When my health improved, my close relatives and friends were allowed to meet me, as long as they were non-smokers. The doctors had decreed that nicotine was the biggest danger to my convalescing body and forbade smoking in my presence.

I had been a smoker since my youth. I had been in my eighth class when I started. A rubber-tapper, who stayed at our place, would start his work before sunrise and I was the one who accompanied him with a small kerosene lamp so that there was just enough light for him to tap the trees. I cadged beedis from him occasionally and started to smoke. Although my parents did come to know, when I claimed it was to get over the early morning chill, they didn't chastise me too much. I also learnt tapping from him. When he had to go back to his place, I took up his tapping work and along with it, his smoking habit.

I quit smoking many times, only to start again. On 31 December 2004, I gave it up with a vengeance and never looked back. Those six years had obviously helped in bringing down the nicotine content in my blood. If not, according to the doctors, the reattached hand may not have survived.

Many of those who visited me brought along home-cooked food. The taste of freshwater fish curry brought by my student Jose Joseph and the beef curry brought by Shaji Joseph of St Albert's College still lingers on my tongue. Prof. Shaji Joseph and I weren't even previous acquaintances.

Dr T.M. Joseph, our principal, too visited me. I saw Father Pichalakkat lurking in his shadow, his posture suggesting that someone was propping him up from behind.

The very next day, Dr Joseph, in his article, 'The Question and Answer in the Controversial Question Paper,' in *Mangalam* daily, excoriated me and branded me a blasphemer. He categorically stated that the question insulted not only one community but all believers equally. What hurt me most was his damnation:

> Those who have been granted the boon of pedagoguery will never commit such errors.

Why was he repeatedly abusing a wounded colleague instead of trying to provide solace? Could it be that, in his opinion, the hurt and harm I had suffered weren't enough?

28

Letters That Changed Hands

On the third day after my surgery, to check if the re-attached hand would still obey me, I gingerly tried to wiggle my index finger. From among my half-curled fingers, that one moved a tiny fraction. Afterwards, I kept watching the state of my nails on that hand. In a month's time, they did grow. I could make out that the reconstructive surgery was a success.

However, the talk of discharge from the doctor took me by surprise. I was still bedridden and had to use the bedpan for excretion. Unable to wear regular clothes, I was wrapped in a single sheet all the time. My resemblance to a new-born would have been complete had there been a feeding bottle.

'All you need to do is lie in this fashion. The room must be air-conditioned. You should come back in ten days and we will remove the stitches and steel wires from the wounds and put plaster casts on your arm and leg.'

The doctor might have decided to discharge me early considering our finances. It was a blessing on many fronts.

Dr Senthil Kumar, who had come for the last rounds, gave me a final round of instructions, 'Don't smoke. Don't mingle with smokers. Don't become an exhibit in front of people.'

I nodded and asked him only half in jest, 'Can I drink?'

'That is not banned,' he said lightly. I made sure my sister and wife heard him, and heard him well. If I needed to have a couple of pegs on occasion, I could always fall back on his words and use it as a laissez-passer.

When Salomi and my sister went down to complete the discharge formalities, one of the policemen came in and told me that one of the relatives of the patient next door desired to meet me. I gave my assent.

A middle-aged man in a mundu and shirt came in. He stood a little away, silent, and looked at me. I could see tears brimming in his eyes.

When I asked, he gave me his name. He hailed from Vypeen. His skin tone was very dark, apparently from long exposure to sun. He could have been a fisherman but I didn't ask him. Before he left the room, he took out a 1000-rupee note from a bundle of small denomination notes and put it on the bed.

I protested saying there was no need for that. He acted as if he hadn't heard me. As I was completely immobile, I could do nothing more. He went out quickly. I felt tearful when I looked at the gift he had left me. Its value was not printed on the face of that currency note.

I left the hospital on 7 August, after thirty-five days of stay there. Dusk had fallen by the time we left the hospital.

As I could only travel on a stretcher, an ambulance had to be engaged. A friend from Ernakulam sent his car for my family to travel in. With police escort vehicles in the front and the rear, my return trip was a royal convoy. We reached home at around quarter to nine.

As everyone had been alerted by the media, the welcome-home party consisted of a crowd of relatives, friends, local acquaintances and public persons. And, of course, the media.

A blue police van was parked on the road close to our house. A dozen policemen were waiting in our yard.

An air-conditioning unit—bought by my friend Kallarackal Kuriakose for his own use—had already been fitted in my bedroom, as my house had none. I was very gently transferred on to my bed by people known and unknown to me. My homecoming was, albeit stretcher-borne, rather an event full of warmth and affection.

In the subsequent days, a lot of people, both from within and outside my circle of acquaintances, visited me. How do you turn away people driven by sympathy and concern for you? I had to, therefore, ignore the advice: 'Do not become an exhibit.'

After my ablutions and breakfast, Salomi would dress me up by 8 a.m. By that time, the visitors would have formed a queue. Anyone let in was first scrutinised by the police on guard. Many of the people looked at me as they would a corpse. Some of them burst into tears. Some of them kissed my reattached hand. Some of them prayed for me silently; others loudly.

Many came bearing gifts—apples, oranges, grapes, banana, free-range eggs. One poor woman came with a bottle of milk from the lone cow which she reared.

As I lay there accepting gifts and graces, I thought I must not merely forgive my attackers, but thank them as well. For, until then, I had never received so much love and care.

The police also showed remarkable alacrity in ensuring my security. As per the advice of the Muvattupuzha DySP, Sabu Mathew, a battery-powered inverter generator was bought for my house to serve in times of power failure. The Ernakulam rural superintendent of police was T. Vikram, an IPS officer. He not only conveyed his commiserations but also assured me that as a police officer he would do everything in his power to bring the culprits to book. Ernakulam Range IG Dr B. Sandhya contacted me on phone.

Meeting the constant stream of visitors meant I missed my mealtimes. Not wanting to keep my visitors waiting, I didn't have the heart to eat my food, although Salomi and my sister kept reminding and nudging me. I would end up having my lunch at 4 p.m. or 5 p.m. Afraid that my irregular mealtimes may affect my health, my sister stuck up a notice regulating visiting hours. That didn't help much though.

Some people tried to comfort me saying that such things happen when the planets are misaligned. One of my visitors, a retired school headmaster, was a dilettante astrologer. He asked me what star I was born under. I told him it was Kartika. He calculated my age and astrological times and said, 'You are under the influence of Saturn now. You are alive now only because Saturn isn't transiting the fourth, seventh and, tenth signs of the Zodiac.' Known in the vernacular as *kantakashani*, this was spoken of as a period of great calamities in one's life.

A few mavens of vastu, the Indian science of architecture and its effect on human well-being, tried to find causes for my troubles in my house's design and layout. They couldn't find anything wrong in its location or dimensions. Not that it would have caused any misgivings in me. I had decided on the location and layout myself. I was certain that other than the fact that a house should be in consonance with nature, there was nothing else of note in vastu.

The manager, Thomas Malekudi, didn't visit my sickbed. This has stayed in my memory only because I heard that, as his justification for not coming to see me, he had said, 'The college management is conducting an enquiry on him. As the manager, I have to conduct it with the impartiality of a judge. Is it proper for me to meet the accused? What if it hamstrung the carrying out of justice?'

I would have visitors until 9 p.m. It was only when I turned in after my dinner that the pain, which had lurked until then, started at my various wounds like fire-breathing dragons. When sleep became impossible, my sister went to Specialists' Hospital. Dr Jayakumar was chatting with his colleagues in the corridor. He asked her what had brought her there. She conveyed my distress and requested for some painkillers. Refusing to prescribe painkillers, he said, 'Tell sir to have a couple of pegs and sleep.'

Upon her return, she asked me, 'Do you need it?'

I said, 'No. Pain itself is an intoxicant.'

Ten days later, I had to engage an ambulance again to return to the hospital. After removing the stitches and steel wires, I was given plaster casts on my right arm and left leg. All the splints on my left arm and hand were removed. That hand was spared of the plaster cast. To protect the unhealed wounds on that hand, a tubular elastic bandage was used.

With the casts coming on, I was able to sit upright. Clad in a short pants and shirt, while being transported on a wheelchair from the casualty department to the ambulance, I saw the hospital building—which was close to my soul—for the first time. From the next day, I started physiotherapy in a unit run by Specialists' Hospital in Palarivattam.

Those journeys also used to be presidential. At 1 p.m., the police escort jeep would arrive. My nephew drove our car. My sister or wife would be in the front passenger seat. The rear seat was entirely mine. Six or seven pillows were placed around me as dunnage. The trips were thus in the lap of luxury. Only Sundays were off.

Physiotherapy was started on the fingers of my right hand and left arm. Since I had lost all sensation in my right palm, I felt no pain.

However, it was a different story with the left arm. But I bit down on my pain and didn't cry out or scream even if it was agonizing. I lay still.

Although I remained stoic, Mrs Rachel, the physiotherapist, understood the intensity of the pain that I was undergoing. One day, when my breathing became ragged, she pressed my chest and resuscitated me. Sometimes I felt as if the nerves on my temple were shattering. My high threshold for pain and silent sufferance led to such agonies. Rachel madam advised me to take painkillers. I procured them from Specialists' Hospital. However, since the excruciating pain bested them too, I took them only for one day and then stopped.

Every time we reached Palarivattam Junction, close to the physiotherapy centre, I would grow petrified in anticipation of the pain that was to come. Return journeys were calmer on the mind—the next one hour of torture was a full day away!

The 'action heroes' who had come to chop my hand, never had my left hand in their plans. Reportedly, they thought my left was my right. 'When people are doing serious work do they make such mistakes? Isn't my left hand suffering because of the gross negligence on my attackers' part? So, even if I declaim that I have forgiven them, I must reconsider it in the matter of my left hand,' I joked with my sister one day as we were returning home after physiotherapy.

The police had apprehended some of the heroes who had done the butchery. A few, they brought home and took my statement. I looked at them dispassionately. Their eyes too reflected the same dispassion and apathy.

On 19 August, a day after my limbs were put in casts, I received an envelope via post from the manager of Newman College. There was a show-cause notice and the enquiry officer's report in it. I was to give them my reasons as to why I should not be dismissed from the college service. I assumed that this was a mere formality for the college's documentation purposes because even the common man knew the truth behind the question paper; as soon as I provided them with my supporting arguments for my retention in the employ of the college, my suspension would be withdrawn. My reply, dictated and transcribed, was handed over to the manager on 25 August.

Salomi and Amy went to Bishop House to deliver the letter. When the manager realized that they were my wife and daughter, he flew into a rage. He spoke to them in harsh tones, raining down invectives on them and demanding to know why I couldn't have named the character Thomman or Mathai or whatever else, and why I had to name him Muhammed. Apparently, the enquiry commission had already cost them Rs 2,50,000. Although he grudgingly accepted the letter, not only did he not show common courtesy to two ladies, but also behaved quite boorishly with them.

We decided that we would not take the tale of the manager's tantrums to the media. The Taittireeya Upanishad dictum *satyam vada* (Speak the Truth) doesn't enjoin the listener to shout out every kind of truth; it only means that what is spoken should be the truth.

The next day's newspapers reported that my reply to the show-cause notice had been submitted. If the report in one of the papers was to be believed, the college manager, the vicar-general of the Kothamangalam Diocese, Monsignor Thomas Malekudi, had asked after the welfare of the teacher whose palm had been chopped off and had sent off his wife and daughter with words of consolation. I asked no one in particular, wasn't this what he ought to have really done?

The chop aimed at my left wrist had ended up almost severing the last three fingers of that hand. Another hack had smashed the last joint of my ring finger. The only two fingers that were capable of even minuscule movement were the index finger and thumb. Rachel madam probably realized that I would never be able to write with my right hand again— which is why she advised me to start writing with my left hand. As if I were a child taking his first writing lessons, she pressed a pen between the fingers of my left hand. My fingers had no strength to grip the pen.

In a brand-new notebook, she drew an unbroken line that had interlinked shapes which resembled the Malayalam letter ഥ (tha). As my homework, she asked me to fill the entire page with similar lines and bring back the book the next day. Rachel madam became my second writing guru. I remembered Sister Pausthinamma, my first teacher in my first standard, who had made me draw a string of zeroes on my slate.

It was 1 September 2010. When I got back home, thrilled and triumphantly bearing the notebook given by Rachel madam, a messenger from the manager was waiting for me. As soon as I was transferred from the car to the wheelchair, I was handed the envelope.

It was my dismissal order.

29

Off with Their Heads

Not in my worst nightmares had I dreamt that I would be dismissed from my job. Even when the manager had threatened to punish me, I had assumed that it would be confined to my removal as the head of the department or docking a couple of my annual increments. But as soon as the attack on me took place, even the man on the street understood that it was a concocted controversy and even Muslims had turned sympathetic towards me. I was confident that even minor disciplinary actions wouldn't be initiated.

It took me some time to believe that this was really happening and to reconcile myself to the awful truth. When I accepted the reality, I underwent tremendous stress and panic. A darkness overwhelmed my mind. There was no light at the end of the tunnel.

A friend and his daughter were waiting for my return after physiotherapy. A practising lawyer in Erattupetta, he read the order and tried to console me saying that any court would throw it out. I too didn't doubt it, but when would that be achieved? Until then, handicapped as I was, how would my family and I survive?

As per the university's rules, there are seven types of punishment. Warning is the first; dismissal is the last. Someone who is dismissed cannot be employed in any college in the university. He will also not be eligible for pension, gratuity and other end-of-service benefits.

The one just below dismissal is compulsory retirement. That also is tantamount to termination of services. However, the eligibility for pension and other benefits are not vitiated. Nor is employment in any other college banned.

Even the people who protested against the question paper only demanded my transfer from Newman College. If the management didn't want me in any of their affiliated colleges, they could have imposed compulsory retirement as a punitive measure. I would have collected pension for the rest of my life and avoided a life of penury. I was hurt inside and grieved silently.

We could not bring ourselves to tell anyone about my dismissal. The next day I didn't go for physiotherapy, as I lacked the will to do anything. Although the day after that, my sister forced me to go with her, I had no interest in pursuing the writing exercise. What was the point now in learning to write?

As Rachel madam insisted on my doing the writing exercise, I thought I should tell her about my dismissal. However, a sense of shame held me back. When there was no official press release about my dismissal, I hoped in vain that there would be a withdrawal of the order.

However, on 5 September, Teacher's Day, the news about my dismissal appeared in all the newspapers. In the press meet the day before, Monsignor Malekudi had declared that it wasn't a punitive action and only a disciplinary action. I am still trying to understand the difference between the two.

Most of the newspapers judged the management's action as cruel and deplorable. In *Mathrubhumi* daily's cartoon column Crow's Sight, my sorry plight was depicted through the caption, 'Newman College teacher dismissed. Another *adhyaa . . . pakadinam*,' wherein, by splitting the Malayalam word for teacher and attaching its tail to the Malayalam word for day, they made it read 'Vengeance Day'.

That was the day I received the maximum number of phone calls wishing me for 'Teacher's Day'. Every call pushed me deeper into sorrow.

The office bearers of the All Kerala Private College Teachers' Association (AKPCTA), of which I was a member, also arrived that day, to bring me the Rs 7,00,000 fund which they had collected for my treatment. The generous donation and their words of consolation did ease my tensions to some extent.

The students of Sanjo CMI Public School, Koduvely, came to meet me bearing a much bigger gift of love. Father John Palappally, their principal, accompanied them. They had brought a compilation of letters written by the students, from the first standard to the tenth standard, in a beautifully bound book titled, *Signature*. They also showed me a poster with the legend 'We Are With You' under which their kindergarten students, who hadn't yet started to write, had dipped their tiny hands in multiple colours and placed their handprints on the poster.

The letters all spoke to me with respect and sympathy and revealed that the children were wholly against religious fundamentalism. They were pained by the attack on me and were praying for my family and me. They were inspired by my readiness to forgive my attackers. They were happy that I had been proved innocent. They were also glad that the surgery was successful, and they wished me a speedy recovery. They also wished me success and fame in my vocation of teaching.

The letters were penned before my dismissal. The ideals and perceptions that had gone into the letter must have been inculcated in the children by their teachers and especially Father Palappally—none of whom were my acquaintances. I therefore accepted what they had written through the children as unbiased public opinion and that gave me a lot of happiness.

I thus experienced wholly Father Palappally's words in the foreword,

> This *Signature* is a remedy—an unadulterated, herbal medication concocted by the children to apply on his wounds.

On 6 September, the *New Indian Express* put out an editorial condemning the dismissal. It opened by comparing me to a Shakespearean tragic hero who was forced to undergo undeserved punishment for crimes he had not even dreamed about. The explanation by the question-setter had clarified that there was neither blasphemy nor disrespect to the Prophet.

> It was the twisting of facts by the rumour-mongers that led to an impression that he had committed 'blasphemy'.

The editorial titled 'Rubbing salt into teacher's wounds' said,

> Today there is better understanding of the whole incident
> and, therefore, greater sympathy for the teacher . . . Only a very
> insensitive body of people could have overlooked these extenuating
> circumstances and dismiss him from service when he has a wife and
> two children to support. The management of a college, named after
> Cardinal Newman of 'Lead Kindly Light' fame, should not have
> stooped to the level of those who cut Joseph's hand by cutting off
> his livelihood.

I could only see that editorial as a reflection of the effectiveness of the
media interactions I had had while I was in the hospital and away from
home. At least a few people had realized my innocence. That was good
enough for me.

Although the Communist Marxist Party leader, C.P. John, had
promised to intervene with the college management to reinstate me,
his attempts could not even take off due to the sheer cussedness of the
management.

Dr Thomas Mar Athanasius, metropolitan of Kandanad Diocese,
Malankara Mar Thoma Syrian Church, came home to meet me, pray
for me and provide me with solace. He contacted the authorities of the
Kothamangalam Diocese and asked for an appointment with Bishop
Mar George Punnakottil to discuss my reinstatement. The messenger
from Kothamangalam conveyed to him that this was an internal matter
and other churches trying to interfere in such matters would lead to them
getting distanced. And that was the end of that.

I read some of the social and cultural leaders' comments on my
dismissal. Although a few were not ready to give me a clean chit,
they were unanimous in their opinion that the punishment was not
commensurate with the crime. Although Father Paul Thelakkat,
spokesman of Syro-Malabar Catholic Church, had declared that the
college management's decision conveyed the right message, he too held
the opinion that the severity of the punishment was not warranted.
Four or five years later, he had to recant his statement and also say that
the management's decision was wrong.

Prof. M.K. Sanoo, my professor and litterateur, said,

> I can't see that the teacher has committed any wrong. He
> inadvertently used the Prophet's name. He has apologized for
> that. The right thing to do is for the management to reconsider the
> matter properly in all perspectives and reappoint the teacher.

Allow me to quote from two more educationists:[1]

> The dismissal of Prof. Joseph is an example of the start of remote-
> control rule by communal forces in Kerala. This is injustice. He has
> done no wrong to deserve dismissal. It's only natural that religious
> leaders' names are found even among teachers, fish-sellers, and
> lunatics . . . the explanation given by the teacher in this matter is
> entirely credible. The responses given by Joseph make it clear that he
> has all the qualities to be a teacher. Yet if he is being dismissed, it only
> shows the management's cowardice.
> —Prof. K.G. Sankara Pillai (Poet)

> The dismissal of Newman College lecturer T.J. Joseph is unjust. He
> should be reappointed. The stance taken by the management is an
> overt attack on academic freedom.
> —Dr P. Geetha (Writer and College Professor)

Among other cultural and literary icons who condemned my dismissal
were Justice V.R. Krishna Iyer, Justice K.T. Thomas, Anand, Paul
Zacharia, O.N.V. Kurup, Sugathakumari, Vaisakhan, George
Onakkoor, P. Valsala, U.A. Khadar, Ninan Koshi, Father A. Adappoor,
Pazhavila Rameshan, Dr K.S. Radhakrishnan, Swami Agnivesh, and
Joseph Pulikkunnel.

The observations of Dr K.N. Panicker—historian, ex-vice chancellor
of Sree Sankaracharya University of Sanskrit, Kaladi, and vice-chairman
of Higher Education Council—on the question-paper controversy, the
ensuing incidents, and the management's actions were the most balanced.
The conclusions in his articles that appeared in *Frontline* and other
publications revealed the sagacity of that doyen of higher education.

My colleagues at Newman College protested my dismissal by taking one day's mass leave. It's another matter that many of them were coerced by the management into signing on the attendance register in the later days. The students declared a strike and marked one day as a Black Flag day.

The education minister, M.A. Baby, announced that the government would directly intervene in this issue if required, as the dismissal was harsh. Mahatma Gandhi University wrote to the college management to re-examine the dismissal carried out without following the proper procedure.

M.J. Shaji, an autorickshaw driver and human rights activist, went on hunger strike for nine hours in front of Newman College, kneeling down and holding a cross, demanding that the unjustly dismissed teacher be taken back.

More than a hundred Catholics from Vannappuram marched to Bishop House, met the bishop and the other leaders and made emotionally charged appeals for my reappointment. Catholics under the leadership of the Joint Christian Council conducted a protest march to Bishop House, declaring the dismissal as unjust. Another protest march—under the aegis of various teachers' organizations in which thousands took part—went to Newman College. Many organizations conducted dharnas in various places against the dismissal. In the protest rally held in Ernakulam, my guru, Prof. Sanoo, appealed in the name of Jesus Christ to the Church leaders to reinstate me. Letters from all over the world asking them to take me back in my job reached Bishop House.

I submitted a mercy petition to the manager to repeal the dismissal order on humanitarian considerations.

All these efforts came to naught. Not only that, Kothamangalam Diocese declared war on me.

To counter the public opinion and to placate the faithful, Mar George Punnakottil issued a pastoral letter titled 'Question-Paper Controversy—Disciplinary Action' to be read out during the Sunday sermon in the one hundred and twenty churches and institutions under the Kothamangalam Diocese on 12 September 2010.

Some of the senior priests were not ready to read out such an un-Christian and falsehood-riddled pastoral letter that tried to justify my dismissal by denigrating me and branding me as a culprit. Some others left out parts they considered as outright lies, and acted as if they had carried out the bishop's orders.

The bishop who had declared his 'honesty of purpose' at the beginning of the letter by stating, 'As you will be desirous to know why the teacher was handed out a harsh punishment and I have a responsibility to clarify this' told barefaced lies to the faithful.

The reverend stated that, 'a commission consisting of senior high court advocates to conduct a full enquiry had been appointed,' when they had appointed only one lawyer to conduct the enquiry.

As far as I was aware, at that point in time, the two recent cases of college teachers being dismissed were that of Prof. Joy Michael of St Joseph's College, Moolamattam, and Prof. Sebastian Antony of St Albert's College, Ernakulam. The enquiry officer had been the same in those two cases as well.

His amateurish attempts to damn me in the report—by tarring me as a blasphemer and derogator of the Prophet—would have shamed any self-respecting person. In the impugned question, the only two characters were God and Muhammed. To misconstrue the name Muhammed as Prophet Mohammad, the enquiry officer had used Allah instead of God throughout his report. As it would take me much more than a meagre chapter or two to describe this person's mean, iniquitous ways, for the sake of brevity, I desist from doing so.

The part, '. . . it is highly questionable and moot why a dialogue between God and a lunatic—from P.T. Kunju Muhammed's "Screenplay: Discoveries of a Believer", not part of the syllabus—was adopted, and the word lunatic was replaced by Muhammed while creating the question . . .' in the pastoral letter was written with the invidious purpose of misleading the faithful to believe that the test question was on a topic which was out of syllabus and something that the students didn't have to study, and that it was prepared with an ulterior motive.

'The teacher didn't pay heed to the DTP operator pointing out the inappropriateness in the question,' was another brazen lie. The DTP operator—a temporary employee on daily wages at the mercy of the management—was a poor girl who had fully imbibed God's word that one should not bear false witness. Although she had been put under immense pressure, her statement to both the police and the enquiry officer was that she had only smiled when she had read the question.

I had come to know later that she had become mentally disturbed when falsehoods were foisted on her and publicized in order to crucify me. In order to regain her equilibrium, she had to undergo counselling.

I shall not go into similar inanities contained in the pastoral letter.

The pastoral letter cited my unwillingness to accept my mistake as the paramount reason for my dismissal.

I had prepared the question paper. No one else was responsible. I had owned up to this at every turn. I had expressed regrets and apologized for the question being twisted, misinterpreted, and being used to create trouble by miscreants.

This statement of apology was the one which the manager had transcribed and made me sign. This was appended in the enquiry report as my confession statement.

Did the reverend father want me to confess that I had done this to create religious discord? Would I have been taken back into the university's faculty if I had confessed to a crime I hadn't committed? I didn't need anyone's charity from claiming to have done something that I hadn't.

The above were the reactions I had given to the media when they wanted mine to the pastoral letter.

Anand, a reputed novelist in Malayalam, had written a piece titled 'A Sliver of Light' in one of the prominent Malayalam dailies lauding my stand. That acted as a wonder drug and strengthened my mental fortitude.

The pastoral letter was read out in most of the churches. It was accompanied by a paper titled 'Question-Paper Controversy: A Ledger of Enquiry' by Thomas Malekudi. Many of the younger priests not only read these out, but they also badmouthed me.

Whether directed to do so by the bishop or not, in the following days, nuns from the various convents under the diocese visited the homes of believers and started to spread rumours that I was a wife-beater and neglected to take care of my mother.

Various publications owned and controlled by the Church were filled with broadsides against me and encomiums for the college management, both in the form of articles and opinion pieces.

Not merely religious groups, even INFAM (Indian Farmer's Movement), a farmer's group run by the Catholic Church, printed and distributed leaflets and announcements, denouncing me and supporting the Church's actions.

Anonymous letters abusing the elderly and virtuous Father Adappoor—who had deplored the actions of the Church and the college management in his various articles—and spewing lewd vulgarities about my sister, although a nun, were sent around the state through mail.

Their efforts met with commendable success. The crowds stopped visiting my house. None of those who had prayed fervently for me ever came home after that. Most of the Roman Catholics stopped interactions with us. Even close relatives stopped coming home. They too needed to prove they were true believers.

I am a Roman Catholic under the Kothamangalam Diocese. The college I used to work in belongs to and is managed by the same diocese. As a part of the diocese, theoretically I am also part of the management. I believed that to act against the interests of the college or its management is tantamount to acting against my own interests. In which case, why were the diocesan-powers-that-be waging war against me—condemned as an accused in a crime I didn't commit, and crippled by the attack on me? Who were they trying to appease? A question I—and plenty of others too—have asked ourselves many times over.

The answer to this can be found in the autobiography of Assistant Director General of Police Dr Sibi Mathews, IPS, who was, at that time, second in the Kerala Police ranking, and head of its intelligence wing. As the head of the wing, he had kept a close watch on the question-paper controversy and its fallout. It should be noted that Sibi Mathews was a devout Catholic and had good contacts with the Church's leaders. In the autobiography entitled *Nirbhayam* (Fearless), the relevant portion about the case goes as follows:

> Newman College gave him initially a suspension order and followed it up with dismissal from service. The college management, including the Kothamangalam bishop, did things with a vengeance and vengefully, to appease the Muslim community. Such excessively punitive measures were unwarranted against Prof. Joseph, a Roman Catholic and brother of a nun. Some extremist youths, realizing that his own Christian community was ostracizing and isolating him, chopped off his right hand in a manner ordained in the Sharia law.'[2]

I am only trying to explain here, in brief, the kernel of this fearless revelation.

The Church authorities and the college management had decided to denounce me on 26 March when there was trouble in Thodupuzha town by communalists. From that point onwards, I had only been blamed, cussed at, and generally demonized by all of them.

The police discovered that the planning for the attack on me had started from 28 March. Until all the arrangements were ready, the attackers kept calling Bishop House regularly. They wanted to know the Church authorities' stand on my case. They sought replies to not only what the Church would do to me but also to what the authorities would do if they did something to me.

I had been told of the calls by the manager when I had met him with my reply to the memo of charges on 5 May.

Even if blinded by faith, the extremists were not unintelligent. They sussed out the Church's stance in my case very craftily. If the authorities had clearly said that I wouldn't be denounced and protected as a member of the flock, they would have never had the courage to mount an attack on me.

I realize now, even if late, that the friendliness that the bishop and the manager showed to me when I had visited Bishop House was consideration for a man marked for death.

I was suspended on 26 March 2010. The university rules require all the enquiry formalities to be completed in three months and action taken. The enquiry officer was appointed by the manager with instructions to submit the report by 15 June 2010. Although the report was submitted in time, the manager delayed action.

The news about my attack reached on 4 July. Monsignors Thomas Malekudi and Francis Alappatt, Fathers Joseph Koyithanath and Kuriakose Kodakallil immediately mounted a fact-finding visit to the site to evaluate the situation. They met police officials and held discussions. They came home and consoled my mother and others present.

Father George Pottackal, our parish priest, told my family that Bishop Mar George Punnakottil would be visiting them shortly. Perhaps it was because I didn't die that the bishop gave up on that idea altogether.

The attack on me was condemned even by Muslim organizations. The Church authorities alone remained silent. The very next day, in the meeting of the office bearers of the Old Students' Association held at Nirmala College, when some of the people pointed out the need to protest strongly, Monsignor Malekudi showed little interest. His comment, 'It would've been better if he had been killed,' revealed what was going on in his mind.[3] Mounting pressure from the leaders of believers' organizations, priests, and the faithful compelled the Church authorities to condemn the attack. The bishop wrote a pastoral letter. It reminded the faithful that protests must be restrained. Silent marches were held in Thodupuzha, Kothamangalam, and Muvattupuzha.

The bishop, Monsignor Malekudi, and Monsignor Alappatt, along with other inmates of Bishop House, held a religious-harmony meeting in a hall in Muvattupuzha, which included some maulvis and hajis. There was no audience, yet they distributed panorama-sized photos to newspapers and news agencies.

After all these charades and farces, they removed me from their employment. Then they held press conferences in which they stated that I would be taken back if the Muslim community requested that they do so. When they don't have the grounding of morality and ethics, what else could they have done?

That the attack on me didn't go to the desired and logical end was what aggravated the Church authorities' frustration. Because of that, they had to fire me and earn general opprobrium. This frustration was blatantly reflected in an article in *Mangalam* daily in 2010, penned by Father Noble Parackal, a postgraduate student in Newman College and then a novitiate brother. Its title said it all: 'Decapitate senseless heads'.

30

Case Diary

In case you are curious about the plan hatched by my attackers, and what happened to them post the attack, I shall give you the police version of it.

I have been told that the gang that attacked me made was made up of active members of an organization called Popular Front of India (PFI) and its political wing known as Social Democratic Party of India (SDPI). The police never investigated the higher levels whence instructions were given to these cat's paws. Due to many reasons, the investigations stopped at the door of a district-level leader of the PFI. Accordingly, the mastermind was the one listed as the twenty-eighth accused in the Sessions Case No. 1/2013 (NIA).

Another active member was the supervisor, the eighth accused. Although I know the names of not only the master-planner and the supervisor, but also those of their accessories and accomplices, out of consideration for their and their families' futures, I am not recording them here.

On 28 March, two days after the rioting in Thodupuzha town, the master-planner, the supervisor, and three others met in Seema auditorium in Perumbavoor and conspired to mount an attack on me. It was also decided to form separate groups under the supervisor to work out the actual plan and the logistics, collect money, make preparations, carry out the attack physically, destroy evidence, and flee to boltholes.

On 3 April, the master-planner, the supervisor, and fifteen others met in the Kerala Water Authority's Inspection Bungalow in Muvattupuzha and laid detailed plans.

On 6 April, another meeting took place in Revenue Tower, Kothamangalam, under the stewardship of the master-planner, followed by one near the Taluk Office on 10 April, and on 19 April, near the gate of the sub-station.

On 4 May, convened by the master-planner, those co-opted into the attack gang held a meeting in the Municipal Park and selected one of them as the leader. The master-planner arranged funds, weapons, explosives, vehicles, mobile phones, and SIM cards, all of which were procured using fictitious identity cards made available to the attack gang.

As instructed by the supervisor, an autorickshaw driver, a member of the logistics gang, prepared a map of the route to my home. Another two men, under instructions from the master-planner and supervisor, did a reconnaissance and verified the route map.

On 6 May, the six-member attack gang headed to my home. Including the supervisor, six men of the support group waited at various points to receive the vehicles, weapons and blood-stained clothes used in the 'operation', and destroy the evidence.

By the time they arrived, I had left for my colleague T.A. Joy's home. They were the ones my sister had invited to come into the house and wait for me, as they had come to request for an article for a college magazine.

On 17 May, the master-planner, the supervisor, and four others turned up purportedly to seek medical aid for the gang leader's daughter but shelved the attack plan as I had stepped back into the house and shut the door, and they noticed that there were other people in the house.

On 28 May, they came again. Two of them even trespassed and searched for me inside my house. My stepping out to go over to my neighbour's house derailed their plans that day.

Since, after the last incident, we had started locking the gate and door, realizing it was not easy to get at me inside my home, they decided to attack me out in the open. Realizing that their motorbikes were inadequate to intercept and waylay me since I invariably travelled by car whenever I went out, they bought a Maruti Omni van from a Christian in Thrissur at the asking price, through a broker called Mani. As someone had to drive the vehicle, the gang co-opted one more person and their number swelled to seven.

After a month of preparation, on both 2 and 3 July, they lay in wait on the road for me to emerge. The support gang of six also waited along various points to render post-op clean up. Although I had travelled by car on both days, as I had used different routes to head out and return, they couldn't ambush me.

The two men on the motorbike who tailed me on our trip to Bishop House on 2 July were the ones who had verified the route map and were charged with monitoring my movements. After using the Chalikadavu bridge on the way there, we had switched our route through Muvattupuzha town on our way back.

On 3 July, they all met up at Kakkanad. They spent the night at the mastermind's house, where the role assigned to each one was reiterated, and they were given more money, weapons, and explosives. The supervisor was contacted by phone and made to confirm that the post-op arrangements were in place as planned.

Early in the morning on 4 July, the five of them left their master-planner's home in the Omni; two others joined them at Karikkad junction. After reaching Muvattupuzha and learning from the supervisor that I had gone to church, they waited near my home. A man was stationed near the Muvattupuzha police station to report on police movements.

The lookouts near the church and near my home alerted the attack gang when I left the church and neared the destination. They intercepted me and carried out their mission.

As they drove away, they deposited all the weapons that they had used in the attack in a bag. The bag was handed over to the man waiting for them at a place known as Varappetty. At Irumalappady, on the Kothamangalam-Perumbavoor route, they got into other vehicles waiting for them. The Omni van was driven by someone towards Perumbavoor; at a deserted place, he removed the false number plates and threw them into the Periyar Valley canal.

My son Mithun's 'intervention' had caused injuries to two of my attackers. One of the wounds was deep. As instructed by the supervisor, they were taken in separate cars to a house in Aluva, changing cars twice on the way. A dentist was brought there along with medicines and bandages and the two were administered first-aid.

All the members of the attack gang were then sent to various safe houses and shifted from one to another frequently with the help of many sympathizers.

My daughter, Amy, in her call to the police station, had informed them that the attackers had come in a white Maruti Omni van. At the time of the call, the Aluva rural superintendent of police, T. Vikram, was conducting a mini conference known as SATA with his subordinates through police wireless sets. When the SATA was on, the wireless sets in all the police stations under the rural SP had to remain switched on and one officer had to be in attendance.

The Muvattupuzha officer attending the SATA immediately told the SP that the attackers were travelling in a white Maruti Omni van. The SP in turn alerted all the police stations to check all the Maruti Omni vans on the road. He informed the IG, B. Sandhya, and the DGP, Jacob Punnoose. Sandhya relayed the alert to all the stations in Ernakulam and the neighbouring districts.

Although a Sunday, the police came out in full force everywhere. Some sixty white vans were detained by the police on that day, throughout the state.

Around 9 a.m., when the sub-inspector of Perumbavoor police station, C. Jayakumar, inspected a white Maruti Omni van that had come out from one of the side roads, he found blood stains on its floor. Although the driver had a Muslim name, a sticker of the Holy Family on the windscreen increased his suspicions.

When questioned, the driver claimed he was delivering the van to another man from Irumalappady as per his friend's instructions. The police found the name and the phone number of this person on the driver. The van and the driver were taken into custody. Using the number, the police got to the man who was supposed to receive the van and hide it, and arrested him.

Having come to know that two of their men had been arrested, PFI members led protest marches to the Muvattupuzha and Perumbavoor police stations demanding they be released as they were innocent. Although the crowd was on the verge of turning violent and pelting the police at Perumbavoor with stones, the police didn't quail. However, this made the police certain that the arrested men had a role in the attack.

Interrogation revealed that they were engaged by the supervisor. They found out that the van had belonged to a Lawrence from Thrissur and got the name of the person who had bought it from him. Investigations based on mobile phone locations and calls also continued. The premise on which the police looked for links was—on the morning of 4 July, there would have been a caller near my home reporting on my movements; the gang in the Omni van would have received calls or messages from him; the ones who waited down the road in Irumalappady or elsewhere too would have had mobile phones.

They used the cyber cell to trace the calls in the vicinity and the possible routes the Omni van could have taken and discovered calls from previously unused SIM cards procured using false IDs. Then, thwarting the best-laid plans of the master-planner and his supervisor, when they decided to use new SIM cards to avoid detection, they found the IMEI numbers of the mobiles in which these SIM cards were used, and the previous SIM cards used in these phones, and from there the investigation moved on to the owners of those SIM cards. From them they received enough pointers to the master-planner and the members of the attack gang. The police then started to pick up the men from their lairs. The police couldn't track down some of the men.

DGP Jacob Punnoose has said this was the best-planned criminal attack in Kerala and if the police hadn't found the vehicle within an hour of the crime being committed, this would have added another item to the list of unsolved crimes in the state.

Our own small precautions and actions also contributed to the success of the police's prompt and excellent actions. The police numbers we had pasted near the phone enabled Amy to call them with no loss of time and for them to alert their stations. The blood spotted by the SI in the van came from one of the attackers who had been hacked at by my son, in an attempt to save his father. Amy and Mithun can be proud that their presence of mind and bravery helped capture those who had attacked their father for no reason.

31

Don't Ever Give Up

Realizing that more than an attack on my person, this issue had far-reaching social repercussions and dimensions, E.P. Unny, a cartoonist and writer, wrote a piece titled 'Testing Tolerance' in the *Indian Express*, published on 10 October 2010.

After coming down from Delhi, he met not only me, but many others connected with the case. However, Monsignor Malekudi was not ready to give any explanation. 'Enough has been written against us . . . who cares?' were among the curt words he used to dismiss Unny.

Even if Prof. Rajan Gurukkal, the vice chancellor of the university, made statements such as: 'Newman College is a government-aided institution, not a pontifical seminary teaching catechism'; 'the government is the pay master'; 'we'll use the implied powers in the University Act'; and the minister, M.A. Baby, declared that, 'if the order is not withdrawn, the government will intervene', who was going to heed them?

Prof. M. Leelavathy, my teacher and famous litterateur, has revealed the truth behind the arrogance of private college managements in her article titled, 'The Matrilineal System in Colleges' in the *Mathrubhumi* daily of 7 November 2010.

The government pays the teachers for the work they do; the management of the educational institutions don't. The power to punish can only be with those who protect. It's only in Kerala,

God's Own Country, that God protects and the Devil punishes . . . the managements have the best of all worlds. They can appoint whom they want. They can take bribes as they please. They can insult or dismiss or do whatever they please to whomever they appoint. The government is a mute witness. Because all rules are made in their favour. Fearing that the minorities will go on the warpath, the governments that come into power by turns, maintain this status quo.

I, therefore, didn't fall for anyone's bluster. My only refuge now was the courts. As per the university's regulations, I could have appealed to the MG University Appellate Tribunal against my dismissal. Its office is in Thiruvananthapuram and is presided over by a judicial officer at the level of a district judge.

Any appeal against the decision by the tribunal would have to be made to the high court. After that comes the Supreme Court. The final decision would come from there.

It is not easy for an employee to get a favourable judgment from the courts once he is dismissed by the management. On many occasions, I have personally heard Monsignor Malekudi boasting that no one should be so presumptuous as to think that he or she could litigate against the management and win. The management is an institution. Therefore, money that has to be spent on a legal case is of no concern to them. Where would an individual get that kind of money was his question. They had already launched the legal battle. I had received notice of the caveat filed by the management's lawyer on the same day that I was dismissed. A caveat is an anticipatory appeal filed to prevent any appeal from the other party being decided on without hearing the caveat appellant's side.

I was in no position to stand up, let alone walk, during those days. My friends had engaged a lawyer to file the appeal to the tribunal. I could meet my lawyers only months later.

The initial expenses for litigation were met with the donations received from some well-wishers.

A retired headmistress from Thrissur, Saudamini teacher, sent me Rs 10,000 with a note, 'Only truth has eternal victory.' Such actions and generosity were a great relief and fortified my self-confidence.

Two or three articles written by me appeared in *Mathrubhumi* and *Kalakaumudi* weekly magazines. Some of the readers who learnt my side of the story became sympathetic towards me. Surya TV had me interviewed by Anil Nambiar and sent out an appeal for financial help. All these helped bring in money for my treatment and for prosecuting the case.

Bank employees showed me more sympathy than any other group. The next in line were government employees. The common man came next. The fact that teachers came last in that list did cause me some disappointment.

I decided that I should be frugal with the money given by these kind-hearted people. For the first time in my life, I started writing down my daily spend, which Gandhiji had recommended would help control expenses. I had no idea when my means of livelihood would be restored to me.

Both my children had taken educational loans. Some generous, benevolent people were ready to pay Amy's fees and related expenses; we could therefore shift her instalments to our living expenses kitty.

I was determined that I should regain the strength in my limbs and went every day to Ernakulam for physiotherapy. The taxi fare was Rs 1000 and therapy charges, Rs 250.

After the plaster casts were removed, gritting my teeth through the excruciating pain, I worked on my left hand and left leg. However, there was no improvement in my right palm, which had lost all sensation; its fingers refused to obey me.

I would receive letters from empathetic strangers those days. I could only search out their telephone numbers in those letters to call and thank them. Thanks to Rachel madam's zeal, I continued to practise with my left hand and when I discovered that legible letter formation was within my powers, I had an urge to write to someone. The news of O.N.V. Kurup being awarded the Jnanpith award became an inspiration.

Although he had never taught me, I had attended his lectures and speeches. In 1988, I attended a college teachers' orientation course conducted by the Staff Academic College at Thiruvananthapuram. O.N.V. Kurup had taken classes on poetry. As the person charged with receiving and attending to the guests, I had got introduced to him. On many occasions when I taught his poems in my class, the poet seemed to have possessed me. I did manage to write out a congratulatory note to him:

> To my O.N.V. sir,
> This is a left-handed note by someone who has lost the trove of letters kept treasured in his right hand. Like every Malayali, I too am elated that your imagination that has soared up to Jnanpith like Fireflies, from Salt[1] encrusted letters. I bow to you, the master poet.
>
> Affectionately,
> T.J. Joseph

Since signing the note was not possible, I had affixed my thumb impression.

A week later came his reply:

> To T.J. Joseph With Love
> I have to hand the laudatory note
> Writ with your trembling left hand, my friend;
> As I saw the thumb print on it,
> Tears tumbled down from my brimming eyes.
>
> I once wrote: Someone who hasn't sinned
> Is being crucified somewhere;
> When I think it was your turn yesterday,
> Your pain pervades my heart too.
> Even when I pray 'Father, forgive them',
> My heart tells me they will not receive absolution;
> They are not men who do things unbeknownst
> Isn't God the mercy that resurrects victims?
>
> Standing at shores of the ocean of tears
> Shed by tortured souls, I am imbued with its salinity.
>
> With Love,
> O.N.V.

I am praying for your quick recovery. May the belief that all lovers of humanity are one with you strengthen your resolve.

A cheque for Rs 10,000 was enclosed with the letter.

The attitude of another 'lover of humanity' was diametrically opposite. After reading E.P. Unny's article and feeling for my plight, C. Antony Louis, a social worker from Mumbai, had sent me a letter offering free legal services from Maharashtra Litigants' Association, which he was part of. He had enclosed a demand draft for Rs 5,000 as financial aid for me. Since he didn't have my exact address, he sent the letter and draft to Sukumar Azhikode, an academic and writer, requesting that they may be forwarded to me. He replied to Louis that he would not be able to forward the letter and that he had torn up both the letter and the draft. That erudite man of letters must have thought a cheque and a draft were the same.

I later received a letter from Antony Louis describing all this along with a copy of the letter sent to Sukumar Azhikode registering his protest at his lack of common courtesy and decency.

CPM Secretary Pinarayi Vijayan, and Ministers Kodiyeri Balakrishnan and Kadannappalli Ramachandran had visited me during that time.

Uzhavoor Vijayan, the chairman of the Kerala State Handicapped Persons' Welfare Corporation, after visiting me, had met Monsignor Malekudi at Bishop House and had asked him, 'When it's our bounden duty to reserve jobs for handicapped people and help them earn their livelihood, was it ethical to remove from his existing job someone who has been left a cripple by the forces of evil?' As if he were someone who would be swayed by such arguments!

When the press was going to town about the hand-hacking case and the dismissal story, in Mithun's college, only a handful of his classmates and teachers knew that he was my son. A new teacher was going through the usual introductions that happen on the first day. When Mithun said he was from Muvattupuzha and had graduated from Vishwajyothi Engineering College, Vazhakulam, the teacher, said, 'The manager of that college, Thomas Malekudi, is my uncle. He has become famous now with the firing of a teacher of Newman College.'

Mithun didn't enlighten him that his own father was the cause of his uncle's world-level fame. One of his classmates, recognizing the conflict in that dramatic moment, defused it by steering the discussion in another direction. Later, the teacher came to know who Mithun was and apologized to him and consoled him.

While returning from my physiotherapy sessions, I would buy fish from a stall near Kakkanad. If I asked for half a kilogramme of fish, they would give one kilo, and take only the price for the half kilo. One day, I had checked out two types of fish and then asked for half a kilo of one of them. They handed over half a kilo of both. I declined to take both but they insisted; and accepted payment only for half a kilo. I do not know their religion or their caste.

The fish-seller in our area in Muvattupuzha was a Muslim. Earlier, if we asked for half a kilo, we would receive exactly half a kilo. That has changed since: when we ask for half a kilo, we get at least three-fourths of a kilo.

I also used to buy fish from a place called Adoopparambu near our house in the evenings. When I was bedridden, if my son or nephew went to buy fish, the seller would refuse to accept money and sent them back with the fish, saying he would take the money from me. Later, even when I went in my car to buy them myself, he refused to accept money. He said he would take money when I was able to walk to his shop. Only when I threatened to stop buying his fish if he didn't accept payment did he, very reluctantly, start to accept money from me again. He was a Muslim.

Second-rung writers and cultural activists came to meet me often. They gifted me many books. Those good-hearted people may have thought that since I was stuck at home, I should use the time to read and get enlightened.

I was invited to the public convention conducted by the leftist teachers' associations at VJT Hall in Thiruvananthapuram on 16 November 2010. Pinarayi Vijayan, who had come to inaugurate the convention, helped me on to the stage, holding me by my hand. The crowd gathered there raised slogans supporting me; it was a new experience for me. In his inaugural address, Pinarayi Vijayan said that the whole of Kerala was on my side and that there was no difference between the extremists from PFI who had chopped off my hand and the church diocese that owned and managed the college.

I used the occasion to thank everyone who had kept my spirits up through empathy, comforting messages, prayers, and monetary and other help.

I was garlanded by leaders such as Pannyan Raveendran, Prof. Ninan Koshy, Prof. Puthussery Ramachandran, K.E.N. Kunjahammed, Aloysius D. Fernandes, and many cultural activists; others honoured me with *ponnaada*s and shawls; and yet others gifted me books. Overwhelmed by such love and honours, I got off my high only sometime after returning home.

The daily taxi fare for physiotherapy was bothering me; the doctor had said I would need two years of physiotherapy. I knew that, at this rate, I would become too penurious to complete it. Therefore, one day, I limped into the driver's seat of my Wagon R. I pressed the clutch pedal with my left leg. Although I felt the pain, the pedal did go down. Using the three fingers of my left hand that had been regaining some of their strength, I engaged the gear. The right leg needs power for braking, and that was in a better shape anyway. I drove the car up to our neighbour, M.C. Joseph's house and returned. It was the shot of confidence that I needed. The next day, in the company of Mithun, I drove seven kilometres to Vazhakulam town along the highway and back. From then on, I drove myself to Ernakulam for my physiotherapy.

One day, I drove to Kalayanthani near Thodupuzha to attend a funeral. My friend, T.A. Joy, and my personal security officer came along. While we were returning, we saw two nuns waiting at the bus stop. One of them was a retired Malayalam professor from Nirmala College and the other, a teacher in a school near Muvattupuzha; both my acquaintances. As we could accommodate two more passengers, I stopped the car and asked, 'Would you like to come with us?' They looked at each other, wordlessly. Then, a few seconds later, as if they had come to a decision, they climbed into the car.

From the backseat, they kept glancing at my reattached right hand, and the maimed and reconstructed left hand. When we were nearing Muvattupuzha, I asked them, 'Why did you hesitate to get into the car? Couldn't you have thought that having driven up to Kalayanthani, I could also drive back in the same manner?'

'We did think that way and found courage to get in,' said the schoolteacher nun, with disarming honesty.

Many others to whom I offered lifts were reluctant to accept it and excused themselves giving improbable reasons.

During this time, my driving licence expired, and I engaged an auto consultant to get it renewed. However, when the application for renewal was taken to the doctor for certification, he recognized me in the photo and refused to certify it. I took back my application from the consultant and went to the same eye-specialist myself. He checked my eyes and spectacles and confirmed that my sight was good. On my physical capability, he wrote that my hand had been maimed but I was able to use it. I went to the Regional Transport Officer; he referred me to a Motor Vehicle Inspector, a Muslim from Thodupuzha. We spent an hour in friendly conversation, and, when he asked me about it, I narrated the backstory of the question-paper controversy. Then he asked me, 'Did you drive yourself here?'

'Yes.'

'Then, let's do a test drive.'

I drove around within the grounds of the Muvattupuzha Civil Station. After he was satisfied with my driving, he signed the papers. I felt proud that I had done it the proper way.

For some time, I had given tuitions for high school and plus two students in Mother and Child Foundation, a charity organization for orphans and handicapped children in Mailakombu near Thodupuzha. Dr S. Sankararaman from the physics department of Newman College also used to give tuitions there.

There were eight to ten students from each class, and they would be placed in different rooms. On my first day, I was shown around by Afrid, a seven- or eight-year-old North Indian boy, who was gradually picking up Malayalam. After showing me each room, he would say, 'Edaa, let's go,' as if I were his peer.

Some of the police officers assigned as my personal security officers would also teach there. We would go there at night; the security officer would always remind me that travelling so late was a risk. More than that, it was my depleting funds that made me call off the tuition classes; the daily expense on petrol to Thodupuzha and back was Rs 150.

A poster beneath the glass top of their office table attracted me very much. A crane was shown swallowing a frog, with the frog's head almost entirely in its mouth. The frog, with its rear legs flailing in the air, had, with its little hands, a stranglehold around the crane's neck. The caption under it was 'DON'T EVER GIVE UP'.

Joshy Mathew, the manager, told me that he had downloaded it from the Internet and taken a printout. I downloaded it into my heart; and then, etched it there—Don't Ever Give Up.

On 23 March 2011, I again went under the surgeon's knife in Specialists' Hospital, because eight months' physiotherapy hadn't shown the desired results. My right forearm was opened along its length and two finger joints on my left hand were operated on. The microvascular surgery lasted more than six hours.

This was followed up with physiotherapy. However, other than making me suffer increased pain and more expenditure, it did very little to get my hands functioning again. After a year of daily physiotherapy, I decided to make it on alternate days. The primary reason was lack of funds.

The next year, I underwent surgery again, or more correctly a series of surgeries. A steel rod each was removed from my left leg and my right forearm. Six nails were inserted in my fingers to keep them in a bent position. A keyhole surgery was done for inguinal hernia.

Two weeks later, the nails were removed, and physiotherapy was restarted. Still the last two fingers in my left hand showed no improvement. Nor did the fingers of the right hand. The last four fingers of my right hand were willing to bend only so far as if they were trying to curl around the handle of something I was trying to lift up.

However, I now owned the motto 'Don't Ever Give Up'. I offered to be operated on again. The doctors weren't enthusiastic. They knew the location of all the nerves and veins in a normal arm; in a mangled and remade arm, all these would be in a tangle. If they snipped one or the other by mistake, I could lose even the limited movements I had in my arm and hand. I concurred; I could not afford to lose whatever little I had.

Dr Jayakumar gave me the name of Christine M. Kleinert Institute, in Louisville, Kentucky and said, 'If you get yourself treated here, your right hand may improve.'

While I was struggling to get to Ernakulam for my physiotherapy, here was someone suggesting I go to the USA for treatment. I made small modification in my 'Don't Ever Give Up' motto. I changed it to 'Be Happy With What You Have'.

My mother had the right to live in our ancestral home at Variyanikkadu and be the beneficial owner of all the agricultural produce of the land attached to it. We had rubber trees, half of which had been planted by my own hands. They were due for replanting. Some of the trees were still young and productive. Since we never got someone to tap the latex, the place was like a small jungle now, overrun by undergrowth.

I wondered whether I should go there and start tapping. To tap, the right hand must hold the handle of the tapping knife and keep pressing it down, while the left hand stays on the metal blade, guiding the direction of the knife. I took up a tapping knife. Three fingers on my left hand had movement which was enough to guide the knife. However, the inflexible fingers of my right hand were not able to grip the handle.

I then fitted a 15-cm-long PVC pipe over the tapping knife's handle. I screwed on an elbow at the other end and fixed another pipe perpendicular to the first one. I held the knife's blade in my left hand and placing the upright pipe in the web between my thumb and my index finger of my right hand, I pushed. I realized that if the need arose, I could still do rubber tapping.

The next day, accompanied by my wife, sister and mother, we left for Variyanikkadu with the aim of restarting our traditional trade. My sister's leave had been extended for a year.

The policemen who were guarding us, dropped us there and returned. Our Variyanikkadu house was within Thidanad police station limits. Two policemen from that station came in as our protection officers. Salomi got busy with cleaning up the place and cooking. My sister and I started to remove the undergrowth to clear a path to the rubber trees. Since two fingers in my left hand still couldn't grip properly, the chopper often flew out of my hand as I tried to hack at the plants and bushes.

I was able to tap the trees. However, I was not able to drive into the tree the metal strip that guided the flowing latex into the collection vessel. That my sister had to do.

One day, as I was washing up after the tapping was done, I found the skin and some flesh on the middle finger of my right hand was sheared off. I must have injured myself when I tapped one of the old trees and scraped my finger against one of the metal strips already present in the tree. As I had no sensation on that part of the hand, I never felt the pain.

We had no dining table in that house. One day, holding the stainless-steel plate in my right hand, I was eating puttu and chickpeas curry with my left hand. After I lifted the plate, I saw that my entire right palm was one big blister. My plate had faithfully transferred the heat of the chickpeas curry on to my hand, and my insensate hand remained mute. More than the burn, the fact that it was not getting conveyed to my brain hurt me. To make it worse, the doctor had explicitly ordered that until my hand regained its sensation, I should not suffer burns or cuts.

We spent two weeks there and when everything was toted up, there was no net gain. After feeding the policemen, since there were no eateries near our place, and our own expenses, nothing was left in the purse, and we decided to return home.

The money given by my association was used for foreclosing the mortgage on my house. The legal cases were the biggest drain and there was always some unexpected expenditure for that. When the kitty was gradually getting depleted, and we started to wonder what next, someone would turn up out of the blue with financial help. The critical expenses were being met somehow.

At one time, having run out of funds, when I was at the end of my tether, Yukthivadi Sanghatana (Rationalists Organization) turned up with the money they had collected for me. I asked myself, why would they need other gods when they are themselves playing the role of God?

More than the earning of money, we needed to learn how to spend it more effectively. Many people continue to be destitute not because they do not earn, but because they do not spend wisely. I had written an article titled 'Thrift' for the value education classes in the college. I now implemented, with an iron hand, thrift and frugality in our family's economy.

The cooking gas stove was replaced by a wood-fired stove. As a smokeless stove used up more firewood, when it wasn't raining, we would cook al fresco using a conventional wood-fire stove. Ration rice was available at Rs 2 a kilo for low-income families. We had been buying that for a long time. Compared to the ration rice we used to get during my childhood, the two-rupee rice was of superior quality. So that gave me no sorrow. However, it was not so for the rest of my family, however uncomplaining they were.

We cut down on our plentiful diet of meat and fish. We found out the prices of the various vegetables and bought only the cheapest. We went to the land and started to use papaya, moringa leaf, tarvine leaf, colocasia leaf, elephant yam leaf, banana blossom and its floral stem, tender jackfruit, ivy gourd and its leaf—all freely available to us.

Our general health improved; I lost ten kilos. Hypercholesterolemia, diabetes, and hypertension had been knocking on my doors. My cholesterol fell from 210 to 150; blood sugar from 125 to below 100.

When I went to attend the funeral of a friend's father, an ex-colleague from our college met me and surveying me from top to toe, he said, 'Joseph, you are looking fit.'

I couldn't but help make a wisecrack, 'Come evening, I'll be more "fit",' fit being the Malayali's euphemism for getting sozzled.

32

Four Suits

During the years between 2010 and 2014, after the expenditure and long hours spent on medical treatment, most of my time and money was spent on legal cases.

One of the cases didn't set me back by much. Nor did the outcome give any benefit.

We had petitioned the Kerala State Human Rights Commission (HRC) seeking redressal for the illegal detention and torture suffered by my son Mithun and his maternal uncle, Saju. Based on the complaint e-mailed by Mithun, HRC had instituted case no. HRMP No.1314/2010 against the Thodupuzha SHO, Sub-inspector Shinto P. Kurian. Learning of it from news reports, Human Rights Protection Council of India also filed a complaint of violation of Mithun's rights; based on that, another case, HRMP no. 1950/2010, was instituted by the HRC.

The HRC started its procedures in the second half of 2012. Hon'ble Member R. Natarajan examined the case and sittings were held in Thodupuzha Government Guest House. I would attend the sittings out of curiosity. The majority of petitioners were poor people and Dalits. The defendants were almost always police officers.

In Mithun's petition, only Shinto Kurian was mentioned. However, during his examination and from his description of the torture he had undergone, the commission found DySP Kuriakose also culpable and suo motu included him in the accused list. When he appeared after receiving its notice, and saw me there, he scowled at me. He griped that he was being put through this despite behaving decently with me on the day of my surrender.

While the evidence collection was going on, Kuriakose came home and asked us to not to press the case against him. When I didn't show any such inclination, he went so far as to give me a veiled threat, 'We all are living in this place.'

Based on evidence, the commission discovered that from 27 March to 30 March 5.30 a.m., Mithun and Saju were in illegal detention. As the only witnesses to the torture were policemen and their appearances to bear witnesses against one of their own was next to impossible, there were no eyewitnesses to corroborate the torture. Although Dr Navas of Idukki District Hospital had certified the injuries on their bodies based on his physical examination, and this certificate was presented to the commission, despite its summons, Dr Navas refused to depose before the commission. The commission therefore didn't rule on the torture.

The gist of the ruling of the commission is as below:
The petitioner, Mithun, and his uncle, Saju, were not involved in any crime. Nor are they suspects. In an attempt to track down Prof. T.J. Joseph, the accused in case no. 327/2010 of Thodupuzha Police Station, these two were detained illegally in the said police station, threatened, humiliated, and subjected to egregious behaviour. Their fundamental rights were violated by the arbitrary and illegal detention. The two police officers are guilty of extreme violation of human rights. As government servants, the government carries indirect liability for their wrongdoings. The government must, therefore, pay the petitioner Rs 25,000 as compensation. This amount should be recovered from the offending officers equally. The State police chief should also institute departmental action against these officers.

These proved to be lines writ on water.

The police officers found guilty by the commission immediately engaged top criminal lawyers and filed writ petitions in the high court to quash the commission's order. They procured a stay order against the execution of the commission's decree. And that was the end of that. Until the time of writing this, that was where things stood.

The denouement of most of the judgments pronounced by the HRC was the same. Those who lacked the wherewithal to approach the courts were the ones who turned to the HRC. Even if they got a favourable judgment, they would get no benefit. The defendants went to court with their own appeals. Where do the poor people have the time or resources to prosecute them in the courts?

In my opinion, the HRC in Kerala is no better than a scarecrow. None of their findings or orders finds fruition. Other than wasting poor people's time and the treasury's funds—in effect the public's money— what is achieved? My experience has taught me that, in reality, the commission's activities are ineffective, ineffectual, and infructuous.

The next case stemmed from a group of imbeciles trying to kill me. That I didn't die turned to be a curse for them, me, and a number of other parties. The day that I had had a providential escape from them for the third time, I had submitted a written complaint to the Muvattupuzha DySP. Although I had categorically stated that they had intruded into my house with the intent to attack me and that I should be given protection, if the police authorities didn't even file a criminal case, how can we blame them? Didn't they have much more important and valuable work to attend to, to be bothered about a rashly foolish teacher's life?

Only after the imbeciles had achieved their goal, and I had been rendered immobile and bed-ridden, did the police wake up. Be it at the hospital or at home, I was provided heavy security.

Within hours of the attack, the police had definitive information about the attackers and their controllers. There were rumours that the police and the attackers and their backers had reached a certain understanding. The intelligence wing had expressed their displeasure at the pace and turn of investigations. There were voices of dissension between investigating officers.

Reports of external influences sidetracking the investigations appeared in the media. Reporters even reached out to me in my hospital bed, asking for my views on the progress of the investigations. What could I tell them? I facetiously offered to tell them about the progress of my various aches and pains.

A case which had started off with charges that cited only relatively weak sections of the Cr.P.C. had rapidly transformed into that of a terrorist act. The investigating officer was upgraded from circle inspector to DySP. External pressure hamstrung the investigations. The police filed a charge sheet in the court without apprehending the main culprits. After a few days, considering the extremism angle and the foreign connections of the culprits, the National Investigation Agency (NIA) took over the investigations. The NIA's southern regional headquarters was in Hyderabad, from where high-ranking officials—DIG, ADGP, and SP—came and met me.

My attackers had only been obeying orders—mere cat's paws. As much as I held no grudge against the axe used to maim me, I held no grudge against those who wielded the axe either. I had already stated that I had forgiven them. However, they were the main accused in the case. Could I withhold my statement from the police? Even if our fundamental rights as citizens were denied, we cannot stop doing our duties as a citizen, can we?

After the initial rounds, when I had thought I was finally rid of the nuisance of giving statements, came the NIA's entry into the scene. A Muslim DySP from Hyderabad was in charge to prevent any religious animosity influencing the investigation, as all the accused were Muslims. On the first day itself, I had explained the backstory of the question to him. The next day, when he returned after meeting the principal and Father Pichalakkat at Newman College, he declared:

'As a Muslim, I can't countenance your act of insulting the Prophet. But that shall not affect my carrying out my duties.' He said this to me in private and in a harsh voice.

This proved to be an empty avowal. Kerala Police had recorded eyewitness statements, including mine. The NIA had to record only that which had been left unrecorded by Kerala Police. However, the DySP asked us everything all over again and when our statements were put on record in English, the sequence of events had changed, creating loopholes for the defence attorneys to exploit conveniently.

The SP who followed the wounded-heart DySP discovered that the case had been weakened. The DySP was excluded from the investigation, and he himself took over the investigations. Then he looked for another

Muslim DySP and gave him the charge. He was a Malayali with a progressive and secular outlook.

I cannot, with any confidence, say that the NIA's investigation was any more rigorous and energetic than that of the local police. They seemed content to wait for the suspects to turn themselves in rather than actively hunt for them.

When my own neighbours, who were eyewitnesses to the attack, showed reluctance to become prosecution witnesses, NIA officers asked me to persuade them. I refused. I told them that neither my family nor I wanted the accused to be punished, and we all were ready to be witnesses only because we were doing our duty as citizens. Finding other witnesses didn't figure in our duties as citizens, and we would not do it.

After receiving summons from the court, my family and I went to Viyyur Central Prison to identify the suspects. We were separated and made to sit in separate rooms. We were allowed to meet one another only after the identification parade.

The identification had to be done in the presence of a judge. The suspects were made to stand between men who resembled them. Only two or three suspects were included in a group of about twenty and placed well apart. Neither my family nor I had any problem in identifying my assailants.

A few days before the hearings were to commence in the NIA court, relatives of two of the accused came to meet me. Two of them were the parents of the person who had made the route map to my house. The father was an ex-government employee. The parents wept and sought my forgiveness for the wrongs of their son. They begged me to give no statement in court which could end up convicting their son.

They were accompanied by the wife of another person who was in the support group of the actual attackers. She was carrying an infant and had come to plead similarly for her husband.

'I have not seen your people in person, nor know of them in any other manner. There will be no need for me to say anything about them in the court. Nor will I.' I sent them off with that assurance.

The judge was a middle-aged man; the public prosecutor, a relatively young man; and the principal lawyer of the defendants, a very old man. All three were from North Kerala and mutual acquaintances. We had in-camera proceedings as requested by the prosecutor for the safety of the witnesses. The court proceedings, therefore, were not reported in the press. From what I saw and experienced, in-camera proceedings benefitted the defendants more than it did the witnesses.

The defence lawyer's attempts to get the accused off the hook were based on a fictitious entry in the logbook of the police telecommunication office in Aluva. The entry showed that at 8.37 a.m. on 4 July 2010, a wireless message had been received that a professor of Newman College had been attacked by two masked men and that the men had escaped in a white Maruti Omni van bearing registration no. KL-07-AD-7201. This record was the result of a conspiracy, with or without the blessings of police officers, to lead the investigation away from the right track. The defence lawyer used the conflicting statements of the witnesses to fill in the gaps in his outline story of two masked protestors from the riots in Thodupuzha being the real attackers and used that to get his clients acquitted. The basis for this had been created by the first NIA officer who held charge of the case.

The first prosecution witness was my wife Salomi. I was the second witness. We were examined and cross-examined for five and six days, respectively. To stand in the witness box for so many days for the entire length of the court hours was not easy to do, to put it mildly.

The witness box was to the right of the judge. The bench-clerk sat beneath the judge's podium. In front of him, on the first row, were five or six defence lawyers and the public prosecutor. Behind them were the investigation officers. Behind them, the thirty-one accused men arranged like schoolchildren. The charge sheet had thirty-eight; the investigation team failed to find seven of them.

My chief examination was on a hartal day. I was taken by a police van to the court. As the public prosecutor had given me a heads up that the wounds on my legs and arms may need to be shown to the judge, I was in a mundu and a shirt. The hon'ble court couldn't have been less bothered about the wounds. The impression given was that the wound certificate produced would be studied and everything understood from that. The cross-examination that lasted another five days was the most excruciating. I have heard it said that a cross-examination is like a chess game between a grandmaster and someone who doesn't know the rules of the game. This is because the match is between the lawyer who has studied law and the examinee who hasn't.

Most of the lawyers use the tactics of getting the witness emotionally upset, engender inconsistencies in their answers therefrom and strip precision from their responses. The defence lawyer used the same tactics against me. He mocked, insulted and railed against me. The accused sat there enjoying the show as their lawyer rode roughshod over me.

The proceedings went on in a manner that made me wonder whether I was the witness or the accused.

The defence counsel read out a part of statement, which the first NIA officer had mangled and asked me if I had given such a statement. At first, having listened to the part which was part truth and part lies, I said that I hadn't. However, since part of it was true, in a moment of indecision, I corrected myself, 'Yes I did say that.'

Instead of advising me, 'You can't keep changing your answers like this. You must answer after careful thought,' what the judge snarled at me was, 'I will remand you and send you to the sub-jail. The cross-examination can continue after you take rest there for a week.'

The public prosecutor and NIA officers were stunned. The judge's words saddened me, but didn't scare me. I had lost the fear of jail long ago. I stood unperturbed in the witness stand. After a while, the judge regained his equanimity and the cross-examination continued.

The judge's outburst was not missed by the Special Branch and Intelligence Bureau. The SP from the Special Branch called me from Thiruvananthapuram and advised me to consider giving a petition, either by myself or through the public prosecutor, to change the judge, citing that, despite being the victim of the attack, the judge was not allowing me to give my statements freely, was browbeating and threatening me with incarceration during cross-examination, and consequently I had lost confidence in the court. I excused myself saying that that was not needed, and that it would only lead to complications.

My family members too suffered at the hands of the defence counsel. They were harangued, browbeaten, ridiculed, and abused in equal measure.

The accused seemed to be cheerful both inside and outside the courtroom. While the hearings were going on, ten of them were under judicial custody. The court had given them exemptions from the normal restrictions imposed on accused prisoners—when the lunch recess was on, family members of these prisoners were allowed to meet them freely and they were allowed to eat together in the court canteen.

Those in judicial custody were brought from the sub-jail in a police van. One day after the court session, while being taken away, harried by the policemen, one of the prisoners in handcuffs was hurrying to keep up with the others. His young son, maybe four or five years old, was hanging on to his handcuffed hands, and scurrying along on his little legs, prattling on all the time. Carrying an infant, the man's wife was also trying to keep up with them—a scene that pained me much, and is still fresh in my memory.

With so many accused and witnesses, proceedings in the NIA court made me feel it was interminable.

Next came the appeal given by the University Appellate Tribunal against my dismissal. At first, I didn't consider it a legal matter. It could have been resolved at any time with the ease of a son—ejected by the father from the family home without cause—being heard and taken back in. Or a simple reconsideration on the part of the parent. However, thanks to the enlightened views of the Church's elders, nothing of that sort happened.

A leading lawyer, K. Ramkumar, agreed to represent me pro bono in the tribunal. The appeal was filed at Thiruvananthapuram by advocates P. Vijayakumar and Baby Kuriakose. The college management filed their affidavit. Although the preliminary filings were over, on each hearing date, the college management filed a new petition or request for extension and kept prolonging the matter. For taking an extension one day, the reason the defence counsel gave was—it was his mother's death anniversary!

The judge was transferred out and a new judge came in his place. However, on every hearing, the management's counsel did his job well—they kept asking for adjournments. They perhaps knew that if the hearing did happen, the dismissal would be set aside.

Once I was able to walk, I met the bishop and the manager. The main objective was to show them that I was still fit for the teaching job. For, in an article in one of the Church's publications, an aged professor had expressed his doubts on how Prof. Joseph, with a wounded heart and patched-up, disfigured body, would be able to teach students.

I thanked the bishop for his visit to the hospital and exchanged pleasantries with the manager. I didn't ask to be taken back. After having prostrated myself at their feet and being spurned, my dignity and sense of pride didn't allow me to genuflect before them again.

In the hearing on 1 September 2012, we weren't expecting more roadblocks. We took Ramkumar to Thiruvananthapuram the previous day, put him up in the Kerala state government guest house, and took him to the tribunal on the dot. When our case was called, the judge asked, 'Can't you try to resolve this through conciliation?' My lawyer agreed. Their lawyer said he would inform the court after checking with the management. And we went our respective ways.

That was the second anniversary of my dismissal. Instead of hearing this old appeal and passing his judgment, what was it that persuaded the judge to suggest a conciliation? In the next hearing, the management said that they were ready for conciliation and the court appointed a mediator.

By that time, Thomas Malekudi had made way for Monsignor Francis Alappatt as the manager. He, along with the corporate educational secretary, Father Kuriakose Kodakallil, appeared before the mediator. I had gone there mentally prepared to give up my seniority, my position as the department head, etc. They were only willing to change the level of punishment to compulsory retirement instead of dismissal.

Realizing that they would never again have me as a teacher, I agreed to accept voluntary retirement. If I did that, when my pension was calculated, my full service would be considered. The management had nothing to lose by agreeing to this. However, for me to submit the voluntary retirement request, I should be in service; for which I should be allowed to join for at least a day. The management refused to let me do that.

Mediation and conciliation went up in smoke. Reconciliation vaporized.

With the hope that on the next scheduled date at least the hearing would happen, we took advocate Ramkumar again to Thiruvananthapuram. Since the management's lawyer had filed an additional petition, there was no hearing. This became the standard practice and the lawyer kept making sure that the case was never heard. One day, after many adjournments, when in October 2013, I fancied that the hearing would take place, the judge had gone for Haj pilgrimage.

Mar George Punnakottil retired and Mar George Madathikandathil was anointed as the new bishop. Although I had visited him at Bishop House, as it was our very first meeting after his elevation, I didn't have the heart to request him, as the patron of the college, to reinstate me in my job. However, since Father Adappoor insisted, on the very next day, I sent a written appeal to him by post, seeking my reappointment. I never received even an acknowledgment for it.

After a while, Sister Marie Stella met the bishop and requested that my dismissal be revoked. He said that since it was a decision taken by his predecessor, he could not interfere in it. Later, he did come to my house to pray, but he never reopened the door to my livelihood.

After I was attacked and maimed, I appealed to the state chief minister and home minister to withdraw the blasphemy case filed by the police against me of their own accord. The government had no will or courage to withdraw a case they had got instituted for communal appeasement. I filed a petition in the high court to have the First Information Report (FIR) quashed.

By then, a new government had been sworn into power. Although initially they informed the court that no case was pending against me, they later changed the story. The government pleader informed the court that the investigation was over, and the police were waiting for the government's approval to file the charge sheet.

My quash-the-FIR petition was dismissed by the court with the advice to file a discharge petition when the charge sheet was eventually filed. I was told by an IPS officer in the NIA that the judge had quietly washed his hands of the whole thing, much like his predecessor.

The Thodupuzha police station filed the charge for crime no. 327/2010 at the Chief Judicial Magistrate Court in 2013. When I received the summons, I went to the court and took bail. As the case was groundless, I filed a petition in the court seeking dismissal of the case and to declare me innocent. Advocate Ramkumar appeared on my behalf. The court decided that the case against me under sections 153A, and 295A, and 502 (2) was baseless and I was cleared of the charges.

The court had followed my reasoning in the case. The order stated that the controversy was created by some Muslim brethren who misunderstood the name 'Muhammed' used in the question as that of Prophet Muhammad. An action cannot be evaluated based on the words of fanatics or senseless people. An act doesn't become a crime because some people protest against it. Citing the Supreme Court, the court also mentioned that we should develop a sensible reading habit.

The order came out on 13 November 2013 at around 11.30 a.m. The phone was ringing off the hook. My friends came over, bearing sweets to celebrate the news. The print and TV media approached me for my reaction. I told them, 'I'm happy about the order. And happier to be alive to hear of it. I thank all of you.'

33

Royal Proclamations

When I returned from church on the Sunday following the court order, Salomi was seated in front of the TV, hanging on to every word. Apparently, Monsignor Francis Alappatt had announced that I would be reappointed by the college. It was on TV. She was thrilled.

T.A. Joy had informed her over the phone that it had been announced in one of the channels. From that moment, she had switched on the TV and hadn't moved from there or had her breakfast and was lost to the world. I also joined her in front of the TV. In an answer to a question, the manager had stated that since the court had cleared me, there was no objection to my being taken back. Although there was no categorical 'we will take him back', it looked like a good beginning and I thought my reinstatement wasn't too remote a possibility.

I had crossed three years of unemployment. We were facing financial difficulties. Most of Salomi's gold ornaments had been pledged to the bank for loans.

Amy was employed in Medanta–The Medicity in Gurgaon as a staff nurse. She had started to send Rs 10,000 every month. We used that money for Mithun's expenses at the Kerala State Civil Service Academy where he had joined for coaching.

Salomi was ready to work in a shop or a beauty parlour. I had stopped her because of my mother's age and condition. One day, when she saw women cleaning the sides of a road under the Rural Employment

Guarantee scheme, she said enthusiastically that she could join them. Their working hours were not too long. However, my heart didn't let me make her do such menial work.

The news of my probable reinstatement reached us at this juncture. Salomi prepared special dishes with the cheerfulness she exhibited on the eve of our church festivals. She invited our close friends and the policemen guarding us for dinner.

When there was no sign of life from the college management even after a week, I went to Bishop House and met Father Alappatt and Father Kodakallil. They said that since the court had found me not guilty, they would consider taking me back. They advised me to meet the bishop as a first step, which I did two days later, since he was not there on that day. After half an hour of pleasantries, he asked me to meet the manager to sort out the re-appointment matter. I didn't let the matter rest and on the same day, at 2 p.m., I met the manager at the Vazhakulam engineering college. My retirement date was 31 March 2014. He agreed that I would be taken back before that. He also asked me to get my lawyer to draft a compromise petition to be submitted to the tribunal.

On 16 January 2014, I submitted the copy of the petition drafted by my lawyer to the manager. The manager took it saying that he would have to show it to their lawyer first.

One month went by. On 14 February, I met the bishop, who again asked me to meet the manager. Since he was absent, I had to go the next day, only to be told that the advocate wanted some changes made in the petition. I had no other choice but to agree and came away that day.

Five days later, I received an envelope from the manager through a messenger. It was a compromise petition redrafted by their advocate.

As I opened it and read it with great excitement, I felt as if someone had beaned me with a heavy cosh. There was nothing in it about reinstating me. The dismissal had been downgraded to compulsory retirement—something mooted by them two years ago at the conciliation meeting and turned down by me.

The next day I went back to Bishop House. The manager was not in his office, and I went to the first floor of another building, where I knew he could be, and knocked on the door. He must have been expecting me. He was very lackadaisical; after asking me to sit down, he looked at me blankly. When I asked why my being reinstated was missing in the petition, he simply nodded and said, 'The advocate begs to disagree. In his opinion, if you are taken back, it may be prejudicial to the management.'

'It's only a compromise petition that is being filed in the tribunal. The decree will be issued by the tribunal. Then where is the problem?'

'The lawyer says that he won't do anything damaging to the management after accepting such a large fee from us,' he replied.

'How much have you paid?' I asked, instinctively.

'I don't know how much was paid earlier. But now, for every hearing he goes to, we pay him Rs 30,000.'

I did some mental math. There had been over forty hearings. So on his travel account alone, the guy had netted over Rs 12 lakh. It was no wonder he didn't want to be the one to kill the goose that laid golden eggs.

I was at a loss for words.

The manager—perhaps aware that I wouldn't accept the compulsory retirement mentioned in their lawyer's draft petition—said, 'Let the order of the tribunal come. That's my opinion. Only that's going to work.'

It was 21 February 2014. There was no question of a judgement coming before 31 March 2014 from the tribunal on a case that it had not even heard. I walked out of that set of buildings—which, in the vernacular, is called palace—that make up Bishop House, abandoning all my hopes of retiring as a college professor.

When the majority of the teachers in Newman and Nirmala colleges went to the bishop with a signed petition seeking my reinstatement since I had been found innocent by the courts, he had welcomed them with a tongue-lashing.

The next day, I met my lawyer, Vijayakumar, at Ernakulam and told him that the management did not intend to take me back. Although I had given him a copy of the court order clearing me of the charges, he hadn't submitted it to the tribunal. The naïve lawyer had apparently thought that since the management was going to reinstate me of their own volition, what was the need to file the order in the tribunal.

This was precisely the management's objective. Their false promise of reinstatement was their underhanded scheme to deter me from filing the court order in the tribunal and winning an order to reinstate me. And they succeeded in laudable fashion too.

I asked my lawyer to file the Chief Judicial Magistrate's order in the tribunal without further loss of time. However, before he could do anything, the principal obtained a stay order against it on the case Cr/M.C. No. 1591/2014 which he had filed in the high court, seeking the expunging of relevant portions of the judgement.

The summary of this petition is as follows:

The petitioner is the principal of Newman College. The defendant was a teacher in the same college in the Malayalam department. The Idukki DySP had filed a case against him under sections IPC 153A, 295A, and 505(2). The manager of the college had taken disciplinary action against the defendant on the grounds leading to the aforesaid case, and after following the laid-down procedures, dismissed him from the college's service. The matter is yet to be heard in the University Appellate Tribunal where the defendant had filed an appeal against the dismissal. What is relevant here is that the actions and cause that led to the dismissal and the police case are essentially the same.

After completion of the investigations, the charge sheet was filed in the Thodupuzha Chief Judicial Magistrate Court; after receiving the summons, the defendant appeared in the court and obtained bail. Thereafter he gave a discharge petition C.M.P. No. 5158/2013 seeking dismissal of the charges and finding him not guilty. All the witnesses' statements in the charge sheet are unanimous in stating the defendant as guilty. The court erred wholly while considering the discharge petition and the defendant has been found not guilty. He has obtained a copy of the court order and is in the process of submitting it to the tribunal to negate the enquiry report that led to his dismissal. It's the petitioner's imperative need that the relevant portions of the CJM judgement are expunged. Moreover, the findings of the lower court are diametrically opposite to the facts in the charge sheet and the witnesses' statements.

This was trying to establish that the stereotypical statements of the witnesses nos. 7 to 11 in it were adequate to find me guilty. Witness no. 7

was Father Pichalakkat; his statement said that the impugned question was prepared by the defendant and therefore its whole responsibility lay on the defendant; the impugned question hurt the religious sentiments of Muslims; the question should have been avoided; the handwriting on the prepared question paper belonged to the defendant et al.

Witness no. 8, the principal, only reiterated what witness no. 7 had said.

The tenth and the eleventh witnesses were teachers who merely echoed their two predecessors. The ninth witness was Father Malekudi who had stated that the defendant had a difference of opinion with the management and that the question-paper controversy was created with a motive.

The principal was now arguing that despite all of them speaking in one voice that the defendant was guilty, declaring him innocent was a gross mistake.

There were no complainants against me in the blasphemy case. It was a suo motu case filed by the police. In the FIR, the complainant was SI Shinto Kurian. As it was a criminal case, the government was the prosecutor. The government had a right to file an appeal against the lower court judgement. If, as alleged in the case, the sensibilities of Muslims had been wounded, perhaps they could also file an appeal. Having discovered the truth behind the controversy, none of them had filed an appeal against my acquittal. It was in this context that the principal was approaching the High Court to expunge the order:

> It also prayed that until the high court decides on the petitioner's appeal, the lower court order should be stayed. If the stay is not granted, the order will be produced by the defendant in the tribunal and cause irreparable and irredeemable damage to the college management. The humble prayer of the principal was that the defendant, T.J. Joseph, should be stopped from presenting the CJM court order before the tribunal or any other authority.

If nothing else, that petition and affidavit removed any doubt about the enthusiastically effective role played by the principal in having the question-paper controversy registered as a criminal case, and his decisive participation in the management's action to dismiss me.

The notice of this petition filed on 10 March 2014, reached me only in the first week of April 2014. Many unforeseen events had taken place by then.

34

When it was apparent that the management was not going to re-employ me, the castles in the air that Salomi and I had been building for the past two to three months came crashing down around us.

If I had been able to join back by the end of March as promised by the manager, I wouldn't have merely gained the salary for the month, I would have retired on 31 March and received my salary arrears until then and my terminal benefits. That would have been a handsome amount.

We had to redeem the pawned jewellery; we had to repay our children's educational loans; we had to replace our washing machine and refrigerator, both of which had broken down; we had to paint and renovate the house; we had to build two bedrooms on the first floor; Amy had to be married off—in our minds we had already apportioned the handsome amount of our dreams.

Like a bolt of lightning, the college management's treachery had incinerated, nay vaporized, our dreams and fancies which, after staying withered for four years, were slowly blossoming once more. For Salomi, who had suffered everything stoically until then, this was the last straw. She had nothing left in her to bear up to the blows.

My children being away, only Salomi, my mother, and I were at home. The first change I noticed was her starting to blame me; even for trivial, inconsequential things—retching while brushing my teeth; sneezing loudly; for making noises while eating—she started to call me out and mock me. Although I tried to explain it away with rationalizations such as, 'when one is enjoying one's food, some sounds of satisfaction are bound to come out . . .', I did feel her reactions and judgements were rather odd. Realizing that she was exercised over Amy's wedding, I tried to calm her with an assurance that my provident fund (PF) would suffice for that.

I could have closed my provident fund account when I was dismissed. I hadn't done that perhaps due a petty feeling that it was tantamount to acknowledging my dismissal and a prudent thought that it would remain as savings. In August 2013, I had submitted my application to close the PF account concurrent with my retirement in March 2014. Although the principal had got the monies released for the other teachers who had also applied, he took no action on mine. I again requested the principal to expedite the closure of my provident fund account and have the money released to me as I was in dire need of money; I also asked the manager to instruct the principal appropriately.

After some days, Salomi's fault-finding changed into a guilt trip. She started to feel bad about picking fights with me for trivial things when I had been through so much suffering. I took her to the psychiatry department of Kolenchery Medical College. I was told she was suffering from what was in the past called melancholia and, in modern times, depression. The doctor also warned me that such patients are suicidal and that we should be extra careful. The medicines should be kept by one of us and given to her on time and without fail.

I took out all the pesticides we kept at home and destroyed them. The sharp knives used to slice tapioca were hidden in places that she could not reach. I locked the medicines in a drawer and dispensed them to her myself on time as directed.

Probably because of the effects of the strong medication, she had no energy in the mornings to get out of bed or prepare our breakfast. While sweeping the yard, I always surreptitiously kept a watch on her through the window, as she lay in bed, staring at nothing. When I cooked, I made her get out of bed and sit with me in the kitchen so that she was not left alone.

One day, she told me that she was having indescribable feelings of anguish and on such occasions the wish to die and end it all was very strong. Overcome with fear, I hugged her close and asked her to chant the hymns that we had learnt in the catechism classes. I recited some of them to her as well.

I requested my sister, Mary, to come and stay with us—to have one more pair of eyes to watch over Salomi and to take care of her—which she did. Mithun, studying for the civil services examination, would come home only once in a fortnight. He would always remind Mary to keep a close watch on his mother.

On 14 March, I visited the college to follow up on the PF matter. The college had done nothing about my request. Salomi asked me what was delaying the issue. I told her I was unable to understand the reasons they had trotted out to me. I sent a reminder by registered post to the principal.

Summer had set in. We had had no rain for about three months and the heat was insufferable.

19 March was St Joseph's day and being named after the saint, it was 'my feast'. My neighbour Joseph came by with the payasam oblation received from the church. Salomi had an appointment with the doctor; we called the hospital to check if the doctor was available. He was in, and we reconfirmed the appointment. She showed extraordinary fatigue that day. Mary and I took her to the hospital.

Salomi and Mary met the doctor. My security detail and I sat in the waiting room. In between, we went to the tea kiosk within the hospital premises and had a cup each. I also bought a health magazine that had a cover story on 'Depression in Women'. The policeman kept it with him and kept reading it as we waited.

After getting back home, we sat down for lunch at around 2 p.m. Salomi looked exhausted and after a lot of cajoling by me, ate very little. The tablets provided by the hospital were in her handbag. The cap of the water bottle kept in the bag had worked loose and the paper bags with the medicines had got drenched. I spread them out in another room to dry.

After she had done the dishes, Mary came and told me what the doctor had said. Salomi's condition was not going to get better any time soon. She would be under medication for a long time. Mary couldn't stay away from her own home for that long. I told her that she could leave whenever she wanted and I would make alternative arrangements.

Then I went to Salomi's room, planning to rest for some time. She was not on the bed. I looked at the bathroom; the door was ajar. Assuming she couldn't be inside with the door not shut, I went into the other rooms, looking for her. She was nowhere and I started to panic. I went back into her room and pushed open the bathroom door.

Salomi was leaning against the wall with one end of a *torthu*—the light bath towel used in Kerala—around her neck and the other end fastened to the towel rod. As she had bent her knees, her feet had lost contact with the ground and the noose around her neck had tightened.

The moment I saw her, I screamed out for Mary. I lifted Salomi, holding her up by her armpits to ease the pressure on her neck. Mary came running and, quickly assessing the situation, ran out to fetch a knife and cut the *torthu*. We loosened the noose and took the *torthu* off her neck. Salomi was unconscious. I laid her on the floor and tried to give her mouth-to-mouth resuscitation. I tried to induce breath and revive her by chest compression, pressing on her chest with both my hands.

Mary had, in the meanwhile, brought in the policemen guarding me and they too tried to resuscitate her by CPR procedures. For an instant, we thought she had started to breathe. Two of them carried her out and the other started my car. She was put inside the car, and we sped to Nirmala Hospital in Muvattupuzha.

Her head was on my lap, and I kept compressing her chest. The policeman in the front passenger seat told me to keep doing it as she seemed to be breathing while I was doing the chest compression.

The policemen helped the hospital staff to load her on to the stretcher and wheel her into the casualty department.

As I watched the unhurried behaviour of the doctor in the casualty as he tended to her, I screamed at him, 'Give her artificial respiration, immediately!'

The doctor replied without any emotion, 'There is no point in giving artificial respiration to a dead person.'

I felt my legs go weak. Someone helped me into a chair.

After a little while, another doctor came and took my hand in his. At that time, I had no realization that he was a doctor of that hospital. I thought he was someone who knew me. I told him piteously, 'My wife died . . . now . . . just a little while ago.'

What was I hoping for when I said that? Compassion? Sympathy?

No one else approached me. I sat there, totally defeated and devastated.

Sometime later—I can't recall when—a nurse gave me something wrapped in paper. It contained the ornaments taken off Salomi's body—her chain with the *mangalsutra*, earrings, wedding ring, and toe ring.

By late evening, my friends brought me back home.

Dark clouds blew in, and it rained after nearly four months.

By nightfall, Mithun arrived from Thiruvananthapuram. As I was showing signs of distress, he took me to the hospital, where I was sedated and made to sleep. I was discharged only in the morning.

Sister Marie Stella arrived in the morning from Pondicherry. Amy came home by 11 a.m. from Delhi by air. Friends and relatives were already there. I sat in a room, alone, lost, like an orphan, unaware of what was happening around me, frozen in time and place.

The post mortem was conducted at Alappuzha Medical College. On the previous day itself, I had signed on the paper to donate her eyes. After gifting two strangers the power of sight, she returned home at 5 p.m., wrapped in the wedding saree which I had draped over her head twenty-eight years ago.

As our house was filled with people, a friend from my youth, Pathipallil Tomy, took me into the bathroom to help me dress for the funeral. I recalled my neighbour, Valiplackal Reji, helping me put on my wedding suit.

Although the sky had turned dark and black clouds rumbled overhead ominously, rain stayed away.

My children and I gave her our last kisses and said our last goodbyes. Thousands of people were witnesses.

While returning home after interring Salomi—whose hand I had taken in marriage and made her my partner for life at the church—in the crypt in the graveyard, the sky remained sombre and clouded like my own mind.

35

The Power of the Dead

Salomi's death became a cause célèbre in the visual media. The view that the suicide was caused by the unjust and immoral ways of the Newman College authorities predominated. My relatives and friends were highly provoked and threatened the management with strikes and legal action. Prominent lawyers lending their faces to talk shows and TV news chats gave their opinion that the college management could be prosecuted for abetment of suicide.

The next day, on 21 March, a stream of people came to meet me, including human rights activists. The TV channel reporters also arrived wanting to know the latest on my reinstatement. Who needs a job now? With my mind numbed, I refused to give any reactions. They tried to bring me around. When they persisted, I said apathetically, 'The management can still take me back; but I don't believe they are prepared to do that.'

'This is all we need,' the reporters said, 'leave the rest to us.'

That night, the TV channels went hammer and tongs on the deplorable actions of the management which had refused to take me back even after the courts had cleared me.

22 March. The visitors to my home increased manifold. An increased number of human rights activists and minority rights commission members were among them. Some of them had visited Bishop House before coming to me. Some others headed for Bishop House after meeting me.

Many more went directly to Bishop House demanding my reinstatement. A senior police officer close to the church spent hours there explaining to them the overwhelming cons, rather than pros, of their refusal to take me back and persuaded them to reinstate me.

Social media was filled with posts and posters demanding that I be given justice. There were exhortations to send thousands of letters and emails to the Pope to intervene directly in my matter. The leader of the Opposition in the Kerala Assembly called me on the phone and offered to intercede in the matter of my reinstatement.

This much I had come to know. I don't know what other interventions happened. It was announced on the 8 p.m. news that the college management had decided to take me back. An hour later, the manager called to tell me in person. I was invited to Bishop House on 24 March morning.

On Monday, I reached Bishop House at 9 a.m. The crew of a number of TV channels lay in wait with their cameras. The priests at the reception parlour took me into the bishop's room. Monsignor Alappatt, Father Kuriakose Kodakallil, and Monsignor George Oliyapuram had also arrived.

I was told that I could join duty on 28 March, Friday. Saturday and Sunday were holidays; on 31 March, Monday, I could retire. Father Kodakallil said that the appointment order would be delivered to my home on 27 March. Monsignor Alappatt requested that I should take no legal action against the management. I requested that I should not be ostracized and be treated with sympathy. As the reinstatement was being done unilaterally by the management, and not under orders of the Appellate Tribunal, special approvals from the government would be required to have my salary arrears released. I asked the management to take action on that expeditiously. Father Kodakallil suggested that both parties should cooperate and work together for this.

The reverends didn't forget to advise me that I shouldn't make any statements against the diocese to the media. When I came out and spoke to the media, they were also with me.

Until late evening on 27 March, there were no signs of the order. Naturally, I started to wonder if the management had done their usual somersaulting manoeuvre. Some of the TV channels also floated some trial balloons with this insinuation. However, exactly at 8 p.m. a college attender arrived with the order. He had been waiting at the pastoral centre near my house. He had strict instructions to deliver it to me only at 8 p.m.

On 28 March morning, I went to church, visited Salomi's grave, and got ready by 8.30 a.m. Since my fingers were still not fully functional, my shirt was buttoned up by Sister Marie Stella. I thought this was something Salomi ought to have done and felt a pain in my heart.

When I emerged from the house, two or three TV channel reporters were waiting for me, perhaps thrilled by the major role they had played in seeing my reinstatement through. I drove the car; Sister Marie Stella and Mary's husband, Baby, were with me. Police vehicles escorted us as a convoy, ahead and behind us. In front of the college, another band of policemen, under the Thodupuzha DySP's command, were awaiting our arrival. Inside the campus, most of the TV channel reporters were waiting for me.

The principal had taken some steps in anticipation of my joining that day. By declaring a holiday for the college, he had stymied any possibility of my getting to meet the students in their classes. He arranged a meeting of all the lady professors and lecturers and confined them to a hall. For the remaining male teachers, he assigned invigilation duties, and packed them off, to ensure there was no 'welcome committee' for me.

When I entered the campus, the students from the examination halls across the buildings started to cheer and clap loudly. Some of my old students were waiting for me, having come to know of my arrival on that day.

I was enveloped by a swarm of TV news reporters as soon as I got out of the car. In a few sentences, I told them of my happiness at my return, and my sorrow at losing the one whose loss paved the way for the re-entry.

Although the media wanted to film my signing of the attendance register, they were not allowed into the office. The collapsible grill door was closed and locked; the vice-principal and a group of attenders were holding the fort. They pulled apart the grill door just enough for me to squeeze through and shut it again. They didn't even have the grace to let in my sister and brother-in-law who were accompanying me.

Monsignor Alappatt was waiting in front of the principal's room. I wished him and kissed the hand that had signed my reappointment order. I entered the principal's room and went up to him. He opened the attendance register in which my name had been newly added and placed it before me as he said callously, 'You suffered a lot, didn't you?'

I pretended not to have heard him. I signed on the attendance register with my left hand. As I stepped out of the room, suddenly, a headstrong, and therefore delinquent, professor came running out of nowhere and hugged me.

The Malayalam department was deserted. I stood there for a long moment, looking at the photos of the retired professors on the wall. I wondered whether my photo would appear alongside them shortly. Then I sat down on my official chair. I had nothing to do in particular.

My sister and brother-in-law who had been waiting on the campus grounds came in. They were followed by some local gentry who had come to know of my re-joining and then the reporters.

In the afternoon, I saw Father Pichalakkat near the principal's office in conversation with a nun, a teacher in the English department. I went up to him and asked, 'Father, did you have invigilation duty?'

He shook his head in negation.

'I didn't see you all morning. Are you trying to stay under the radar?' I asked my former student innocently.

'Father is also a priest of a church. He's busy,' the nun leapt to his defence.

My sister and brother-in-law had left early for home. After 4 p.m. I too left with the usual police escort.

31 March was retirement day. Lunch had been arranged by the college council for all members of staff who were retiring that year. I ate along with them.

The send-off event was in the principal's room. There was no ban on media that day. I said my goodbyes as did the others who were retiring. One of the non-teaching staff members came over and kissed my right hand. I was amazed at her courage, considering the possible repercussions of such an act.

Four days after my retirement, I received the high court notice of the appeal filed by the principal and the stay order based on it. The appeal had been filed on 10 March. In view of the changed circumstances, I decided not to discuss that appeal—a prime example of the evil-minded machinations of the management to prevent a favourable judgment from the Appellate Tribunal on my appeal even post-retirement, and thus to prevent me from getting my pension—with anyone.

However, the church authorities surprised me again after a couple of days. On 6 April, an hour or so after I got home from the church, the media descended on my house in full force. In all the churches under the Kothamangalam Diocese, in the middle of the service, a pastoral letter damning me had been read out to the congregation. They had come to get my response.

It was not read out in the church where I attended the service. When I told the reporters that, they gave me a copy.

The Reinstatement of Prof. T.J. Joseph
An Explanatory Note
Dear brothers and sisters vested in the love of our Lord and Messiah Jesus Christ,

The question-paper controversy that had taken place in Thodupuzha Newman College and the consequent actions have attracted everyone's attention and generated varied reactions through the press reports and discussions in the visual media. In this context, the purposely falsified explanations and interpretations given by some about this incident and the college management's actions, have caused misgivings and misunderstandings among the believers of this church. I, therefore, wish to furnish an explanation about all these.

There are people who ask what had Prof. Joseph done to deserve dismissal from service. The act of setting a question that blended blasphemy and religious insult in an internal test for second-semester, BCom students had caused distress to the students belonging to a particular community. One of the students, who had written the test, had made some changes in the question to write out the answer avoiding the portions that reflected insult to her religion; she told the teacher about her alterations. That this slowly became a news item, got branded as a deliberate act leading to many clashes and resulted in the college and its management receiving threats cannot be forgotten at this point. Someone tried to spread a rumour that one of the priests who is a teacher in the Malayalam department was behind this.

However, the handwritten copy of the question paper, discovered later, was found to be in this teacher's own handwriting; he was asked to provide an explanation and since a satisfactory explanation wasn't received, after a detailed enquiry, he was found culpable as per the university's rules and regulations, and disciplinary action was taken. We cannot play down the depth and width of schism that has been created between the various communities of our state by the events that followed the controversial question paper. Almost sixty per cent of Newman College students are non-Christians. The college management is responsible to extend a sense of security and self-respect to them.

Although the police had taken a case against the teacher who prepared the controversial question paper, in November 2013, he was found not guilty by the court. The appeal filed by the teacher against his dismissal was still pending in the University Appellate Tribunal. While the matter was being processed in the tribunal, the management had taken efforts to ensure that the terminal benefits after retirement would be available to him. The management had held many rounds of discussions with the teacher to withdraw all the disciplinary action and retire with all the due terminal benefits. However, all those attempts came to naught.

The management believed that when the order of the tribunal was received, all the issues in this matter including the reinstatement of the teacher would be resolved. However, the procedures in the tribunal got prolonged. The allegation that the management tried to delay the proceedings is not in keeping with the truth. There is clear evidence that it was not the management, but Joseph's own lawyer who had caused the case to drag on. It is not understood why, when it was known that the teacher was to retire on 31 March 2014, the case was hanging fire in the tribunal for four years.

The unexpected death of the teacher's wife as the tribunal hearings got delayed interminably saddened everyone. Moreover, the realization that the management will be unable to do anything on its own volition to help this teacher after 31 March 2014 made this diocese decide to show mercy to him and thus reinstated him in service. It is not true that Joseph was taken back due to the pressure from many people. The only reason that led to his reinstatement was humanitarian consideration.

Even after showing such a humane approach, it is painful to see some individuals and parties with vested interests use this opportunity to denigrate and tarnish the reputation of the Catholic Church and its institutions. In reality, the Kothamangalam Diocese, Newman College management, and the college principal were the real victims of this teacher's senseless and thoughtless act. The unending torments, mental anguish, and monetary losses that the principal and the management had to undergo had not arisen out of any of their wrongdoing.

The stories going around in the media, including social media, are baseless and complete fabrications. Most of the people who are taking part in this debate can see things only from an emotional standpoint. However, the diocese and the college management believe that when decisions have to be taken from responsible positions, discernment more than emotion should drive such decisions.

The diocese, especially the college management and the principal, have been countenancing severe tribulations for the last four years. The decisions taken during such periods of turbulence have also been difficult. The Christian educational institutions and their secular character have been built up over many years through the herculean efforts and sacrifices of many thousands. To this date, there has been no instance of religious discrimination towards any community in the history of Christian educational institutions. With great sorrow have we witnessed the allegation that one of our institutions was in breach of this tradition. The diocese deplores baseless questioning of its actions and teachers—who are also priests—being slandered through character assassination.

The approach of mounting a campaign to victimize the institution, its management, and teachers, using the shield of some unfortunate incidents is not right. It is hoped that this explanatory note helps in understanding the hollowness of the calumny that has been spread against the diocese and the college.

God Bless You.
Mar George Madathikandathil
Bishop, Kothamangalam Diocese
31 March 2014

N.B. On 6 April 2014, Sunday, this circular should be read out during Holy Communion, in all the churches under our diocese and all institutions offering Holy Communion.

What honest intention could have—in contravention to the express instructions of the bishop—stopped this pastoral letter from being read out in Nirmala Matha Church, my own parish church?

Whatever it might have been, I refused to react to this in front of the media on that day.

Even now, I shall desist.

Instead, let me quote verbatim from the editorial in the bulletin issued by the Malankara Mar Thoma Syrian Church's Kandanad East Diocese. This was published and sent to me by post by the Muvattupuzha Bishop House, a few days—to be exact on 15 April 2014—after Syro-Malabar Church's pastoral letter was read out.

The Power of the Dead

Few would have remained not shocked by one of the page-one stories in the newspapers dated 20 March 2014. Even though Kerala has the highest suicide rate in the country, most of the people of the state felt the anguish. The news was about the suicide of Salomi, Prof. T.J. Joseph's wife. As a tragedy that happened in its neighbourhood, the *Diocesan Bulletin* recognizes its responsibility to react to this.

Everyone knows the backstory. In the question paper prepared by Prof. Joseph for the second-semester, BCom students' internal examination, one of the questions was on punctuation. In the passage given in it, he added 'Muhammed' from his side. This was misinterpreted by Muslim extremists as something squeezed in on purpose to insult Prophet Muhammad. They threatened and vowed publicly to take revenge on the institution and Prof. Joseph.

After many days, on 4 July 2010, when, accompanied by his family members he was returning home from the church, some men stopped his car, near his house close to the Hostel Junction in Muvattupuzha, pulled him out, and in front of his helpless wife, aged mother and sister, hacked his right palm and threw it into a neighbour's yard and fled the place. Although his palm was sewn back in the hospital, to this day, his hand is not functional.

It's a matter of pity that the management, only to appease the religious fundamentalists, terminated Prof. Joseph's services. Hospitalization; treatment and convalescence; contempt; derision; every kind of stare from the public at every turn; sympathy that hurt more than comforted; stifling police protection that haunted; altogether, the family's life was turned into a living hell.

With stoppage of his salary, Prof. Joseph and his family were in dire straits. Salomi, who weathered every threat and stood by her husband, even sought work under the Rural Employment Guarantee scheme. The efforts of some of the local social workers in the know of things to get the professor reinstated were defeated by the adamantine and merciless stand of the management. By this time, Prof. Joseph's reinstatement had become a test case of the State's social commitment to secular values and freedom of expression. On 13 November 2013, the Thodupuzha Chief Judicial Magistrate court issued its order declaring Prof. Joseph innocent. The management, however, was unrelenting.

Prof. Joseph and family were living on the hope that he would be taken in at least close to his retirement date of 31 March 2014 so that he would be eligible for pension and other benefits due from the government. However, there was no such move from the management even as the date drew perilously close. This pushed them into abysmal misery. Despair and obstacles pushed Salomi into depression. On 19 March, minutes after the couple returned home with her medicines after meeting the doctor, Salomi hanged herself in their bathroom.

Alas! A controversy over a name added in a minor test question paper had caused the right palm of the question-setter to be chopped off, removal from his employment, and eventually his life partner's sacrificing her life. It's the feeling that the possibility of her beloved getting reinstated and receiving all his terminal benefits was coming to an end that incited her to end her life tragically. The savagery of the Muslim extremists who, accusing Prof. Joseph of blasphemy and destroying communal amity, chopped his right hand and flung it away, and the management's heartless adamancy in not being merciful enough to reinstate him, have played an equal role in the abetment of Salomi's suicide.

Despite their knowledge that Prof. Joseph was due for retirement on 31 March, both Mahatma Gandhi University's Appellate Tribunal, who made no efforts whatsoever to take an expeditious decision and the state government that didn't give it urgent instructions to do so, cannot absolve themselves of their responsibility for this tragedy. The courts should order a comprehensive enquiry into the roles of these four entities in abetting the suicide of Salomi.

The argument of the manager, Francis Alappatt, that the case being sub judice in the Appellate Tribunal was the reason that militated against the reinstatement of Prof. Joseph is not credible in the least. The reason being, the reappointment of Prof. Joseph on 28 March was not pursuant to a tribunal order. Whatever it may be, if the management had taken this decision ten days earlier, Salomi's valuable life would not have been lost.

A simple truth—Salomi's suicide was the only motivation for her husband's reinstatement. Only the management knows whether their conscience, wounded by the tragedy, or their fear of a backlash from the public, or a mixture of both, was the real cause for a change of mind. One thing is certain, a dead Salomi is more powerful than a live Salomi. Because what she couldn't achieve while alive, she could, by dying—bring the management to change their mind.

Congratulations to Joseph master for being able to retire after re-entering the service! Commiserations for the unfortunate delay that led to misfortunes! Homage to Salomi who sacrificed her life to win her husband's reinstatement!

Dear Joseph master, your words in the interview given to Asianet TV channel echo in our minds: 'Won the war, but lost the kingdom.' We wish those who caused the loss should at least realize it. We pray for a reformation of the fanatics. We bow before your noble heart that bears no grudge against anyone. We see the presence of Jesus Christ in people like you.

36

Husband of the late Salomi

One of the traditions of arranged marriages is 'seeing the girl' when the boy meets the girl for the first time in a very formal setting, usually in the girl's house. Salomi was twenty-one when I went to 'see' her. I was twenty-eight.

Recommended by my friends, by that time I had already had three such 'sightings'. All three were schoolteachers. They were closer to my age too. From their conversations, I found all of them very practical-minded. Although I felt respect for them, I didn't feel any affection towards them. It could be because of the romantic in me.

My house was near Pavanatma College. The college was in the line of sight from our house. I hadn't completed a year in my service there.

Salomi's house was in Upputhodu, about six kilometres away from our place. She had lost her father when she was six. She had an older sister and two other siblings younger to her. Her mother brought up the children doing farming with little to spare. She couldn't afford to send them away to study; her two sisters therefore dropped out after high school. Salomi studied up to pre-degree and, at that time, had joined for a tailoring teacher's course.

Thanks to her mother's hard work, when they had built up some savings, her elder sister was married off at an early age into a farmer's family. Her mother was trying to arrange Salomi's marriage too to be rid of her responsibilities as early as possible. A marriage broker had taken me there since I had not insisted that my prospective wife should be employed.

I liked Salomi's simplicity, dressed as she was in a plain long skirt and blouse. She too liked me, as I had gone there in a mundu and a shirt, with no ostentation. Her folks checked and got it confirmed that my job was a permanent one. As my family had no dowry demands, our wedding was solemnized on 11 May 1986.

We were both slim. As I didn't have a thick moustache, I looked young for my age. After our wedding, I took her with me to Maharaja's College one day to visit one of my old classmates there. I showed her around the college. As she was wearing all her ornaments, it was obvious that she was a newly-wed. I walked along the quadrangle, hoping the students would not pass embarrassing comments. However, the comment did come, 'Both are young enough to be admitted to the pre-degree class.'

After our wedding, my parents moved to Variyanikkadu, leaving the Murickassery house in our care. Salomi got busy with taking care of the farming and rearing our children. Her dream of taking a degree in Malayalam without joining a regular college remained unrealized.

In 1993, leaving behind farming and our home, I took a transfer from the college in Murickassery to Nirmala College, since I had an ardent desire to teach Malayalam literature to post-graduate students. When we rented a house near the college and started living there, Salomi found spare time as there was no farming to attend to, and the children had started school. Although she had done tailoring and beautician courses, I didn't allow her to work. I used to come home for lunch. When we constructed our own house, it was close to our children's school, and they too would come home for lunch. I wasn't ready to forgo such small luxuries by allowing my wife to work.

When the children and I were out of the home, she would quickly finish her chores and take books from my collection and read them. Although we never had a discourse about what she read, when I asked her opinion of them, some of her one-liners would surprise me. She took one and a half months to complete the Malayalam translation of Victor Hugo's *Les Misérables*. I asked her opinion and she said, 'It feels like a friend who has been with me for a long time has suddenly gone away.'

The day the zealots chopped me up, her comment to the media was: 'How wonderful would it be if there were a world without religions.' She gained the candour to make such statements through her reading.

She had a likeable personality. She never spoke a cross word to anyone, including me. She was too soft a person to be angry with anyone. She hid nothing from me; she had no inner thoughts that she wished to keep away from me. At the same time, she was so perceptive that she would immediately know what was on my mind. I always wondered how she did that.

The only occasions when I had to chide her was when her generosity went overboard. She would feed stray animals and crows with whatever was available in our kitchen. She told me umpteen times that all her organs should be donated after her death.

I had always thought I would be the first to go, since I was considerably older than she was. I would always worry that if that were to be an untimely one, how would my family survive? Therefore, although as an investment it was not lucrative, I had taken a life insurance policy for a decent sum for their benefit. When I completed about twenty years of service, my worry about my family's survival after my death gradually evaporated. I had taken it for granted that they could survive on the family pension, even if I were to die early.

The realization that it was actually her life that had insured my job and terminal benefits—despite all this planning and forethought—was unbearable. Although I had made statements unemotionally such as 'I feel a comrade-in-arms has fallen', inside me, my anguished mind was undergoing spasms.

Among the many consolation letters I had received, one was addressed to 'Prof. T.J. Joseph, Husband of the late Salomi, Muvattupuzha'. I thought that was my true address now. My existence was now as the husband of the deceased Salomi. Her husband had got back the position of a professor that he had lost. Her self-sacrifice had turned out to be his only qualification.

Something that also hurt us badly was that, with Salomi's demise, her own relatives gave up on our children and me. Why should they come to her home or even call and grieve over her absence? Can they be blamed for thinking so? During his holidays, even Mithun was reluctant to come to a home where his mother was not waiting for him.

Salomi's death hadn't registered with my mother who was suffering from dementia. She would walk around saying, 'Where's Salomi? Haven't seen her for some time now . . .' On such occasions, my heart would heave.

Amy returned to Delhi after a month. As my mother and I were alone, Sister Marie Stella and Mary took turns to stay with us. However, they had turned extra solicitous in my case, which I chafed at, and often ended up arguing with them.

I would sit for hours together gazing out through the window; the squirrels and bats that used to suck honey from the banana flower buds became my acquaintances. When I would see the parakeet that perched on the guava tree and the colourful butterfly that landed on the window bars, I would muse that they were reincarnations of Salomi.

My hardy nature, akin to the saying that what has sprouted in fire can't be withered by the sun, helped me tide over many adverse situations. But the grief over my bereavement and the loss of Salomi defeated me. Words of comfort only deepened my grief. I couldn't sleep at night. I didn't want to take any tranquilizers or sleeping pills. I took up reading and let my mind wander through many words to find some temporary solace. Tired from reading, my eyes gradually closed and . . .

37

Gratitude and Respect

Though they had issued the pastoral letter wanting to impress on the faithful that they were on the side of the angels, the power-wielders of the diocese probably dreaded legal action from my side. They got in touch with the head of the Syro-Malabar church, Cardinal Mar George Alencherry and the reverend father gave me a call. Mithun and I went to St Thomas Mount in Kakkanad, his residence. After a few words of comfort, he advised us not to hold a grudge or nurse a malice against the church authorities.

Following Salomi's demise, my provident fund was quickly closed, and I received the money. The alacrity shown by the college management was driven by the fear of legal action. Financial aid from some generous people meant that financially things eased up.

Amy resigned from her job in August 2014 and returned home. She wanted to take the IELTS examination and go abroad. Mithun had lost interest in his studies and didn't clear the Civil Service preliminary examination. He also returned from Thiruvananthapuram. With their return, and the end of my solitude, I started to get back to normal. I became more engaged with their lives and found a new sense of responsibility. Mithun was employed as a manager in a firm in Ernakulam. Amy joined an IELTS coaching institute in Thodupuzha.

I submitted a counter affidavit in the high court against the petition filed by the principal for nullifying the court order that had found me not guilty. Since the management had taken me back, I had withdrawn my appeal in the University Appellate Tribunal. However, the principal's lawyer used to periodically obtain court-mandated stays that stopped me from presenting before any authority the court order that had exonerated me.

The manager had given my reinstatement order—four years after my dismissal—cancelling my suspension and dismissal orders, as if there was no break of service and making me eligible for my salary and all terminal benefits. Since that was a unilateral action by the manager, to make it effective and bring to fruition, the university's and the state government's approvals were required. On the other hand, if both parties had filed a joint conciliation petition in the tribunal and got an order released, none of this would have been required and there would have been no procedural roadblocks.

Although the Church authorities had said both parties should cooperate to get the arrears and pension released expeditiously, there was no move of any sort from their side on this score. I was told by the superintendent in the office of the deputy director of collegiate education that the proposal sent by the principal to regularize my service seemed to have been made with a mind that it should never get the approval.

Not wanting to leave things half-done, in addition to my salary arrears bill, he had also sent the salary bill of the guest lecturer who had been my locum for those four years. This is notwithstanding the fact that, when the management reinstated me after cancelling my suspension and subsequent dismissal, it had taken upon itself the responsibility for paying the guest lecturer's salary. In that context, what should the principal's attempt to get the government to bear two salaries for the same post be seen as other than a malicious move to get objections raised and the proposal blocked?

The deputy director's office in Ernakulam sent back my salary arrears bill without passing it. The application for service regularization was redirected to the director of collegiate education's office in Thiruvananthapuram. That got orphaned in the collegiate director's office and in the higher education department with no decision being taken on it.

Amy got through the IELTS examination and started the process to go to Ireland as a nurse.

The media published reports about my misfortunes—non-receipt of my arrears and pension despite passage of many months after my re-entry into the service and retirement and despite frequent visits to the government offices and departments. After reading the report, some people offered to advance me interest-free loans. I informed them I didn't need any. Only one person started to deposit a sum of money in my bank account every month, ignoring my nay-saying.

The university took a favourable decision in my matter and lobbed the ball to the state government's court.

Convinced that if things should work as per my reinstatement order, the state government would have to approve it, I tried to organize that. I gave a petition to Chief Minister Oommen Chandy, through the good offices of the Muvattupuzha MLA, Joseph Vazhackan. Then I went to the higher education department in the secretariat at Thiruvananthapuram and met everyone from the clerk to the deputy secretary and submitted a written petition to the Secretary, Higher Education.

Since I had my police security constables with me, most of the guards at the Secretariat entry points saluted me. They must have assumed that I was a judge or a high-ranking official. Considering them an honour in recompense for having been arrested on trumped-up charges and thrown into lock-up and jail, I enjoyed these moments of mirth.

In between all this, under the title *Nalla Paadangal* (Lessons in Virtue), DC Books published a collection of my mini articles, prepared as teachers' aid for value education classes, written while I was the director of the value education cell in Newman College.

On 30 April 2015, the NIA Court found guilty thirteen among the group that was charged with attacking me. Others were let off for lack of evidence. However, the court didn't announce the sentences for those convicted. The media came to me for comments. I said that I had no interest either in the case or the judgement and I had only the same curiosity as any other citizen.

The sentencing order came a week later on 8 May. Ten of those convicted were sentenced to eight years' rigorous imprisonment; three others for two years. Everyone had to pay fines. I was awarded Rs 8,00,000 as compensation from the fine amounts.

The media came to me again. I said I felt no happiness in my attackers being punished. I also clarified that I had no misapprehension that the culprits being punished was justice delivered to the victim.

The media had shown pictures of the culprits emerging from the courtroom with broad smiles on their faces. When asked to comment on that, I told the media, 'I like to see everyone behave happily in this manner.'

The NIA appealed to the high court that the sentence was too lenient. Since the judgement went on appeal, I wasn't given the compensation amount.

On the same day of the sentencing order, the news came out that the government had approved my salary arrears and pension. The next day, the chief minister called to inform me of this.

On 13 July 2015, I went to Newman College to collect the cheque. As he was handing over the cheque, Dr T.M. Joseph asked me, 'Are you happy now?'

It could have been a genuine question. I couldn't think up an answer for it. For me, already the ridges between happiness and sorrow had been flattened.

I have given many interviews and responses to newspapers, radio, and television. I had participated in Soorya Talk Festival at Soorya Krishnamurthy's invitation. Although I have been invited by many organizations to their events, I have been selective and went only to those conducted by some of the cultural organizations.

I was surprised when an NGO called Swaranjali based in Thiruvananthapuram decided to give me their Harmony Award— given to those who are a model for promotion of religious harmony and peaceful coexistence. How much more paradoxical could it be—that they chose someone charged with sowing religious discord and put in a lock-up; who had been maimed, after being accused of blasphemy; who had been deprived of livelihood and accused of sacrilege. I accepted the award, smiling inside. On 21 June 2015, World Music Day, poetess and social activist Sugathakumari presented the award to me in an event inaugurated by music director Ramesh Krishnan at Manaveeyam Veedhi.

In December 2015, Amy went to Ireland. After two months, she started to send money home. All that remained was the heartache that Salomi wasn't there to share my happiness that our days of privation were ending.

The plan for additions to our house on the first floor had been drawn up when Salomi was alive. That was completed. Then I started searching for alliances for my children. That wasn't easy. Once the parents came to know Amy and Mithun were my children, they backed off. Who would like to marry into a house that had twenty-four-hour police presence? Furthermore, which believer would send their son or daughter to a family that had been destroyed by the depredations of a hostile Catholic Church? Who would be ready to court the displeasure of the Church's leaders?

Amy, however, found her life partner herself. She fell in love with Balakrishna, a Telugu Hindu whom she met in Ireland. He had gone to Ireland to study MSc Nursing. Religion or other denominational differences didn't prove to be a hindrance in their relationship. An alliance with Liss Maria, a postgraduate engineer from Kalayanthani, was finalized for Mithun. His wedding took place on 16 April and Amy's on 7 May 2018.

The absence of Salomi, who would have been by my side on those happy occasions, left a searing wound on my soul.

Only after fulfilling my primary paternal responsibilities and finding some peace of mind, did I find energy and inclination to complete my memoirs. After I had started to write with my left hand, and started on the memoirs, many things intervened and interrupted it. In a way, that didn't detract from it and even improved the narrative. A denouement did come much later.

I had completed the second part of this life story first: My life before the question-paper controversy. Since you have travelled with me this far, I am inviting you to read that too. When you read that, you may begin to appreciate the eccentricity or the difference in my way of thinking.

I thank you. And I wish you well.

PART 2

38

Farming, Hunting and Me

'Very fertile soil, isn't it?' murmured Father Paul Thelakkat, surveying the lush, produce-bearing black pepper and bitter-gourd vines that had twisted themselves around the coconut palms and fruit trees. He had come along with my teacher, M.K. Sanoo. They must have strolled around the garden because, as an avid gardener himself, he was very interested in horticulture.

Elephant yam and other vegetables also grew plentifully in my plot of land in addition to the coconut trees and fruit trees. I felt proud. I had planted, watered, and tended to all these plants, trees and vines, using my slashed, mangled and reconstructed hands.

There was another reason for my gratification. I had not forgotten what my neighbours had told me while I was planning to buy that piece of land. One of them had said, 'It's good enough to build a house on, but not for farming; it's just quartz.'

Another lady neighbour, a government servant, had said, 'You've been had. Who pays this kind of money for this block of rock?'

I was not discouraged or deterred by their warnings. I had a good idea about how to convert that piece of land. What Father Thelakkat was looking at now, I had envisioned then. My background in farming had prepared me for this.

My forefathers, who had been migrants to the eastern high-range regions from the western end of the Meenachil taluk of Kottayam district, had moved up into the middle class by buying land with money earned from their sheer hard work. The ancestral house of all the family names such as Paraparakath, Purathe Muthukaattil, Panakkakkuzhiyil and Thenganakunnel was the same.

At the age of sixteen, my paternal grandfather had moved to Variyanikkadu—where I was born—for *dehandam* from Amparanirappel near Bharananganam. Dehandam in the vernacular literally means physical labour. The Hindu overlords use the derived word *dehandakkaran* for cooks. The Christian overlords use it for tenant farmers who tilled the earth and worked on it.

The valley that my grandfather had chosen to farm on belonged to the Vellukkunnel family. This vast land in Kondoor village had been gifted by the Thiruvithamkoor (Travancore) Maharajah to their forebears. It still bears the name Pandaarapaattam in the revenue records. Until the beginning of the twentieth century, the land, especially in the hilly tracts, had been ploughed and farmed on exclusively for rice cultivation. The land would be left fallow for twelve to fifteen months after one harvest. By that time, the whole area would be overrun with undergrowth.

At the beginning of the summer, these shrubs would be cleared and before the monsoon arrived, the dry coppice would be set on fire and the land made ready to receive the seeds. As soon as it rained enough for the water to seep deep into the earth, the seeds would be sown by one person with ten, or even twenty, people following him and tilling the field lightly. They would be singing the ploughing songs passed down the generations through oral tradition. This seed tilling was turned into a celebration with copious supplies of toddy and arrack.

Rice was the main crop—half of the harvest went to the landowner, who would annually let out different plots of land to Christian sharecroppers of Meenachil taluk to cultivate upon. After each year, the farmers moved on to another piece of land allotted to them.

From the second decade of the twentieth century, the landowners decided to let out lands on the plains for sharecropping, mainly for commercial crops and for longer duration. Christians from Meenachil were once again the volunteers. One of them was my grandfather.

Mainly commercial crops such as areca nut palms, coconut palms and black pepper were planted. Fruit trees such as mango and jackfruit and annual crops such as elephant yam, colocasia, tapioca and plantains were also grown. Half of all the harvest still went to the landowner except that now the agreement was that when the perennials such as coconut and areca nut palms reached maturity, that is, after twelve years, half of the land would be given to the sharecropper and registered in his name.

Our elders would say that both virgin earth and virgin bride were alike. Both could be hewed in any way a man wanted. The men who came as sharecroppers loved their land just as much as they would love a woman. They worked on their land with passion; turned the earth over; used the boulders they dug up to build ridges and turned the land to flat terraces and stanched erosion; built fences to keep away animals and protect their crops.

From the first light until darkness fell, they worked the land. On moonlit nights, they worked late into the night. When the single torthu which they wore became sodden in their sweat, they would wring it dry and wear it again. As soon as the household chores were over, their women joined them in farming, helping in weeding, breaking clods, and tilling.

Irrigated by their sweat, the land bloomed. The coconut palms shot up; the fruit trees vied with each other in their produce. The pepper vines embraced all the trees—some planted and others naturally sprouted—and their peppercorns strung up splendidly.

The landowners were regular churchgoers, Roman Catholics like the sharecroppers. Notwithstanding that, the exploitative mentality of feudal lords pervaded here as well. When the jungles were turned into fertile fields, their thoughts turned to how to get rid of the sharecroppers. Using lame excuses such as that the sharecropper's dog barked at the landowner, or his five-year-old son didn't show enough respect to the landowner, the sharecroppers were evicted.

Those who refused to accept the pittance, decided as compensation by some lackey intermediary of the landowner, were beaten up, their homes set on fire, arrested by the police on trumped-up charges; some murdered in cold blood. Even the ones who resisted at first fled for fear of their lives. The owners sold the land vacated by these farmers at handsome prices.

However, some fortunate sharecroppers like my grandfather were not made to leave. His landowner maintained a benevolent relationship with his sharecroppers. Nor was he avaricious.

My grandfather was hardworking. He was good at everything—cutting trees, blasting rocks, building fences, and everything that had to do with farming. Compared to other sharecroppers, our land always grew every crop more plentifully and exactly half of that was given to the owner without fail.

My grandfather wouldn't dream of keeping for himself even one coconut more than was his due. He believed that if we showed any dishonesty, it would be turned into *uthirippukatam*—an obligation of restitution. If we expropriated anyone else's property, that would remain a lifelong obligation. And if we were to die without repaying that debt, we would be denied entry into heaven; or so believed the Christians of that era. It was common in those days for old men on their deathbeds calling upon their scions to repay such debts.

My grandfather always showed patience and humility in his dealings with the landowner. When policemen or government officials cut down the trees—which we had planted and tended to—on our land for use in the houses they were building, my grandfather didn't object. He consoled himself with the thought that, in comparison to other landowners, his own was a much better human being.

In addition to the six acres he had started out with, the landowner gave my grandfather five acres which someone had abandoned. While he was managing those eleven acres, my grandfather purchased outright another ten acres upon a hill in a place called Njarakkad and started farming there as well.

Unfortunately, our landowner also failed to honour the commitment to transfer half of the land to our grandfather upon completion of twelve years. Forty years went by with him enjoying fifty per cent of our land's produce, the fruits of my grandfather's toil. When the land reforms act came and it looked as if all the farmed land would go to the sharecropper, the landowners showed an unholy hurry to give the fifty per cent of the sharecropped land.

Although those who knew the law advised my grandfather, 'You don't have to let go any part of the land you have toiled on for forty years; it's all yours,' he agreed to divide the land as per the original pact. Only man's laws change; God's remain constant. My grandfather wasn't ready to incur an obligation of restitution.

On 7 February 1955, the landowner commandeered the second piece of five acres and registered the title deed of the initial six acres on which our house stood in my grandfather's name.

My grandfather had two sons and five daughters. The eldest among the boys, my father, could study only up to the fourth standard, as there were no secondary schools in the neighbourhood. Therefore, he joined his father in tilling the land.

Hunting was an inseparable part of farming those days. To a great extent, to protect their crops, it was essential for farmers to kill wild animals. The meat-loving Christian sharecroppers couldn't spare money to buy meat. They hunted the animals in the forests around them and ate their fill.

Hunting was also an entertainment for the men who toiled hard from dawn to dusk. Even kings would revel in their royal hunts. Hunters of wild animals were feted, and always had a halo of heroism around them. Manufacture and ownership of guns was just as illegal then as it is now. Nevertheless, the police and other law-keepers turned a blind eye towards it and were rather lax. Therefore, the farmers who liked to hunt had guns at home.

My grandfather and father were accomplished hunters. However, by the time my father attained adulthood, the animals in that area had either been hunted to extinction or had started to give the area a wide berth. I grew up listening to stories of my grandfather's hunting exploits. One night, he shot a huge wild boar which had come to uproot our tapioca tubers. Although he injured it, the boar managed to run away. He reloaded his gun and set off after his quarry, tracking its trail of blood. He had a headlamp strapped to his forehead. Squealing loudly, the boar burst out of the bushes and charged at him, its lethal tusks lowered. My grandfather leapt up, grabbed at a low-hanging branch of a tree and hauled himself up in the nick of time. The irate boar, in its rage, bit viciously into the butt of the rifle that he had dropped. Then it started to patrol around the tree, intent on getting at my grandfather.

My grandfather whistled to direct his younger brother—who had joined him in the hunt—towards his tree. His brother moved towards the boar, his gun aimed at it. The implacable boar squealed open-mouthed and charged at him too. Only to be shot dead through the mouth.

The sharecroppers had a quirky style of animal husbandry. Most of them kept cows, but not at home. The cows were let out to graze in the forest; when they were about to calve, they would be brought back from the forest and cared for all through their lactation period, after which they would be dropped back to the forest. And no one would take away the cattle from the forest, for most of the farmers abided by the tenth commandment: 'Thou shall not covet.' However, tigers and leopards didn't care much for Moses and his commandments. So, occasionally a cow or two would disappear. When the bull calves were sufficiently grown, one of the men would shoot them and divide the meat between the families.

One day, my grandfather went into the woods to retrieve a barren cow. He had to search for it until noon. He shot it down and returned home for lunch. After lunch, he and his younger brother went to skin the cow and bring the meat home. The sight that met them was terrifying: a tiger was tearing away at the udder of the dead cow. Although he had his gun with him, the rounds in them were too small, actually only pellets to shoot birds or small animals like rabbits.

The tiger was frightened away by the sound of human voices, but my grandfather was certain that it would come back. He returned home without approaching the dead cow for fear of spoiling the spoor. He got rid of the pellets and reloaded the gun with heavy rounds. He went back to the carcass, climbed a tree close to it, and concealed himself among the leaves, with the gun pointed at the carcass.

The tiger did return. My grandfather swivelled the gun, drawing a bead on the ear of the tiger, the soft point of entry into the skull for the round. The rustle of the leaves caused the tiger to look up at my grandfather, but by that time, he had squeezed the trigger. The round penetrated the skull and the tiger fell dead on the spot.

He and his cronies skinned the tiger and paraded the skin in a procession to Erattupetta, about ten kilometres away. He had to stand them a treat and bought toddy and arrack, spending all of Rs 2, a princely sum then. This was a tale he would often recount.

Although done to show off his heroism, it turned out to be an ill-advised parade and led him to a series of troubles. Even though there was no case against him for killing the tiger, one of the policemen from Erattupetta station coveted the gun which had killed the tiger. It was an unlicensed gun and it was a time when the police had unlimited powers.

One night, as my grandfather set off with the loaded gun for his hunt, a mountain of a man approached him and asked for directions to Myladi. The man was wearing trousers and a shirt and the very sight of him made my grandfather wary. He gave him the directions, but instead of going on his way, the man grabbed at the gun. It was my grandfather's proudest possession with a pedigree and one he valued more than his own life. No way was my grandfather going to give it up without a fight.

The gun was loaded with enough powder to shoot a round that could fell a wild buffalo. As both men grappled for the gun, my grandfather pointed the barrel at the sky and resting its butt on the man's tummy, pulled the trigger. The gun went off with a deafening crack, completely unexpected by the gun grabber. The recoil sent the man mountain sprawling and he lay curled, clutching his abdomen. My grandfather didn't wait for him to straighten from the foetal position and came away with his precious gun.

The next day, my grandfather and his brother were rafting down the Meenachil river near their ancestral home when he saw three or four policemen waiting on the banks. He immediately understood that they were waiting for him. He instructed his brother to leap out and start running as soon as the raft drew close to the bank, which he did. The police gave chase and caught him. Only then did they realize that he was the wrong man and not the one they were looking for.

'Why did you run?' asked the policemen.

'I was frightened seeing you, sirs,' my great-uncle told them unctuously.

In the meanwhile, my grandfather made good his escape. Eventually, the landowner had to intervene, broker peace, and extricate him from the case of shooting and propelling a policeman.

Now back to my own story.

As the eldest son in a farmer's family, I was co-opted into working the land at a very young age. Even as a five-year-old, I had to pull up wild growth with my tiny hands and separate weeds and wild growth from the earth tilled by my father. A good part of our land was coffee plantation, and picking the berries was one of my early chores. We had tall coffee trees with berries growing at the tip. One day, my father had climbed a coffee tree and the pole he was using to grab the berry bunches at the treetop fell from his hand and hit my right forearm as I stood beneath the tree, gathering fallen berries from the ground. As the end of the pole had been sliced at an angle, it was pointed and sharp, and pierced my arm. I was in second standard then and my injury provided me with a week's leave. One of the identification marks for my secondary-school leaving certificate book was the scar which that pole left on me.

The second scar was a gift from my younger brother who had been in second standard then and me, in the eighth. Together we were clearing the undergrowth in the rubber plantation. As I hacked my way through the bushes using my right hand, my left hand which was hanging loose was slashed by my brother's chopper. As he was still a kid, and my own hand was slim, the damage wasn't much—it required only four stitches.

At a very young age, I had learnt the primary lessons of rubber-tree tapping, mixing the latex with coagulants and ammonia, rolling it into sheets, etc., but I got promoted as a full-blown tapper only when I was in the eighth standard.

By the time I got my right to vote, I had become an accomplished member of our farming family—I could climb coconut trees, areca nut palms and jack fruit trees and deliver their produce and green and dried foliage; weave coconut fronds; use that and palmyra fronds to thatch houses; do the masonry for firewood storeroom and latex machine room; pick tea leaves and coffee berries; dig up and till the land; excavate pits for planting rubber saplings; build platforms for rubber planting; plant, water, and care for vegetables; erect fences and much more.

About half of our land in Murickassery was paddy fields. We had cleared the swamp ourselves, pulled out the stumps of dead trees, and converted it into fields. We had only our muscle power; we had to root out every deep-running root physically until none of it was left. I learnt to build ridges along the field and plaster them with mud for stability. Following in the footsteps of my father, I learnt to sow seeds in the waterlogged paddy field. We ourselves did the weeding, harvesting, threshing, and drying in the beginning.

When I became a college teacher, I didn't stop loving the soil. I was determined that, as long as I had the physical strength, I should earn enough for my daily bread by the 'sweat of my brow'. It's that belief that still makes me take up the *thoompa*—a long-handled, hoe-shaped spade—and although my reconstructed hands can't grip it tightly, it still hits the earth hard.

By the time I was born, opportunities for hunting didn't exist. Even if they did, I doubt if I could have ever become a hunter, because even when I listened to these tales of daring hunts, the primal fear of the hunted animal would often surge to the fore in my imagination and haunt me.

However, I believe that a fearless heart is genetically inherited. That readied me to face the many hunts which took place against me.

39

What's in a Name?

'What's the boy's name?' asked the headmistress, opening the admission register for class one.

'Ouseph,' said my father, who had brought me along to the school.

I was hearing the name for the first time. I was called Appachan by my folks. Although this was an appellation used in many places for father or father-in-law, among the Christians of Central Travancore this was a popular pet name.

When children with epithets such as Appachan and Pappachan were enrolled in school, the name used is the one given at the time of baptism. The name given in the school ends up as a person's official name.

The first-born male child in a family is almost always named after his paternal grandfather at the time of the baptism. That is how I was christened Ouseph. My father was also Ouseph because his grandfather was also Ouseph. In short, my lineage was a series of eldest sons.

Until a generation or two ago, a person's father's name came first and then his own given name. However, by the time I joined school, the European style of one's own name as the forename and father's name as the surname had come into vogue. As both my father and I had the same names, this ordering didn't matter to me. My father had given my name as Ouseph.

My father's official name too was Ouseph. He was however, universally known as Pappachan.

The headmistress who admitted me into Little Flower Lower Primary School in Chemmalamattam was a nun. She didn't pencil me in as Ouseph. She said it was too old a style. Names such Ouseph and Youseph were the Syro-Malayali versions of Joseph. According to her, the modern style was Joseph. The headmistress turned me and my father into Josephs. She considered my name as Joseph, son of Thenganakunnel Joseph in the English style, and shortened it to Joseph T.J. in the admission register.

Upon reaching home, of his own will, my father changed his father's name Ouseph and restyled his name also into T.J. Joseph. Except in the title deed documents, which he had inherited from his father and which continued to show him as Ouseph, he lived as T.J. Joseph for the rest of his life.

Most of the people in and around our area were Roman Catholics. If the most common name among the Muslims was Muhammad, among the Christians, it was Joseph. In every class I attended in school, Josephs were in the majority. In a class of forty, at least ten would be Josephs. Thomas and Mathew were next most common.

Initials became essential to distinguish between the many Josephs. The teachers used the name with initials; our classmates made do with only the initials. When the initials were also the same, they resorted to nicknames.

Students of my generation revelled in the use of nicknames. There was hardly any teacher for whom the students didn't coin a nickname. The sobriquets were seldom born out of fondness. Ridicule and lampoon were behind all of them. However, sometimes the inventiveness and imagination that went into creating the names were amusing and had to be marvelled at.

We had a teacher who used to write a lot on the blackboard. He wrote more than he spoke. The children honoured him with the nickname Ezhuthachan (literally the father of writing; also the short name by which Thunchaththu Ramanujan Ezhuthachan—considered the father of modern Malayalam—was universally known).

Another teacher used to ramble on with no rhyme or reason. By the time his classes ended, the students would have lost whatever comprehension they had of the subject they were being taught and be in a state of confusion. He was dubbed Confucius.

My class teacher in the eighth standard was nicknamed Shastri. Someone who interacted with the students with serenity and paternal love, he was a slim, bald man who resembled Lal Bahadur Shastri.

I have never used nicknames, not for the teachers, not for anyone. The only occasion I have used them was when my interlocutor couldn't place a person, and I had to use it to identify him. I have always felt pained when the nickname was based on some deformity or physical handicap. I have even fought with other students over this.

One day, when I was in the eighth standard, we were playing tag in the school ground during the lunch interval. A student who had lost his sight in one eye due to some eye disease was among us. His eye looked almost necrotic. One of the boys called him 'Pus-eye' and ridiculed him during the game. I didn't like it and told him not call him such names. He rushed at me shouting, 'What'll you do if I call him names?'

What followed was something between a punch-up and a wrestling bout. The details are scarce. One of the school peons passing by separated us. Wins happen to the righteous; therefore, I must have won. I was none the worse for wear. His shirt was in tatters. A good chiromancer could have read my future from my opponent's reddened cheek.

At that point, my future looked bleak. When the first period started after the break, the attender came to our class and asked me to report to the headmaster's room. My adversary was already present there. The sight of him—like a young banana sapling which had survived a hurricane— evoked sympathy in me.

The case didn't go to trial on that day. However, the sentencing was done, and an extreme one. The headmaster ordered, 'You can attend classes only after your father meets me.' I was scared to tell my folks that I had been suspended from the school. Therefore, for the next two days, although I did leave home on time, I spent my day loitering outside without going to school. A week-long holiday for Navratri followed, during which time I was sent as our family's representative to attend my cousin's wedding in Murickassery. I had accompanied our other relatives and returned after a week. By then, my mother had learnt of my suspension from one of the schoolteachers. My father was supervising the farming at Njarakkat hills near Enthayar at that time.

I explained my moral position to my mother. The next day, I went with my mother's letter to the school and handed it over to the headmaster. My mother had humbly requested him to let me attend the classes as my father was away at Enthayar, and as soon as he was back, he would meet the headmaster. That cut no ice with our headmaster. I was sent back home with the letter.

My mother immediately sent me to meet my father. After changing buses thrice, by 5.30 p.m., I reached a place called Elamkadu, about forty kilometres away. Our homestead, on a high hill, was about three kilometres from there. I could see no one else going in that direction.

It was the north-east monsoon time. All through my bus journey, it had been raining quite heavily. By the time I alighted, the rains had abated, but it was cloudy and, since it was October, the light was failing fast. I had to cross a big stream that channelled the water flowing downhill. Murphy, the Britisher who owned the Enthayar Estate, had built a motorable bridge over it during his time. It had been washed away in one of the floods, leaving only its pillars standing. Along the pillars, the stream was shallow but wide. People would ford the stream at this point. When the water was low, sometimes trucks would also cross over at this point.

There were big boulders upstream from the bridge and nimbly leaping from one to the other, a person could get across without getting one's feet wet. I was hurrying to reach our homestead before nightfall, but when I reached the stream, I was dumbfounded. The water was flowing in a torrent and the stream had breached its banks. The low point where the bridge used to be, was a lake of swirling water, its depth unfathomable and the strength of the current there inestimable.

The location of the boulders could be discerned from the waters swirling around their tops, although the banks had already been breached further upstream as well. The stream was about twenty feet across at that point and there were no boulders there. Drawing upon my memory of previous crossings, I estimated that the depth would only be up to my neck and decided to cross from there. Convinced that I needed to be as far away from the boulders as possible, I had walked about thirty feet upstream.

My estimation of the water depth was correct; but of the current, not so. Fighting its unexpected strength, I swam, treaded water, and waded through it as it swiftly bore me downstream; by the time I could get across, I was very near the boulders. By the time I crossed twenty feet, I had been swept thirty feet downstream. It was providential that I decided to go that far upstream before entering the water, otherwise I would have been dashed against the boulders and wouldn't have lived to tell the tale.

By the time I climbed the hill and entered our house, it was dark. I was completely drenched. My father was dumbstruck when he saw me. His first question was, 'Eda, how did you cross the stream?' He was able to estimate the volume of water in it from the torrential rains that had fallen. He was also sure that even adults would find it hard to cross at that time.

I gave him a bowdlerized version of my experience. However, I could see that it hadn't allayed his fear. For a long time, he stood there, gaping at me.

He had seen and heard of many lives lost in those turbulent waters. There had been one incident when a cloudburst had resulted in a landslide and as the water cascaded down the hillside, my father had seen a corpse that had got snagged on the branch of a tree by the stream.

I told him of the scrap in the school ground. He didn't seem to be overly bothered about it. In the mental state that he was in, fights among schoolchildren would have seemed trivial.

The next day, we started from there. The water in the stream, which had been in spate the previous night, had gone down. Even so, my father held my hand tightly as we waded across.

We went directly to the school before going home. The headmaster was on leave and a teacher we had nicknamed Poovanpazham (after a type of fat plantain, as he was fair-skinned and stout) was holding the fort. Childless, he had a lot of affection for all the children. At a time when caning and corporal punishment was the norm, this teacher never beat any of us.

The attender fetched my antagonist from the class. The substitute headmaster conducted the hearing. It didn't seem to be of any great import to him. He told my father, 'This is all very common among kids. Don't bother too much about it. However, this boy's shirt has been torn and he is from a poor family. Can you buy him a shirt in its place?'

'Would it be enough if I pay money instead?'

'Yes, that should do.'

The teacher calculated the cost of the fabric and stitching charges and set the amount at Rs 5. In those days, a decent shirt could be tailored for that sum. My father happily handed over the money to the teacher. Tapping of the rubber trees grown by us was done by my mother and myself; of the 250 trees, 150 fell under my remit. The prevailing wages in those days was one paisa per tree. The wages of five hundred trees went towards my attempt at restitution—I did some quick mental arithmetic. The other inconveniences and losses were extra.

Still, it was a relief. If our original headmaster had been there, things would have ended very differently. He was my namesake, including the initials, but had been given a nickname as well. He was known as Kochusir (little or junior master) among the public, but with this penchant for peppering every conversation with 'da' (look here), his nickname was Dakochu among the students.

I was well aware of the conclusion of such trials of fights among children. At the end of it, in the presence of the accused's guardian, the culprit would receive four strikes of the headmaster's cane on his buttocks. No more, no less. I considered it fortunate that the headmaster was on leave that day; not because I was spared the pain of the caning or the shame of being caned in front of my father, but because I thought my father was spared the humiliation of seeing his son being caned.

I am not yet done with nicknames. Although I never used nicknames for others, my own classmates calling me by my original name was rare. I was given many monikers. Even when the nicknames used were derogatory or intended to ridicule me, I would answer to them, as if they were my own names. Although, at that time, I had not heard of the Shakespearean character who asked, 'What's in a name?' or Goethe who had said, 'I am what I am, so take me as I am,' I had a similar ethos from the time I was a child.

The first time I was given a nickname—Pakki—was when I was in my seventh standard. I am not sure whose imagination had taken wings to dub me that. Pakki is a corruption of *pakshi* or bird in Malayalam. We used it for small birds such as house sparrows. I used to be very slim in those days; and not very tall. I may have weighed around twenty-five kilograms. My stature may have provoked my friends to call me by that name. It was many years later that I came to know of the legendary brigand and Kerala's Robin Hood, Kayamkulam Kochunni's comrade, Ithikkara Pakki. When someone called out Pakki, I would answer, considering it as my pet name. When others used the name to mock me, I still responded, neutralizing the ridicule and taunt in those calls.

When I was in the eighth standard, during the School Youth Festival, we presented a one-act play under my tutelage; I was the writer and the director. I had chosen a whodunnit plot, since, those days, detective novels were my passion.

The plotline was something like this: a gang of bandits, whom the police had failed to bring to book, is running riot; an educated, but unemployed, young man runs into this gang during his travels; he confronts them, braves their lethal weapons, and floors all of them; the police arrive and take them into custody; the protagonist receives a special reward from the police department and a job in the criminal investigation department. All's well that ends well.

Since I lacked the personality to feature as either the protagonist or the antagonist or the police inspector, I took on the role of a lowly gang member. We had rehearsed the fight scene. The direction given was that the verisimilitude of the fight was the responsibility of both the giver and the receiver.

When the play began, all my blow-by-blow stunt-scene direction of feinting at the first punch, blocking the follow-up punch with the left hand and the rest of it failed to materialize on stage. The first slap of the robber chieftain landed a painful blow on the protagonist's cheek. How could a hero be seen to quail? He retaliated with a full-blooded slap. From there it rapidly degenerated into a barroom brawl. I too received quite a few punches. My fake, turned-up moustache flew through the air to land at the edge of the stage. I followed its trajectory, pretended to stagger and fall close to it and tried to paste it back on. However, the damn thing refused to stick to my upper lip. Therefore, I decided to continue to lie there, as if I had been knocked out.

The play ended eventually. Only some members of the audience realized that what they had witnessed was a real fight scene and not a simulation. In those days, there was a great interest in one-act plays. The senior students would stage some good skits. This would bring the parents also to the school. Someone from our area was in the audience for our play as well. He had caught on that it had turned into a free-for-all and carried the tale to the whole countryside. For a long time, whenever I ran into him, he would take the mickey out of me saying that the blow had withered my insides and made me look emaciated like a consumptive.

Thengai Srinivasan was a well-known actor in Tamil films during the '60s. His name had got the prefix *Thengai* (coconut) after he acted as a coconut-seller in a play named *Kal Manam*. As my family name was Thenganakunnel, I was nicknamed as Thengai Srinivasan. For a long time, the people in our place would rib me with 'Story and Direction by Thengai Srinivasan.' Thengai Srinivasan was then truncated to Srinivasan and, subsequently, Sreeni. Whenever I would take part in amateur plays, I chose Sreeni as my stage name to be printed in notices and publicity material. Even now, there are many people in my hometown who address me as Sreeni.

My pre-degree course was in a private, non-regular college in Parathode in the high-range, a seven-kilometre walk from our homestead in Murickassery. My classmates were from Parathode and Vellathooval schools. They found my alma mater, Achamma Memorial Higher Secondary School in Kalaketty, droll, especially the name of the place which literally translated into tethered ox. That gave me my next nickname, which was not only used by the students but by the teachers as well. I happily accepted that name and went above and beyond the call of duty—in some of the skits presented locally, I used the pseudonym J. Kalaketty.

To do my degree course in St Thomas College, Palai, I stayed alone in my ancestral house that had been lying locked up for two years. Although I continued my rubber tapping and farming activities, I was gripped by an existential angst at that time. Reading novels by O.V. Vijayan and M. Mukundan had led to this. Ravi of *Khasakinte Itihasam* (The Legends of Khasak) and Dasan of *Mayyazhippuzhayude Theerangalil* (On the Banks of the Mayyazhi) entered my soul. I wore my hair long; I turned up at the college shabbily dressed, in what was then called 'hippie' style. I would be shrouded in silence and solitude, seated in the last bench in the classroom, and I came to be known as 'Swami' or ascetic among my classmates. I accepted that too with equanimity and blessed them all. Although in the second year, I had my hairstyle changed to a step-cut, and got rid of the existential angst, I continued to be Swami to all.

When I joined Maharaja's College in Ernakulam for my post-graduation in Malayalam, everyone called me Joseph. There was no other Joseph within a mile. Joseph was a powerful name in the literary scene of that time—the Josephs in Anand's novel *Aalkoottam* (The Throng) and in Balachandran Chulikkad's poem 'Mappusaakshi' (Approver) were icons of determination and self-sacrifice. Most of the Josephs in literature traced their lineage to the just and noble Joseph in the tale of Jesus Christ, whose wife's Immaculate Conception was taken in his stride without any marital acrimony.

I started to like my name from around that time. Truth be told, I liked being called by my various nicknames until then.

With my limbs maimed and mobility impaired, when I lay on the Specialists' Hospital's ICU bed like a felled banana plant, the State's education minister honoured me by calling me a moron. He had later said that it had been his instinctive reaction.

I told my friend who wanted to know my reaction to the moron-calling, 'The world-famous novelist, Fyodor Dostoevsky wished to create a character—a paragon of morality or "the positively good and beautiful man." The creator of that Christ-like character felt that a guilelessness bordering on fatuousness was essential to that character. In his novel titled *The Idiot*, the protagonist Prince Myshkin was referred to as the "idiot" by the other characters.'

While I had none of the sterling qualities of Myshkin, that feeble-mindedness or fatuity was present in copious quantities in me. I had scribbled down these lines at the time of my self-realization:

'Fool.

I am a cretin.

An imbecile.

An unmitigated moron.

And my monumental imbecility—realization that I am a fool.'

40

The Munificent Maharaja's

A lethal disease, that fortunately didn't end up as fatal for me, was the reason I became an alumnus of Maharaja's College. I came to know it was rheumatoid fever only many years later, that too from an Ayurvedic doctor.

The year was 1981. However, that too has a backstory.

In school, my preparations for examinations would start only on the previous day. When I came to college, things improved a little—they started from the time I received the timetable of the examination. After taking my examinations thus without needless stress and strain, and ever undergoing the dreaded exam fever, in my final-year BA, I was left dumfounded by one of the papers. Where I had assumed I would be able to gobble up *Kerala Panineeyam*—the treatise on Malayalam grammar—within a week, the book proved to be a nightmarish can of worms.

I hadn't picked up the textbook even once or attended the Malayalam grammar classes. After appearing for the examination without studying that text, I decided to 'cancel' the paper—that is, annul the test taken and its scores, and opt for a chance to reappear in the betterment examination. Our syllabus was constructed in such a way that this would automatically annul all my elective papers for both my first and second years. Although it was a conscious decision, later I did find it to be a foolish one.

In the following year, as the syllabus had been changed, I had to sit for examinations for six papers and I didn't get to study *Kerala*

Panineeyam properly even then. It required at least a month of assiduous work to have even a reasonable grasp of its contents. Since I couldn't find the time and mental space for doing that, I convinced myself that I could compensate for it with better marks in my other papers in order to qualify for admission into the post-graduation course.

It came to pass the way I had imagined it, and in a euphoric high, I applied for the MA degree course in five colleges—NSS and St Berchmans colleges in Changanassery, Maharaja's College in Ernakulam, and University College and Kerala University's Karyavattom Campus in Thiruvananthapuram. I submitted the applications in person in all these institutions. Due to shortage of funds during these journeys, I couldn't take a room in these places and had to sleep in railway stations or bus terminals. Within a week of my return from one of these trips, I came down with high-grade fever.

I used to live alone in our house at Variyanikkadu, working the land and teaching in a tutorial college in Erattupetta. Fortunately, two days after the fever started, my father came down from Murickassery by chance. He took me to a small hospital in Pinnakkanadu, where, when they saw my condition, they admitted me. The doctor said I had contracted typhoid and would take some time to recover.

However, after a week, my condition worsened. I suggested to my father that I should be moved to Kadamapuzha Hospital in Kanjirappally. Perhaps due to his faith in the doctor's prognosis and fearing the expenses at a bigger hospital, he didn't pay heed to my suggestion. I used the good offices of an acquaintance who had been admitted in the same hospital with influenza to prevail upon my father to shift me. We went there with a referral letter from the doctor. Another week went by with no improvement in my condition. They too treated me for typhoid. When I didn't respond, they decided to change tack. The new treatment brought some relief.

Since my father had not returned as promised, my mother came in search of him. Eventually, tracking us down to the hospital, she remained to take care of me. One of the elderly men from Variyanikkadu who had visited me, reported back to my folks at home that I was on my deathbed. That prompted some of my kinsmen to visit me.

I received interview cards from all the colleges I had applied to. My father fetched them from our Variyanikkadu house, where they had been delivered. My first preference was SB College since it was only a two-hour bus journey from home. As I scanned through the interview cards, my heart leapt into my mouth. The interview dates were over for the first four of them! The fifth was from Maharaja's and the interview date was the next day. I let out a long sigh of relief.

I had completed three weeks' stay in hospitals. My health had started to improve. The IV infusions had been stopped for the past two days. I had started to take broken-rice gruel. I informed the doctor of my need to go to Ernakulam to get my admission done and on the condition that I would return to the hospital, he let me go, as there was no other option. Although I could just about manage to stand on my feet, I was still extremely weak and fatigued. Yet, due to the natural perversity of youth, I didn't agree to my father's suggestion that he would accompany me. For all times, for every young man, the starting point of his lack of liberties is his father.

The next morning at 5.45 a.m., my father put me on a direct bus to Ernakulam from Kanjirappally. I reached Ernakulam at 10 a.m. for the interview slated at 11 a.m. However, the college office told me that the interviews would take place only in the afternoon as they clashed with the 'Meet the Candidate' event as part of the college council elections.

I found Maharaja's College to be a festival land minus the celebratory sounds. Girls and boys were seated on all the available steps in mixed groups, chatting. There were isolated pairs engaged in private conversation. No canes of prudery, intolerance, or discipline were chasing them away.

Although I wanted to walk around and admire the *nalukkettu* style architecture that screamed out old glory and the quadrangle in the middle, in my weakened state, I didn't dare to do it. I sat leaning against one of the big pillars near the Malayalam department and hung on.

The pre-election event was held in the quadrangle. The first chairman candidate to address the students was a slim boy doing his pre-degree course. Dressed in a shirt and a mundu and standing with a bent stance, he was not a member of any student organization. I enjoyed his satirical speech made with remarkable felicity and filled with outlandish campaign promises such as—if he were elected the chairman, he'd build a helipad on the campus to improve the transportation options of the students; all the classrooms would be air-conditioned; ropeways would be built over the quadrangle for teachers to go from one class to another, etc. None of the official candidates who followed him could match his oratory.

I cannot but write a little more on this worthy. One day, this wise guy had come for an elocution competition in which I was also taking part. He spoke well and stuck to the topic; it was apparent to me that he would walk away with the first prize. When the bell went off, indicating the end of the allotted time, he continued to speak. So, they switched off the microphone. That didn't crimp his style; he kept talking without the mic. When it became obvious that nothing else was going to stop him, the organizers got on to the stage and bodily carried him away. As he was being frog-marched out, he was still gesticulating and fulminating . . .

It was a competition to select participants for the University Union Youth Festival. It was a masterly performance of an anarchist who wanted to cock a snook at the authorities and tell them no one was bothered about their awards and honour lists. In my mind, I honoured him. Citing indiscipline, they gave the first place, which was rightfully his, to another boy. I was in the second place.

Much later, a prominent daily reported that he had died. Like Mark Twain denying rumours of his own demise, this man also had to, after reading his own obituary, walk into the principal's room to deny he was dead, even as discussions were going on about giving the college a holiday in honour of the dead student. Who is to say that it wasn't his black humour that inspired him to insert his own obituary in the daily? Whatever it was, the next day the paper printed an apology for the wrong report of his death. I wonder what became of that little genius.

By the time the interview and formalities were over, it was 5 p.m. When I hit Thodupuzha, it was late night and the last bus for Kanjirappally had already left. I was compelled to take a room in a lodge and spend the night there. Since I had no appetite, I had eaten very little on that day—one vada and glass of tea from the college canteen was all I had. My supper was a glass of tea and another cocktail of medicines.

Around 2 a.m., I started to feel such severe discomfort that I imagined I was at death's door. I cursed myself for forbidding my father from accompanying me. I lay helpless on that bed, without even the strength to get up and drink from the water jug on the table.

In the morning, when the room-boy knocked on my door, I was still alive. I had him fetch me a glass of tea and that put some energy back into me. This proved sufficient to make the fifty-kilometre journey to Kanjirappally and get back to the hospital. I had to spend another two weeks in the ward and continue the penicillin injections and other medications for another week.

Following election-related violence, Maharaja's College was closed indefinitely. By the time it opened after a month, I had found sufficient strength to attend college. However, I had to keep taking a handful of pills. After two weeks, I returned to Kanjirappally hospital for a check-up. The doctor who had treated me was no longer working there. After checking my records, the doctor who had replaced him asked me if I had had tuberculosis. Although I denied it, he wasn't ready to take my word for it. I had been given anti-TB drugs all along. He had my x-rays taken. There was no patch, and I was cleared. However, the doctor advised me to have my ESR checked regularly, and to continue the medications. The sad truth remains that many of the doctors do not go beyond prescribing medicines to show the sensitivity to inform the patient what ails him or her and why the medicines have been prescribed.

My family's finances were in dire straits at the time I joined Maharaja's College. Our pepper plants had come to the end of their productive life and all that was left was some paddy production in our land in Murickassery. Rubber had been replanted in half of our Variyanikkadu plot; in the remaining area, many of the trees had been squeezed of the last drop of latex, and were now ripe for cutting down. Only some eighty clonal root stock trees were yielding any latex. A rubber tree has a productive life of about twenty-eight years during which the tree can be tapped four times starting from the top to the bottom. Often there is one final slaughter tapping, after which the tree could only be cut down to be sold as timber. The slaughter tapping also used to be my duty.

The practice of using plastic sheets for protecting the latex during the monsoons hadn't started in those days. Therefore, from June until September it was lean season for tapping. I used the time to teach at a private tutorial college in Erattupetta. I had set aside the money I had saved to do my post-graduation. However, I had burned through that amount for my hospitalization, which eventually cost us much more. I had to take a loan from a rubber trader to join Maharaja's.

As I no longer lived there, my father moved into our Variyanikkadu house to continue rubber tapping. I moved to Ernakulam in November; in the middle of January, I went to Variyanikkadu to take some money from my father. It was around 2 p.m., and my father was still at work. I felt bad that he had to live alone and toil because I had gone away to study. Since the weather was unseasonably warm and the trees were all at their slaughter-tapping stage, the yield was meagre. Therefore, I asked my father to give up tapping and return to Murickassery. He asked me where I planned to get the money for my hostel fees and other expenses. I assured him I would find some way to manage that.

In my time, Maharaja's, unlike many educational institutions, was never strict about students' attendance. My plan was to work part-time or even full-time in some hotel. Unnikrishnan, a friend who was doing his MSc in mathematics, told me that a parallel college at Thevara, near Ernakulam, had a vacancy for a Malayalam lecturer. Unni used to teach there sometimes to tide him over his financial difficulties. I joined there as a teacher at a salary of Rs 300 a month. After finishing up there every day, I would return to Maharaja's.

At the start of my second year, my father gave me Rs 3000, half of the sale value of the trees which had been felled after their slaughter tapping. That enabled me to give up my part-time teacher's job. In all my life, that was the only year I could dedicate entirely to studies, without having to work on the side. I was eligible for scholarship under the Kumara Pillai Commission Report (KPCR) scheme, under which the government gave a grant of almost Rs 1000 a year. The first-year's amount was spent almost entirely on books.

My first experience of staying in a hostel was in Rama Varma New Hostel of Maharaja's College. P.K. Shaji, my classmate, and I were allotted what was nicknamed the 'dark room' of the hostel as the only windows it had opened into the corridor and none to the open area outside whence natural light could come in. Even during the day, we had to switch on the lights; if there was a power failure, we had to light candles. Although it had little ventilation and light, there was free passage to the multitude of mosquitoes, and mosquitoes have always been extremely partial to me; there could be a crowd around me, but I alone would be chosen to receive their dedicated and undivided attention. I would swaddle myself completely in a sheet with only my eyes showing to escape from their special love. Then they would try to bite my eyelids!

Anti-mosquito coils were not popular then. Given the parlous state of my finances, I didn't even think of investing in a mosquito net. To escape from the blood-sucking swarm, there were days when I would sleep in the 'common room' which had a ceiling fan in the middle of the room. Anyone could go and sleep there—even non-hostelers and non-students! I saw a man once who, having come to Ernakulam and possibly having no money to stay in a hotel or lodge, had slept in our common room and left the very next morning. He later became a famous movie director.

When it wasn't raining, I would sleep on the hostel terrace which was laid with terracotta tiles. The strong sea breeze kept most of the mosquitoes away. However, unexpected showers would rudely wake us up from our precious sleep sometimes. On other days, I would crawl into the mosquito net which Shreedharan, who was doing his MA in politics, had strung up in one corner of the common room, and which he seldom used.

The ground floor had all the juniors, the pre-degree students; the first floor, the undergraduates; and the top floor, the postgraduate students. In my second year, I got salvation from the dark room to room ninety-nine, near the staircase. Davis, doing his post-graduation in applied chemistry became my roommate.

Maharaja's hostel was spared of the ragging or hazing which was the nightmare of junior students in many other college hostels. There was fraternal love among the inmates. The juniors would address the postgraduates respectfully as *mashe* (teacher).

The inmates had all the freedom they wanted; no one lorded it over them. There was a warden for namesake; a kindly professor who would come once in a while, mind his own business, and leave unobtrusively; he had a room too, but it was vacant most of the time.

The students preferred to go for late-night movies, since evening shows meant missing dinner. As the main door would be locked by 10 p.m., upon their return, the moviegoers had to clamber up a drainpipe at the back of the building and squeeze in through a window, the bars of which had been removed long ago by someone with great foresight and consideration for cine-lovers.

Since we would study late into night and preferred to have tea or coffee or light refreshments to keep us going, one day I asked the watchman whether it was necessary to lock the collapsible main door every night. Although I hadn't much hope, surprisingly it brought about a change. From then on, the door remained open through the night, which was a blessing for the night-owl cinephiles and tea-drinkers.

Now and then, I would be barred from the mess for non-payment of hostel dues. Thereafter, only room rent, water, and electricity charges had to be paid. If those weren't paid, thankfully one wasn't evicted from the hostel, they would be marked down as arrears and would continue to accumulate in the account books.

Whenever I was barred from the boarding, I would cook gruel in the room using a stove. I brought rice grown by us from home. Most often this was the accompanied by sautéed bitter gourd and green grams. Although I would make enough for all three meals of the day, on most days I would get to have it only once. My friends would polish off the rest. However, they were also kind enough to make sure I never starved— someone or the other would stand me dinner and lunch.

By the time the study-leave for my final-year examinations started, my funds had run dry. When the KPCR money was delayed, some days were a real struggle. I had to cadge small loans from my friends to tide over those days. One day, when I had neither money nor rice to make the gruel, due some inexplicable, unknown rage within me, I couldn't bring myself to ask anyone for a loan. However, I didn't let my studies suffer. When I felt famished, I boiled some leftover barley powder with water and drank it—the remnants of the barley grains I had bought when I was down with fever many months ago. Then I went back to my studies.

That evening, Joju T. John, a student of BA Malayalam and secretary of the Malayalam Association of the college, came into my room and dropped a twenty-rupee currency note into my shirt pocket without saying a word or my asking for it. It was his pocket money given by his father, a schoolteacher, but it was enough to feed me for three days. Students like him were the reason why Maharaja's College always had the enviable reputation of fraternity and bigheartedness, which only kept increasing over time.

Although some students tried to rope me in into fighting the college union elections, I avoided that whirlpool. I was at the fag end of my student life and this was the first opportunity I had had to be a full-time student. I was quite aware that any slip-ups and my future would become inextricably linked to rubber trees and tapping knives. However, I did participate in all the cultural activities in the college.

During my first year, Dr M. Leelavathy was our department head. She loved us like her own children. The next year, she was promoted as the principal of Brennan College in Thalassery and her place was taken by Prof. M.K. Sanoo. As a man of convictions, who was steadfast and uncompromising in matters of principle, he resigned from the service ahead of his retirement. However, he was so committed to his vocation that he found a place outside the campus and made time to meet us there and complete the syllabus. Even Dr Leelavathy came down during weekends from Thalassery and took classes for us in linguistics and other papers.

Going by my graduation marks, in our class of thirty in my post-graduation course, I would have ranked as ten. With a vengeance, I not only mastered *Kerala Panineeyam* but lapped up other grammar treatises and critiques. More than the desire to score high marks, my impetus was my desire to have the conviction that I was truly a 'master' in my chosen subject and not merely in the degree that would be conferred upon me. I wanted the marks to be a by-product of that mastery. In any case, during both years of my post-graduation, I topped my class.

After thirty-five years, Prof. Sanoo in an interview given during his ninetieth birthday celebrations had reminisced about his teaching days and stated that, while he was fond of all the students he had ever taught, he had a special regard for the last batch of students. And that he would not be able to forget Joseph who was one among them. Isn't this accolade from a revered teacher the greatest honour his student could hope for?

41

Let the Rat Feast on the Cassava Today

After my post-graduation, I was invited to join some of the non-regular colleges as a teacher. I didn't accept any of them as I would have had to stay away from Variyanikkadu. The two years I had spent away for my post-graduation had had a telling effect on the farming. In over an acre, mature rubber trees had been cut down after slaughter tapping. That area should have been replanted in the previous year. I decided it had to be done immediately as otherwise the income from the land would get delayed that much more.

I cleared the undergrowth and drove in stakes as markers. I dug pits, planted the saplings, and built the ridge around it for damming the water. I dug up the rest of the area one-foot deep. Since the land had an incline, I built mud walls at various points to prevent soil erosion and planted nenthran banana plants and tapioca as intercrops.

The rubber trees in over half the area were not ready for tapping. There were only a small group of trees that could be tapped, but they were the less-productive clonal trees. Since I was doing the tapping, there was some margin; I also had to transfer money home after meeting my personal expenses. Therefore, most of the work I did alone except for making the mud walls.

By the time I had sent in my application for the BEd course to NSS Training College, Changanassery, my hands had once again become callused; all the saplings I had planted had taken root and were growing luxuriantly. However, I had not taken a firm decision to join the course when I had applied.

My wish was to enrol for the MPhil course in Madras University. However, since I didn't have the wherewithal, BEd was a compromise. When the admission card was received, I was in a dilemma for two reasons—I never aspired to be a schoolteacher for one; the other was that I was worried that my farming activities would be affected. On the other hand, if I didn't join, that would be a blunder too. Not too many colleges had Malayalam BEd course those days. I was assured of a high schoolteacher's job as soon as I got my degree. What is known as management seats—a proportion of the sanctioned seats the management of private colleges sells to the highest bidders—were in high demand and were going for Rs 15,000–20,000 for BEd Malayalam course, quite a substantial sum when you consider a teacher's salary was only Rs 500–600 in those days. Given these circumstances, would it be advisable to forfeit the seat I had won on merit? I asked myself many such questions. In the end, I decided to join the course.

Since I couldn't abandon my farming and living expenses in Changanassery would be high, I decided to commute from home. I knew the sixty-kilometre-one-way commute was not going to be easy, especially with no one at home to help me. However, I decided to take the bit between my teeth.

I needed no alarm to rise at 5 a.m. After my ablutions, I would prepare some simple fare for breakfast and leave home at 6.30 a.m. The nearest bus stop was three kilometres away. At 7.25 a.m., I would board the private bus which plied between Erattupetta and Changanassery and get to my destination at 9.30 a.m. I would duck into a teashop, wash my face, have a cup of tea, and walk to the college, which was about a kilometre away in Perunna, and arrive in time.

During my MA days, I could write up to thirty pages in an hour. However, after a year's toil wielding the hoe, pick, and spade, my hands had grown stiff and callused. Initially I found it hard to take down notes during the lectures at speed. My palms had grown so rough and prickly that I feared I might score my face while washing it.

My main meal of the day was lunch from a restaurant near the college. When the class dispersed at 4 p.m., I would walk to the bus terminal, take a bus up to Kanjirappally, and change buses to Pinnakkanadu, which was my stop. In the morning too, I had to buy the ticket in two stages. According to the rule, students' concession was only for forty kilometres. Therefore, I had to buy a full-fare ticket up to Kanjirappally, and the rest of way at the concessional charge.

My raiment conformed to India's ancient virtuous prescription that a student should wear poor clothes—mine was a polyester mundu that needed no ironing and shirts made of coarse fabrics. Although I used to carry a file, since I had the aspect of a daily labourer or farm worker, whenever I asked for a student concession ticket, the bus conductors would look askance at me. To add to their suspicions, I was twenty-seven years old at that time, and older than most of the conductors. Most of the time, they would demand to see my concession card. I was always mindful to keep on my person both my student ID card and the concession eligibility card given out by the private bus-owners' association.

One day after he checked my card and verified that I was a student, a conductor asked me contemptuously, 'Isn't it time that you stopped all this, big brother?' I said nothing and only smiled at him.

Around 6.30 p.m. I would alight at my bus stop. I would have tea and snacks from a nearby teashop and get them to pack two bondas. Those were not for me. Receiving some high-quality intelligence—I don't know what their source was—that I was growing tapioca or cassava, rats and greater bandicoots in the neighbourhood had beaten a well-worn path to my land. They had no patience; by the time the tubers started to grow, they would start boring their way in. Since I had dug up all the land, they had it easy. Every day, at least five or six tapioca plants would be uprooted and the tubers gnawed out of existence.

I had turned into a rat exterminator in the night. The bondas were used to deliver the poison. I would divide the bondas into four quarters; in each piece I would scoop out a small hole with the point of my knife, fill it with poison, seal the hole with the scooped-out piece and leave these four pieces in the path taken by the rodents. Although in this manner I must have dispatched many of them to meet their maker, they were quickly replaced by their descendants. Mine was a war of attrition and went on for a long time.

I would reach home at around 7.30 p.m. planning to make some gruel for dinner. Then either tiredness or laziness would deter me from such exertions. So, I would take one of the bondas meant for the bandicoots and eat it. Often, one thing led to another and I would be tempted to eat the second one too. Then I would make a momentous decision, 'Let the rats feast on the tapioca today.' I would get a sound sleep reserved for a ruthful proponent of non-violence.

42

Pasteurized Milk

As I couldn't make the one-hundred-and-twenty-kilometre commute to Changanassery and back every day, I missed classes on quite a few occasions. On the days that I was in class, I made it a point to make my presence felt. Raising doubts was the way I did this, calling attention to myself. That and later, indulging in a bit of polemics. I shall narrate one such instance.

Although every one of us had specializations in our BEd course, there were general subjects which all of us had to study. These classes were held in the auditorium and the teachers addressed us from the stage and used a PA system.

Our 1984–5 batch had 187 students. We had congregated for the first class of 'Education in India'. Prof. Philippose was taking the class. He asked our opinion on Indian education insofar as its current theory— that the curriculum should be designed and classes structured after assessing the knowledge levels of the students—was concerned.

Who's going to give any opinion? Everyone sat there silently, disinterested.

'This is the fundamental flaw in our education system. We have no capacity to react, to respond.' Citing examples of lacunae in the Indian education system, he started off, 'All of you are either graduates or postgraduates, highly educated. Most of you are silent not because you have no opinion. But because you don't have the boldness or the nerve to state them.'

He had questioned our self-respect. I started to rise slowly from my seat, when I saw a namesake of mine from the natural science department also getting to his feet. I let him have the first shot.

'Indian education is now at different levels. My opinion is that there should be a coordination in the field of education.' He said as much and sat down. The professor gestured to me to say my piece.

Initially I had stood up planning to oppose what the professor had said, but that was when my namesake gave his opinion. I thought I'd cover both in one go.

'I don't agree with either the opinions I heard here just now. Why . . . ?' I paused and looked around the class. I had everybody's attention. I continued in a firm voice, 'I can still recall a lesson in a text book I had when I was in the second standard. Amma gives me pasteurized milk. If I don't drink it, amma will weep. Why does amma cry? I should grow up to be like my father. That's what amma wants.

'I have heard from a lady professor that the wife of the professor who wrote that lesson would cry if her own children refused to drink milk. She knew both the husband and wife. This lesson is appropriate for those children or other highborn children like them who would understand it. The children, including me, learnt this text when a majority of people in Kerala were struggling to slap together one square meal a day.

'Since my father was a farmer, he would toil on the side of some hill, plant tapioca, elephant yams, and greater yams and provide his children three meals a day. However, when I was doing that lesson, I had no idea what pasteurized milk was, what then to talk of the starving destitutes? Even the children who lived in slums and hovels—for whom even gruel is hard to come by—are forced to drink this 'pasteurized milk' in their textbooks. If they don't drink, reportedly their mothers will cry! And why are the mothers crying? Because they should grow up to be like their fathers. That is what mothers want.

'Must I grow up to be like the father who, in his drunken rage, smashes the pot in which my mother has cooked gruel with just the handful of rice she has eked out by washing dishes or dirty clothes at some rich man's house? Does she want me to grow up to be like her husband who grabs her by her hair, slaps, punches, and kicks her? The children reading the lesson are dumbstruck.'

The teacher was starting to look as if he regretted seeking the students' opinion. However, I had to finish what I had begun.

'As long as economic and social differences exist in our society, education shouldn't be unified. On the other hand, it must be deconstructed into several levels. Similarly, in our educational system, we shouldn't let the students' power to react and respond grow; we should try to curb it. Because if we nourish and nurture it, in an unjust social system where the basic needs of men—food, clothing, and shelter—are denied, there are chances they will turn into rebels. If they have to be kept in a servile condition, they shouldn't be allowed to think.'

Then I looked at the professor. He said, 'Yes, yes,' and gestured to me to sit down. I wonder whether he understood my irony. He never reacted.

What came to pass later in Kerala was literally what I had stated oxymoronically then. What was in the public education sphere was privatized and schools of various grades came up offering different syllabi. Using the smokescreen of discipline, they destroyed, and continue to destroy, independent thinking and the power to respond in the students. Children are turned into self-centred and narrow-minded beings. Those with vested interests fill them with false values and turn them into their serfs.

It is a matter of great relief that the economic condition in the state has improved from one of abject poverty to one where the majority of the children are provided with pasteurized milk. At the same time, we also have to welcome maladies caused by overeating, obesity, and toxic foods in place of diseases caused by malnutrition and undernourishment.

43

Men Who Knew Men

The only jobs I applied for are as a college lecturer. Thrice. The first interview was in 1983, at St George's College in Aruvithura, immediately after completion of my post-graduation. One of the candidates was a friend of mine; he had better academic merit than I had. The manager of the college was his uncle and the subject expert on the interview panel was his teacher. That my friend ended up at the top in the rank list was a no-brainer. I was second in academic merit. I too did quite well in the interview, but in the rank list I came third. A teacher in Georgian College, a non-regular college under the same management, had come in second. The first and second rank holders got appointed as lecturers in St George's College.

The second interview was in St Thomas College, Palai, where I had done my graduation. Two of my classmates were already employed there. One of them, with an ear to the ground, had told me that the management had already decided to appoint another of our classmates to the position. I went for the interview only because I thought it was an opportunity to meet my friends and acquaintances who may also come for the interview, since they would have seen the advertisement and applied. My classmates in the BEd course were also there as candidates.

Three of the five panel members were representatives of the management; the fourth member was the subject expert, and fifth, the government nominee. Usually, the government nominee is the revenue divisional office or the district collector. If the management has no vested interest in whom to appoint, the interview will be done properly; otherwise, it will end up as a farce.

The subject expert is chosen for their willingness to toe the management's line and serve its interests. When the interview is a charade, the subject expert and the government nominee are the hatchet men—they have to ask the toughest and most recondite questions to the candidates, save the one earmarked by the management—and leave the poor souls convinced that they are unworthy of even aspiring to a position as a lecturer in a college, let alone being appointed as one. These two often also subscribe to the dictum 'Any fool can ask a question' and its corollary that the fool need not necessarily know the answer. Since their wallets are fattened by generous travel and daily allowances, there are always ready takers for these roles of the court jester and they are willing to carry it out convincingly too.

On that day in St Thomas College, interviews for various disciplines were underway. The subject expert for Malayalam was Joseph Anchanat, professor of Malayalam in SB College, Changanassery. The government nominee was Kottayam District Collector K.J. Mathew. The latter was an alumnus of the college having done his post-graduation in English language and literature from there. As they came out after the interview, I heard the first few interviewees mutter that he was only trying to show off his erudition by asking questions on modern literature. I was feeling cocky—a thrill ran through me that I could indulge in a literary debate with him. Even when I was doing my BEd, I was teaching MA students in a non-regular college twice a week and one of the subjects was modern literature.

As the management's representative, Prof. C.J. Sebastian, head of the Malayalam department, was also on the board. Ever since I was a student, he had been the head of the department. Prof. Anchanat started the interview and most of his questions were based on Malayalam grammar, all of which I fielded well. Next was the collector. Energized, I sat up—modern literature was headed towards me.

'Have you read today's newspaper?'

I was very disappointed by that question from the collector. Forget modern, he was not planning even to touch upon literature per se. He seemed to be testing my knowledge of current affairs. Was I in some interview for the civil services?

Unable to cooperate with the collector's line of enquiry, I turned into a modernist on my own accord.

'No.' I replied expressionlessly.

'Did you read yesterday's newspaper?' he persisted.

'No.' I repeated my answer.

Apparently, not ready to let go of newspaper reading, his next question was asked in a mocking tone, 'So you don't have such habits?'

Pulling up my hands which were until then pressed against my knees, I crossed my arms across my chest and said, 'No, I don't read newspapers.'

I then looked in the direction of my guru, Prof. Sebastian, who sat there flummoxed, as if trying to understand what had gotten into me. Without taking my eyes off him, the newspaper critic in me said calmly, 'We are at a juncture where, after reading four or five newspapers, we have to imagine or suss out what the truth is. Since I have neither the time nor the inclination for that, I have stopped reading newspapers.'

Hearing his student's words, Prof. Sebastian roared with laughter.

I stole a glance at the collector. Quickly getting over his sheepishness, that intrepid guy asked me, 'Not in search of truth, but at least as an exercise in curiosity, can't you read them?'

I felt a new respect towards him; he had understood what I was getting at. Not for nothing had he been selected into the IAS. Let him have his day, but why should I surrender for him to win? I responded with, 'I have lost all such curiosity for a long time now, sir . . .'

That settled it. With that, not just the collector, even the rest of the panel seemed to have had their fill. I was dismissed from their presence.

The interview at Nirmala College was done after my BEd examinations and I had moved to Murickassery. Appointments were to be made in Nirmala, Newman, and Pavanatma Colleges, all under the Kothamangalam Diocese. Two of the positions were for Malayalam lecturers. I had received information that there were many applicants— one post was earmarked for a nun; a few had recommendations from high places including from ministers—but I could try my luck despite all this.

I received the interview card only the day before the date of the interview. I was ailing at that time and had recovered from a bout of fever; but the cough lingered and was set off whenever I tried to talk.

Murickassery had no motorable roads at the time. To reach Muvattupuzha, I had to get up at 3 a.m., walk seven kilometres to Kambilikandam, take the bus that left at 5.30 a.m., and travel three hours. The early-morning walk in the chill of the hilly region, and the cold breeze during the bus journey aggravated my cough. I walked into the interview after spitting out the lozenges I had in my mouth till then.

Since I was still in with a chance, I did feel tense. My only prayer was that my cough should stay away.

The sight of Prof. Anchanat as the subject expert in the panel shook me. It wasn't even three months since the St Thomas College debacle. Would my performance there still be fresh in his memory? I consoled myself saying que sera sera.

I could read an approving expression on the faces in the panel after I told them that my post-graduation was done at Maharaja's under reputed teachers such as Prof. Leelavathy and Prof. M.K. Sanoo, and I was awaiting the results of my BEd course.

Now it was in my hands to project myself. Every question that was going to be asked was an opportunity to showcase my knowledge and intelligence. I decided that my answers should be apposite and creative and not suffer from dry matter-of-factness.

'Recite a shloka from Kumaranasan and interpret it as if we are undergraduate students . . .' Prof. Anchanat said, 'Any shloka from Asan will do.'

Instead of directly starting the recitation of the shloka, I said this as a preface, 'One day, his friends and admirers asked Kumaranasan which were his favourite lines among all the verses that he had penned. He replied that everything that he had penned was dear to him. However, they persisted . . . still, which do you like the most? Then, Asan recited these lines:

> 'karuthiha cheyya vayya, cheyyaan
> varuthi labhichathil ninnitaa vichaaram,
> parama hitham arinjukoota, aayur
> sthirathayumilla athinindyamee narathvam.'
> [One cannot do as the heart desires, nor
> Does the mind adhere to things ordained;
> Unknown is God's will
> Life is but ephemeral; despicable is the human state].

Prof. Anchanat asked, 'Which poem are these lines from?'

'It's from the poem *Leela*,' I replied.

'There is a shloka with similar sentiments in his *Chinthavishtayaaya Seetha* (Pensive Seetha) also. Can you recite it?' the government nominee, possibly the revenue divisional officer, asked.

'oru nischayamillayonninum
varumoro dasha vanna polae pom.'
[There is no certitude; stages in life
Come and go at will.]

By the time I recited those two lines, the government nominee who appeared to be an aesthete, completed the stanza,

'virayunnu manushyanethino
thiriyaa lokarahasyamaarkkume.'
[Man craves for something;
The mystical world is beyond everyone's ken.]

'Where did you read that "*karuthiha cheyya . . .*" was Asan's favourite shloka?' the government nominee asked.

'It's hearsay, I didn't read it anywhere.' I then elaborated on it, 'We had to study this poem for our MA. Prof. Sanoo who taught us mentioned this contextually.'

'Did you believe it just because your teacher said so?' the government nominee was relentless.

'Yes, I did.'

'The students do believe what their teachers tell them,' Prof. Anchanat took my side.

'It's not that. Dr Puthussery Ramachandran has written about this,' the nominee said. It was clear that he was not merely an aesthete, but widely read as well.

Now that the preface had gone down well with them, it was time to interpret the shloka. I tried to invoke Asan's perspective on human life in that shloka, layered as it was by his romanticism that approached life emotionally; his philosophical outlook that revealed the meaninglessness and fleeting impermanence of one's existence; and the farsightedness of a seer who had turned into a poet.

The pleased looks on the faces of the interview panel members told me that my attempt had gone down very well. Whether feeling intimidated by the interview panel or whether due to my prayers, my cough didn't trouble me during the interview. I was confident that I would get into the rank list, and I did tell my friends this.

When I was placed second in the rank list, I went to Bishop House to thank Monsignor Dr George Edathotty, the college manager, and Reverend Father George Kunnamkott, the corporate educational secretary, both of whom were on the interview panel. Father Mathew Thekkekara, the vicar of our parish and local manager of the Murickassery college, accompanied me.

Father Thekkekara had played a significant role in starting a college in the backward and hilly region of Murickassery. His sole efforts had resulted in the creation of title deeds for the lands owned by the diocese in Murickassery which had no title deeds. The electric power line had run up only as far as Karimban, about eleven kilometres away from Murickassery. Father Thekkekara had worked tirelessly to get it extended to our place. When the electricity board could find no contractor ready to tender for pulling the line, he took on that role too and completed the job. He had to arrange the money for all that work on his own and from his inheritance.

The college was only three years old; the construction activities were still going on. The manager asked me for a donation for the building fund. Father Thekkekara promised that this amount would be paid. Since he was aware of our family's financial condition, the manager asked me where I was going to find the money.

'We'll have to sell the land,' I replied.

'No, we don't want you to sell your land and pay,' he said. 'Some of your relatives must have money. Won't anyone of them lend you Rs 10,000? You can pay them back from your salary slowly?'

Even in 1985, that was no small sum and equalled a college lecturer's annual pay. I agreed to pay that sum. Two of my relatives agreed to lend me Rs 5000 each, of which, for one, I didn't have to pay interest. The second one demanded interest at 36 per cent per annum. That was the going rate in the hill regions.

The day before I was to take the appointment order, I received Rs 5000 from the interest-taker. The other man looked at me helplessly. Apparently, the money set aside for me had been used up elsewhere.

Father Thekkekara accompanied me this time as well. We left Murickassery in the afternoon and walked the seven kilometres to Kambilikandam to take the bus. By the time we got to Kothamangalam, it was late in the evening. We stayed the night at Bishop House. After

supper, there was a film show for the novitiates of the seminary—
Koodevide (Where is your Nest?), written and directed by Padmarajan.

Reverend Punnakottil was the bishop in those days as well. We met
the manager after breakfast. I handed over the money in the presence
of Father Thekkekara saying only Rs 5000 could be arranged. He
accepted it without a word and handed over the envelope containing my
appointment order.

Father Thekkekara had always called me Joseph. However, based on
his recommendation, after I was appointed as a lecturer in a college where
he was the local manager, he always addressed me politely as Joseph sir.
He was a decent, honourable man and a great human being.

The college manager, Monsignor George Edathotty, was a
virtuous, righteous priest. He always treated me with a special
indulgence. We have made speeches during school annual days on
the same stage. He would give calm, majestic, and measured speeches
and would always compliment my performance and encourage me.
He passed away before I was dismissed from service following the
question-paper controversy.

Father George Kunnamkott had become aged and infirm at the time
of my dismissal. However, in one of the church meetings he had taken
on Monsignor Thomas Malekudi, berated him and spoken trenchantly
against my dismissal. I was told by the other priests present at the meeting
that Thomas Malekudi had washed his hands of the whole issue with a
lame, 'Bishop asked me to; so I did it.'

Meanwhile, Father Thekkekara had developed dementia and had
forgotten all about my termination. One day, he asked me about my job
and welfare, and I had to tell him again about my dismissal. He was very
upset, 'If you have been dismissed, how will you and your family live?'

I consoled him, saying that everything would work out soon. But, by
the time 'everything worked out' he had total amnesia.

I bow my head in honour and remembrance of Reverend Dr George
Edathotty, Reverend Father George Kunnamkott, and Reverend Father
Mathew Thekkekara. They had not only learnt God's word and knew
God, they also knew human beings and were humanitarians.

44

Retracing My Steps

I

A year after the question-paper controversy and its fallout, I accompanied four of my friends on a trip to Palakkad to attend the house-warming ceremony of our friend, Velappan. Two policemen as my security detail were with me.

I had become acquainted with Velappan while travelling with the movie production companies when I was learning movie-making. Although he had no direct link to the shooting arrangements, he was well known as a public worker in his locality. We were of the same age, yet I used to suffix his name with *ettan* (elder brother) as a mark of my respect and affection.

His house was in a remote village on the banks of the Ikshu river, in the valley of the Nelliyampathi Hills, in Chittoor taluk, a place I have visited many times. When I had gone underground, the police had reached his home also, in search of me.

After we partook of the feast, Velappettan didn't let us leave; so, we had to stay for the night in the new house and start back only the following day.

One of my friends in the group had to go to Chennai to visit someone in Apollo Hospital, therefore, we went all the way to Coimbatore to drop him, before turning back. We were travelling in a Toyota Innova, owned by one of the friends. I drove the car from Coimbatore to Angamaly.

As we approached Palakkad, an idea struck me. Why not make a visit to Sithara Guest House, where I had holed up with the Kerala Police hot on my heels? My friends agreed that it was a good idea. The route from the KSRTC Terminal and Indian Coffee House through a side road to hit Manjakulam Road, wending past the mosque was imprinted on my mind. However, since the road was a one-way street and I had used it only on foot, that too in the wrong direction, we couldn't take that road; we had to take a circuitous route and ask for directions a few times before we reached Sithara.

The six of us entered the reception area. The two people present at the counter leaped to their feet, in a bit of a shock, especially since the two policemen with us were in uniform. I wonder who they thought the rest of us were.

Both men had been part of the staff during my sojourn here, but there were no signs of recognition on their faces.

'I've stayed here before,' I introduced myself. Still no signs of recognition.

'I had used a false name then—Georgekutty,' I said watching them. 'I've come to apologize for it.'

With those words, they were released from their initial shock. The man I was more familiar with emerged from behind the counter and gripped my right hand with both his hands. I had signed in as Georgekutty when he had been manning the reception counter.

He spoke to me like a long-lost friend. Apparently, he had recognized me at the very first glance, but was perplexed because of the policemen in tow and unsure about the purpose of my visit.

He narrated to me the incidents following my arrest. By late evening, a group of policemen had landed there and had asked if someone by the name Prof. T.J. Joseph had stayed there. How could they have known? That name wasn't in their register. They were helpless.

'Reports are coming on the TV. Don't you have one?' one of the policemen had demanded, unable to locate a TV in the reception area.

After the staff had confirmed that they had TVs only in the rooms, the policemen had been taken into an unoccupied room and the TV was switched on. All the Malayalam channels had been reporting on my arrest. The guest house staff had recognized me from the visuals and had admitted that I had, indeed, stayed in their establishment. The policemen had assured them they had only come to verify whether what I had said was the truth and that there would be no other problems. Just as they were leaving, another group of policemen had arrived. When the first group had explained everything to the second group, there was no further interrogation. The owner of the guest house had called a DySP known to him and had ensured that no blame was attached to their guest house.

As we stood around chatting, the entire staff of the guest house gathered around us. Some of them, I knew; some, I didn't. As per their collective request, I rolled up my sleeves and let them see the scars of my wounds. Suleiman came forward and gently touched the scars. I could see women among them tearing up.

'Bad times happen in one's life. What else can be said?' One among them sighed deeply.

To lighten the mood, I asked Suleiman, 'When I had stayed here, did you find anything out of place, anything that betrayed my state?'

'Nothing in particular, but I did notice that you were not going out during meal times.'

When we left after saying goodbye to all of them, I could feel a veil of tranquillity descend on me.

II

Although I had heard of Specialists' Hospital in Ernakulam before, I had never had an occasion to visit it until I was stretchered into it. I actually saw the hospital only after two months of my treatment there. After the initial five weeks, I was brought home in an ambulance. I was flat on my back at home as well for another three weeks. I was brought back to the hospital again in an ambulance and only after the plaster casts were put on both my arms and my left leg was I able to sit up in a wheelchair or on the hospital bed.

Only after that, I switched over from seeing things from a horizontal position and started to see them again as we are accustomed to— vertically. I saw the hospital—the birthplace of my second life—in the proper perspective only then, and its location and elevation started to register in my mind.

A letter written by Justice V.R. Krishna Iyer to the MD of Specialists' Hospital was displayed on its notice board for quite some time. It was a congratulatory letter complimenting the surgeons of the hospital for successfully reattaching the severed palm of Prof. T.J. Joseph.

Whenever I visited the Specialists' Hospital, I was extended VIP treatment. I never had to wait in a queue to meet Dr Jayakumar, who was the lead surgeon and had been in charge of my treatment. If, by chance, he was on his rounds, the hospital authorities would always insist that I wait in the VIP waiting room with all its amenities and comforts.

Dr Jayakumar would always look at my right hand with a special pride and sense of gratification. Although he had reattached the limbs and body parts of thousands of people, in his own words, he had never replanted a human body part that had been 'so damaged'. He had also told me that the improvement that my hand had shown was beyond the doctors' wildest dreams when they had started on the repair work.

Apart from the surgery to reattach my palm, I underwent three more surgeries. After these subsequent surgeries, I was placed in a different ICU, which had other patients as well. After the first surgery, I was put in a small ICU that was meant for only two patients. I wished to see that ICU once more where I had spent eleven days looking at the ceiling, as the pain ebbed and flowed and I swung between agony and relief depending on the quantity of sedatives and painkillers that flowed through my veins. For, strange as it may sound, those days had presented me a kind of mental peace that went beyond physical pain.

When I expressed my wish to Dr Jayakumar, he agreed. A nurse was asked to accompany me and walk me through the ICU. It was empty on the day of my visit. I had lain on the bed on the right side; I touched it with a palpitating heart.

The bed on the left reminded me of the Muslim boy who had lain on it. I refer to him by his religion only because the image of his father and relatives, who had always visited him in their traditional Muslim clothes, has stuck in my mind. The poor boy's ankle, flayed of its skin, had remained an open wound, and was a heart-wrenching sight. The memory floated into my mind again.

I had met him again in the casualty when I had gone to get casts put on my arms and leg. His left leg, crushed by the truck that run over it, had been amputated. He was in casualty to have his wounds dressed.

When we lay side by side in the ICU, I had thought my position was more dire. Where I had come with my palm missing, I went back with it reattached. However, in his case . . . What can be said about the ironies of a treacherous fate?

Three or four months later, I met him again at the physiotherapy centre at Palarivattam. He had put on some weight, perhaps because he couldn't move about or exercise. He had come to the centre to practise walking using the Jaipur foot. When he tried to walk after strapping on the prosthesis to the stub of his leg that extended a little below his knee, he hesitated because of the pain. I tried to encourage him with, 'Standing like this won't do. When you walk a couple of rounds, the pain will go away. You must run with your friends on this very leg.'

'Only run?' Rachel madam demanded, when she heard me. I looked at her. She held him by the chin affectionately, raised his head up and asked him, 'We must climb trees too, no . . . ?'

Biting down on his pain, he took another step forward.

On my way back from the ICU, my mind was filled with images of his face. Somewhere, I hoped, he must be threshing down on his fate with his Jaipur foot.

III

A young man walked across to me in Muvattupuzha town and said brightly, 'Sir, you have taught me.'

'Where?'

'Newman College.'

'What's your name?'

He told me his name. He was a Muslim and had been a degree student in Newman College when the question-paper controversy ran its course.

'What do you do now?' I asked him the usual question I ask my students when I meet them.

'I have a job. In the prison department.'

'In the prison department? What job is that?'

'I am a warden.'

This was the first time that I had heard of one of our students becoming a jail warden.

'Where are you posted now?' I asked with some curiosity.

'Oh, here itself; I am in Muvattupuzha sub-jail.'

'That's wonderful. I was your department's guest there,' I said with some excitement.

There was a reason. I wanted to visit the jail once again. Visiting a jail is not as easy as going to a public place. If I could meet the jail superintendent and request a visit to Cell No. 4, he may facilitate it— after all, I had become something of a 'celebrity' already. Preachers are allowed inside the jail to reform criminals. There had to be a way. It was while all these thoughts and plans were taking root in my mind that I ran into my student, who could be the key I sought to open a few doors for me. My moment of serendipity.

I told him of my wish. He said, 'What's there to ask, you come along any time . . . but do call me before you come.' He gave me his mobile number.

A few days later, I called him and arranged the date and time of visit. When I rang the bell at the main gate, the face that peeked through the small window set in the massive door was my student's. He fetched the key and opened the heavy door for me. The policeman who was my security detail waited in my car parked outside the compound.

I was taken to the jail superintendent's office; he was not there. A senior warden deputizing for him ordered tea for me. I asked them about the officials who had been in charge during my sojourn there. The superintendent who had released me with a Basheeresque 'Now you are free' send-off had retired. Most of the wardens had been transferred out to the central jails at Viyyur and Kannur. All the prisoners who had been good cooks had also been released. The taste of jail food was no longer 'super' as before.

The wardens allowed me to see the spots that were familiar to me. I went and saw the big cement tanks that were always filled with water for the prisoners' baths. I drew close to Cell No. 4. It looked dark inside from where I stood; I could only see some shadows move. Since where I stood was well lit, I was sure that the prisoners inside the cell could see me. I didn't want to move closer and become a spectator of their captivity.

As I walked back to the superintendent's office, the faces of my ex-cellmates flashed through my mind as if on a photo album. Where were they now, I wondered; what battles were they engaged in and in which battlefields of life?

I had read in the press about Jabbar being released and then incarcerated again. He was not charged with burglary this time but was arrested based on a complaint by his wife that he had attempted to molest his daughter. He had filched the song I had written to get it sung by his twelve-year-old daughter and record an album. The senior warden told me that initially he was brought into Muvattupuzha sub-jail but later transferred to Viyyur, and that the woman who had been cohabiting with Jabbar may have filed a false case to get rid of him.

I met only one of my ex-cellmates after being released. Pareethbhai came in search of me one day to my house. It had been about eight or nine months after I had been attacked. The policemen on my security detail stopped him at the gate, chiefly because he refused to identify himself and only said he was known to me. As he insisted that he had to meet me, the policemen summoned me. At first sight, I thought it was a beggar. The lack of recognition must have shown on my face.

He started to introduce himself, 'We were together in . . .' and trailed off, not wanting to reveal any more. By that time, I had placed him. When I confirmed that he was indeed known to me, the policemen allowed him to enter the house.

I made him sit on the sofa in our living room and sat across from him. We were sizing up each other. Where he had looked healthy and fit in the jail, he was now a shadow of his former self and looked weak and frail. He had aged about ten years in that one year. His clothes were shabby. There was a cannula taped on his left forearm.

'How are you now, sir? Are you able to walk and all that?' he asked, looking at me from tip to toe.

I asked with a smile, 'Didn't you notice me walking around?'

'Your hands . . .' he didn't complete the sentence. I moved my hands as vigorously as possible.

His eyes welled up with tears. 'I had told you at that time itself that you should take care . . .' he said that with a little sob.

I tried to smile. 'Now tell me about yourself,' I said to change the subject.

He started his tale. He had been remanded after he was arrested for attacking a local Congress leader in a drunken state. Since the appellant's lawyer had said that they had no complaint, Pareethbhai was released following the next hearing. He was earning his livelihood as an odd-job man when he fell from a jackfruit tree and suffered a hip-bone fracture. He was under treatment for a long time at Kottayam Medical College.

About a week ago, he had joined a restaurant in Muvattupuzha. After two days he felt severe chest pain and was admitted in the taluk hospital. Since it was a government hospital and Pareethbhai was only two days old in his employment, the restaurant owner didn't offer any financial help. Habituated as he was to consuming strong tea and not satiated by the spare fare from the hospital, Pareethbhai had consumed food and tea from a nearby restaurant and run up a bill of Rs 80, although he had no money in hand. He had also been referred to Kottayam Medical College by the doctors in the taluk hospital.

As his own children lived in and around Alappuzha, instead of going to Kottayam, he preferred to go to Alappuzha Medical College. To cut a long story short, he needed money to pay off the debt at the restaurant. And bus fare to reach Alappuzha. When he wondered whom to touch, this old 'roommate' of his came to his mind.

Could all this be true, I wondered. If they were, I thought he shouldn't have to ask another man for help. What if he had none of these ailments? Let him get drunk or do whatever he wants with the money I was about to give him. I would have preferred that he was not a patient. I handed over Rs 400 and asked him if it was sufficient. He said it was more than double of what he needed.

'We may meet sometime, somewhere, if it is fated to happen,' Pareethbhai said, as he was leaving.

At that time, I was thinking about my first night in the jail. I hadn't received the standard issue mat from the jail authorities, since my friends or relatives had not paid the bribes. This was the man who spared half of his mat and spread a sheet next to it so that I didn't have to sleep on the cement floor. I stood there for some time watching him walk away, obviously in ill health and infirm. Each of his hurting steps pierced my heart, which ached with the emotions of friendship.

As I was leaving, my student accompanied me up to the gate. As we neared the gate, I asked him, 'If you were a warden here when I was an inmate, how would you have behaved?'

'I would have arranged as many facilities as possible for you. But I wouldn't have come and talked to you or introduced myself or declared myself as your student.' His response was quick; I liked it for its honesty and sense of pragmatism. I bid him goodbye and stepped out of those forbidding walls.

IV

For getting Amy's passport verification expedited, she and I had to go to Thodupuzha police station one day. At that time, she was a student at a nursing school at Muthalakodam that was under the jurisdiction of Thodupuzha police station. As advised by the officer who had to do the verification, we reached there at around 8 p.m. The following days were not convenient for him and he wanted to avoid delays in getting it done.

My first visit—it would be a misnomer to call it a visit considering that I was taken there in handcuffs with a lot of fanfare and publicity, after I had surrendered at Idukki—to the Thodupuzha police station was a blur and there was no way I could note and remember the way to it. As the policeman assigned as my security detail knew the way, we reached there without asking for directions.

The officer was waiting for us; after verification, he signed the documents. I took his permission to show Amy around the police station.

What is the most important feature of a police station? Its lock-up. That is the integral, inextricable and inseparable part of a police station, the centre point of 'peacekeeping' within our great nation. Amy was seeing a real lock-up for the first time in her life, one hallowed by her father occupying it for a day or so. I reminded her of the fact; I saw no emotion on her face except curiosity.

I peeked into the lock-up. It seemed as if it had had no occupant for a long time. It was dirty, dusty and cobweb ridden. I felt sad; I wanted it to be neat and clean, for, it is another of my memorials.

The large table at which the policemen would sit and dine still occupied its place in front of the lock-up. It was deserted.

With me feeling a little nostalgic, as Amy and I went around, suddenly a terrifying picture flashed before my eyes, like black lightning, blinding me with its intense darkness.

My son, Mithun, leaning against the steel bars of the lock-up door, exhausted and terrorized. He had been brought in because they couldn't track down his father. He was being interrogated and brutalized.

My own breath quickened and became ragged.

It was here that Mithun's nights paled and turned into blinding light, as he sat on a stool in front of the lock-up . . .

It was here that the peacekeepers dragged him over the stairs on the way to the DySP's office on the first floor . . .

It was here that he had been made to sit on the floor with his legs stretched out and then mercilessly beaten with canes on the soles of his feet . . .

It was here that he was made to kneel in front of a seated officer, his head held between vice-like knees and repeatedly pummelled with steel-like elbows on his back . . .

Before my eyes spilled the tears of blood which suffused my eyes, I ushered my daughter out of that peacekeepers' den.

45

The Armour of Humour

One day, I was travelling from Cheruthoni to Thodupuzha. I was seated on the right side of the bus, in a double seat in the second last row. My wedding had been fixed and in those days, for procuring and arranging any number of things related to a wedding, Thodupuzha was the nearest town. From Murickassery that meant a ten-kilometre trip by jeep up to Karimban, another seven kilometres by bus to Cheruthoni, and then another fifty-kilometre bus journey to get to Thodupuzha.

I had to take the lead and also execute all the work related to my own wedding. Repair, maintenance, and whitewashing of the house, printing invitations, distributing them and inviting people in person, all of these fell into my lap since, by then, my father was ailing and enfeebled. My younger brother, employed in Puducherry, could only come down on the eve of the wedding. My neighbour, Reji, was my only help, from start to finish.

My plan was to spend two or three days in Variyanikkadu—where I was born and grew up—to collect the printed invitations and to invite my friends, neighbours, and relatives. By the time I started from Murickassery, it was already afternoon. When I reached Cheruthoni, it was past 3 p.m. Thodupuzha was at least another two hours' journey away. As I had not slept much the previous night, I was very sleepy, and as soon as I sat down, I placed my forearms on the bar of the seat in front of me and started to sleep with my head nestled between my wrists.

I woke up hearing a commotion; we wouldn't have travelled very far. I saw an old woman of around seventy years lurching towards the rear of the bus. Apparently, she was nauseous and the conductor had dispatched her to the rear to do her thing. Before she reached our row, the gentleman seated to my left leapt up and vacated his seat. By the time I realized the peril I was in and could get up and move out of her way, she had entered the gap between the seats, lost the fight to hold it in, and deposited all of her lunch and the supplemental fluids she had used to wash it down on to my shoulder, wherefrom they flowed down my shirt on to my trousers, making them both feel heavy. Generous spatters had fallen on my face, ear and hair.

I slid to the left end of the seat and made her sit by the window. Although she retched a few times after that, there was nothing left inside her to emit and decorate the side of the bus.

Usually, the sight of anyone vomiting was enough for me to retch and feel nauseous myself. I stomped down on my mind; I shut down my senses. I sat there looking unperturbed as if what I bore on my shoulder was a jasmine garland. I was afraid that if I opened my mouth, the spatter on my face and hair would fall in. Still, I managed to ask the crestfallen and contrite woman by my side, who had 'force-fed' me, questions such as 'Where is your house?' and the like, which make for polite conversation in happier circumstances.

The bus was travelling through a forest area at that time. After a place called Meenmutti, the driver stopped the bus near a spring with a small pool of water collected in a depression in the rock. The 'cleaner' on the bus, whose designation reveals his primary duty—his secondary duty being to blow the whistle to alert the driver to stop and start the bus at interstitial stops—fetched a metal bucket kept somewhere in the bus and beckoned me to go with him to wash my shirt.

The bus was parked ahead of the pool. I washed and rinsed out my shirt a few times in the water poured by the cleaner. The cleaner offered to dry it out on the warm metal cover over the engine of the bus. I silently handed over the shirt to him, slipped off my trousers, and dipped it in the water. The cleaner stood by lost and unsure, wondering how I would be admitted back into the bus in just my briefs. I handed over the trousers also to him after rinsing it well. I had a good bath, drawing four or five buckets of water and pouring them over me. I told the cleaner who stood around dithering about what was to be done next, 'There is a briefcase on the overhead carrier above my seat. Can you fetch it, please?'

He heaved a huge sigh of relief. With a relieved smile, he brought me the briefcase. I extracted a torthu from it and towelled myself down and then donned the fresh trousers and shirt that were inside the briefcase. I put the wet clothes in a plastic cover and deposited it inside the briefcase. Many of the passengers showed readiness to share the seat with me when I re-entered the bus, bathed and freshly clothed. They must have been impressed by my stoicism after having been bathed in vomit.

On that occasion, I behaved with serenity not because I was long-suffering or overly patient. I am someone who reacts vehemently when I don't like something. I was able to behave in that restrained manner only because of my sense of humour. When what had to happen happened, my thoughts were: In a bus full of people how is that I was the one who won the lottery? Or drew the short straw? I deserved this, when I had hoped to nap in the bus and see sweet, pre-nuptial dreams. It's that sense of humour that had seeped into me that stopped me from reacting churlishly. Thereafter, in everything I did, I found an enjoyment.

Thanks to my sense of humour, there have been many instances where I acted as if a fall was an acrobatic leap. I shall keep those stories for another day.

My father also had a wry sense of humour. I grew up listening to his wisecracks and jokes. I started to hear my mother's jokes only after she had turned eighty-eight. Did she have a sense of humour before that? I am not so sure . . .

My jocular side came to the fore when I was doing my pre-degree course, especially during English classes. Our teacher was someone called Mathew; his classes were enjoyable. When he taught us grammar, he would make each student say a sentence as an example. My examples were all humorous ones. He would enjoy my brand of humour the most. When it was my turn, everyone would cock his or her ears knowing what was coming. At times, I would make the most platitudinous, blasé, moralistic statements instead. That also would make my classmates laugh. They expected something; what came out was the complete antithesis of it. Aren't such absurd contradictions the source of humour?

However, I was not the clown of the class. I was a grave character. Mathew sir once told me that he had never seen a student with such a solemn expression.

One day, he inspected our notebooks; including me, there were three students who hadn't completed the notes of the lessons taught. He asked us when we could show him the completed work. The other two said that they would submit the completed book the next day—they had only six or seven pages left to do. My case was not the same. My book had twice the number more blanks pages than filled ones. I asked for a week's time, and he agreed.

The notes missing in my book were of the days I hadn't attended class. No one should think it was due to my negligence or because I played truant. As there was no electricity at home and early mornings were chilly, our kitchen started only after day had well and truly broken. Therefore, by the time I had had my breakfast, and set out for college, carrying my packed lunch, it would be 9 a.m. It was a one-and-a-half-hour walk to the college. Even if I ran all the way, I would still not make it in time. The route had steep slopes and climbs. In summers, they were dusty; during monsoons, muddy and slippery. Slipping and falling happened regularly. One fall and I'd cover at least fifteen to twenty feet without having to walk. It also meant that the mundu and shirt would have to be washed in the nearest stream or the Chinnar river. The delayed departure, the treacherous route, the English period being the first of the day, meant that large tracts of my notebook remained fallow and empty.

My other two classmates completed and submitted their notebooks the next day and became paragons of the virtue of obedience.

To copy the notes, I had borrowed the notebook of Alice Mathew, one of the most studious and ever-punctual girls in the class. Despite my best efforts, I couldn't complete the notes within the allotted time. About one-third remained to be done.

Mathew sir had sanctioned me as many days as I had requested for. How could I go and tell him that I hadn't completed it? It had been a week; if he had forgotten about it, I was saved. I went to the college on that day nursing such thoughts.

As soon as he entered the class, he asked me to show him my notebook, as if for all of a week he had been meditating on it, eschewing everything else. What saved my day was a quality I had come across in the

Malayalam text during my high school, days—*prathyulpannamathitvam*, or the ability to think and act in every situation appropriately. I acted in accordance with it—I quickly and insouciantly thrust Alice Mathew's book that was still in my hand into his, and stood back without batting an eyelid.

He riffled through the pages and returned it to me. It took me quite some time to get my breath back. I speeded up the copying and completed it in another two days. The next day, when Mathew sir entered the class, I stood up and offered my notebook.

'What's this?' he raised his eyebrow.

'My notebook,' I said with a straight face.

'But didn't you show it to me the other day?'

'That was Alice Mathew's notebook.' I deadpanned.

His eyes bulged and he pursed his lips in annoyance.

'I did it because I didn't want you to get agitated,' I turned humble.

He gulped down a smile that rose instinctively to his lips and said gravely, 'In our student days we have also done similar tricks. But our disciples outdoing us in such things is something we teachers are proud of.'

Then he laughed out openly.

Mathew sir left teaching and later became a farmer. And I, a teacher. We maintained our friendship. As I lay half-dead with my limbs hacked and slashed, Mathew sir visited me. He came and sat on the edge of my bed and asked me with a sob, 'Da, why did you have to go to such lengths to raise a laugh?'

When I saw him sob, tears welled up in my eyes.

A sense of humour is required to not only create humour but to enjoy it too. Not everyone is blessed with it. It can be dangerous if the listeners are unable to distinguish between what is said as a joke and what is said solemnly. One day, I lamented in passing to my students that my listeners, more often than not, miss the humour in my words.

'We are not like that. We do understand all your jokes,' they said.

'That is true,' I said, 'but my complaint about you is different. Whatever I say seriously is also taken as a joke by you all.'

The one who tells jokes shouldn't laugh. However, those who crack jokes like to see all the listeners laugh. Most of the time, Salomi would never laugh at my jokes. When I claimed that it was because she didn't get the humour behind it, she would say, 'It's not that I don't get it; true connoisseurs laugh inside.'

However, one day, it happened the other way.

Two years had passed after the attack on me. Except for the manoeuvrability of my hands, my general health had improved. After staying back to help us, Sister Marie Stella had returned to her convent after one and a half years' leave. Our visitors' numbers had dwindled. Our children were both in their hostels. Only my mother, wife and I were at home. And outside, the policemen on guard duty.

One day, as we continued to live a quiet, unhurried life, Salomi asked me, 'Shall we adopt a child?' Although I had heard her, I didn't respond.

'It must be an infant; I haven't had enough of bringing up a child.' She was being earnest.

I said as if talking to myself, 'It's when one is unemployed and has no income that such wishes arise!'

'You'll get your job back, won't you? We can do it then.' She was ready to wait. So, I had to teach a class, with her as the sole student, on 'The Difficulties of Child Adoption'. That hit the bull's eye.

'Okay then, we don't have to adopt,' she said, 'I shall bear and deliver a child myself. We can reverse the tubectomy, can't we?'

I was also enthused by the idea, and participated in the subsequent brainstorming. Tubal reversal surgery to re-join the fallopian tubes was known to be done and we could try for a child again. It was a case of let's try, nothing to lose.

'Let's try, no?' she pressed.

'Not at this age. We'll set tongues wagging,' I said, willing my own enthusiasm to take a cold bath.

'What will people say?' Salomi looked at me quizzically.

'They'll say, it's not his hand . . . that should have been chopped off.'

She couldn't control her laughter and got up and went away. Not just that, that day I saw her laughing all by herself a number of times, recollecting the joke.

Once in 1993, she and I went to Pala to attend a wedding reception. As we had no car then, we took a bus. Our children were small and we had left them alone at home. Therefore, we had decided that we would have the food in the first round itself and return early.

It was my colleague's wedding. As I was chatting with the friends when the food service started, Salomi was not with me. As decided earlier, I jostled for a place in the first round itself and had my food. When I came out, she was not to be seen anywhere. Assuming that she would have found a place only in the second round, I looked for her where the food was being served, but she was not there. As I went around asking everyone, 'Did you see my wife?' I was also muttering rather audibly, 'Did some fool kidnap her?'

Even as I was searching for her worriedly, that bit of humour amused me. I found her shortly and we returned home.

Fifteen years later, one of my teacher friends recalled this and repeated my own monologue to me. He had forgotten that I was its progenitor. He roared with laughter, telling me that some teacher had, while anxiously looking for his missing wife at a wedding reception, kept asking himself 'has some fool kidnapped her?' I felt gratified that one of my humorous remarks had survived for fifteen years and stayed in someone's memory that long.

I had no superstition that words said in passing could turn prophetic for oneself and that too to one's detriment. Yet, one big bloody fool kidnapped my wife. Let him take her if he must—what else?

I am not sure if animals and other creatures have a sense of humour. However, it is one of the greatest blessings bestowed upon humanity by nature. It grants the mental strength not merely to triumph over difficulties and crises, but even to forgive one's enemies.

All the lucid thinkers possessed a marked sense of humour. Socrates, Diogenes, Naranathu Bhranthan[1] and Osho Rajneesh were such men.

When Gandhari cursed Sree Krishna, 'You and your race will be annihilated,' he could smile because of the strength provided by the sense of humour which resided in him.

I believe that Jesus Christ, who made disciples of young fishermen with the words, 'Come follow me, and I will make you fishers of men,' could remain serene while facing up to the hegemony of priests and the emperor's henchmen who together conspired against him, and could also forgive the minions who nailed him to the cross, because of the divine power of humour that radiated from within him.

Notes

Chapter 1: A Momentous Question

1. Pokkudan, Kallen, *Kantalkkaatukalkkitayil Ente Jeevitham* [My Life in the Mangroves], DC Books, 2005, p. 41.

Chapter 6: An Affair with Pappadams

1. Guruvayoor is among the few temples in Kerala which still disallows entry of non-Hindus; non-Hindus in the temple premises are penalized by being forced to pay 'cleansing' fees.

Chapter 10: A Police Station Sans Merci

1. Name changed to protect the privacy of the individual.

Chapter 15: New Friends

1. Some names have been changed to protect the privacy of the individuals.

Chapter 16: The Sixth Holy Wound

1. This was a play based on Nikos Kazantzakis's novel *The Last Temptation of Christ*, which shows Jesus's struggle with various forms of temptation, including lust.

Chapter 17: A Song in the Jail

1. Names have been changed to protect the privacy of the individuals.

Chapter 19: Peacekeepers' Sorrows

1. Kerala State Human Rights Commission order in H.R.M.P. No. 1314 of 2010, 12 December 2012 found V.U. Kuriakose and Shinto Kurian guilty of illegal detention and ill treatment of the petitioner. The order was challenged in the Kerala High Court: V.U. Kuriakose vs Kerala State Human Rights Commission and six others, 22 February 2013.
2. Kodungallur Bharani is famous for bawdy songs about the goddess herself and in general. The songs are called *poorappattu* (pooram meaning temple festival and pattu meaning songs).

Chapter 20: The Justice of Caiaphas

1. Interview with a member of the then member of the managing board who attended the meeting.

Chapter 23: Enquiry

1. Chekannur Maulavi (Chekannur P. K. Mohammed Abul Hassan Maulavi) was a progressive Islamic cleric from Malappuram district of Kerala, India. His controversial and unconventional interpretation of Islam based on the Quran made him a lot of enemies among fundamentalists. He disappeared on 29 July 1993 under mysterious circumstances and is now widely believed to be dead.

Chapter 29: Off with Their Heads

1. *Mangalam*, 5 September 2010.
2. Mathews, Siby, Dr, *Nirbhayam: Oru IPS Officerude Anubhavakurippukal*, Thrissur: Green Books Pvt. Ltd., 2017.
3. Interview with an alumnus of Nirmala College.

Chapter 31: Don't Ever Give Up

1. *Agnishalabhangal* (Fireflies) and *Uppu* (Salt) are award-winning works by O.N.V. Kurup.

Chapter 45: The Armour of Humour

1. A character in Malayalam folklore. Considered to be one of the twelve illustrious sons of Vararuchi, he pretended to be mad. His practice of rolling a big stone up a hill and then letting it roll back down is similar to Sisyphus and related allegory.